fine
Cooking
Cakes &
Cupcakes

fine Cooking
Cakes & Cupcakes

100 Best-Ever Recipes

Editors of *Fine Cooking*

The Taunton Press

Text © 2014 The Taunton Press, Inc.

 **The Taunton Press**
Inspiration for hands-on living®

The Taunton Press, Inc.
63 South Main Street
PO Box 5506, Newtown, CT 06470-5506
email: tp@taunton.com

Editor: Carolyn Mandarano
Copy editor: Li Agen
Indexer: Heidi Blough
Jacket/Cover design: Kimberly Adis
Interior design: Kimberly Adis
Layout: Cathy Cassidy
Cover photographer: Scott Phillips
Cover food stylist: Samantha Connell
Interior photographers: Scott Phillips © The Taunton Press, Inc., except for p. 2, 9, 10, 11, 130, and 164 by Amy Albert © The Taunton Press, Inc.; p. 19 © Quentin Bacon; p. 165 by Martha Holmberg © The Taunton Press; p. 200-201 by Steve Hunter © The Taunton Press, Inc.

Fine Cooking® is a trademark of The Taunton Press, Inc., registered in the U.S. Patent and Trademark Office.

The following names/manufacturers appearing in *Fine Cooking Cakes & Cupcakes* are trademarks: Ateco®, Callebaut®, Cap'n Crunch®, Chambord®, Cointreau®, Droste®, El Rey®, Grand Marnier®, Guinness®, Jameson®, Knox®, Lyles Golden Syrup®, Myer's®, Nabisco® FAMOUS® Chocolate Wafers, Pyrex®, Scharffen Berger®

Library of Congress Cataloging-in-Publication Data

Fine cooking cakes & cupcakes : 100 best ever recipes / editors and contributors of Fine cooking.
   pages cm
 Includes index.
 ISBN 978-1-62710-389-3
1. Cake. 2. Cupcakes. I. Taunton's fine cooking.
 TX771.F56 2013
 641.86'53--dc23
                     2013044079

Printed in the United States of America
10 9 8 7 6 5 4 3 2 1

contents

cranberry streusel pound cake
(recipe on p. 25)

snacking cakes

butter pound cake

- 10 oz. (1¼ cups) unsalted butter, softened at room temperature; more for the pan
- 10¼ oz. (2½ cups) cake flour or 11 oz. (2⅓ cups) unbleached all-purpose flour; more for the pan
- 1½ tsp. baking powder
- ½ tsp. table salt
- 1¾ cups granulated sugar
- 2 large egg yolks, at room temperature
- 3 large eggs, at room temperature
- ⅔ cup whole milk, at room temperature
- 1½ tsp. pure vanilla extract

This updated version of the traditional "pound of butter, pound of sugar, pound of eggs, pound of flour" recipe produces a pound cake that's soft and moist, yet still has the classic's buttery flavor and springy texture.

1. Position a rack in the center of the oven and heat the oven to 350°F. Butter a 12-cup Bundt pan, dust the pan with flour, and tap out the excess. In a small bowl, whisk together the flour, baking powder, and salt until evenly combined.

2. In a stand mixer fitted with the paddle attachment, (or in a large bowl, using a hand-held mixer), beat the butter and the sugar at medium speed until light and fluffy, about 2 minutes.

3. On low speed, beat in the yolks until smooth. Stop the mixer and scrape the bowl and the paddle. With the mixer running on medium-low speed, add the whole eggs, one at a time, mixing for at least 20 seconds after each addition. Stop the mixer and scrape the bowl and paddle again.

4. With the mixer running on the lowest speed, add half of the flour mixture and mix just to combine, add the milk and mix until combined, and then add the remaining flour mixture and mix just until combined.

5. Scrape the bowl one last time, add the vanilla extract, and mix at medium speed until the batter is smooth and fluffy, 20 to 30 seconds.

6. Scrape the batter into the prepared pan and spread it evenly. Run a knife through the batter and tap the pan against the counter to dislodge trapped air. Bake until golden brown and a toothpick inserted in the center comes out with only moist crumbs clinging to it, 45 to 55 minutes.

7. Let the cake cool in the pan for 10 to 15 minutes and then invert onto a wire rack to cool completely. The cake will keep at room temperature for 3 days. *–Nicole Rees*

PER SERVING (BASED ON 16 SERVINGS): 310 CALORIES I 3G PROTEIN I 37G CARB I 16G TOTAL FAT I 10G SAT FAT I 4.5G MONO FAT I 1G POLY FAT I 105MG CHOL I 130MG SODIUM I 0G FIBER

Three Easy Pound Cake Variations

Here are three flavor variations: Brandy and Rum Glazed, Lemon-Coconut, and Chocolate Chip. The first two include glazes, which keep the cakes fresh longer and also give them an extra boost of flavor. The third has finely chopped chocolate mixed into the batter. Don't hesitate to experiment with other mix-ins, such as blueberries or cranberries.

Brandy and Rum Glazed

Stir ½ tsp. freshly grated nutmeg into the completed batter. Then proceed with scraping it into the Bundt pan as directed on the facing page.

While the cake bakes, make a glaze by mixing 1¼ cups confectioners' sugar with 3 Tbs. brandy and 3 Tbs. rum until smooth. After the baked cake has cooled for 15 minutes, turn the warm cake onto a serving plate. Using a skewer, poke holes all over the cake. Brush the cake—every visible inch of it—with the glaze, until the glaze is gone. When the cake is completely cool, the glaze will form a protective crust over the cake, keeping it moist for 5 to 7 days.

Lemon-Coconut

Reduce the milk in the recipe to ½ cup, and when you add it to the batter, add ¼ cup fresh lemon juice as well. Then stir 1 Tbs. finely grated lemon zest and 1 cup loosely packed sweetened flaked coconut into the batter, breaking up any coconut lumps. Then proceed with scraping it into the Bundt pan as directed on the facing page.

While the cake bakes, make a glaze by mixing 1¼ cups confectioners' sugar with 6 Tbs. fresh lemon juice until smooth. After the baked cake has cooled for 15 minutes, turn the warm cake onto a serving plate. Using a skewer, poke holes all over the cake. Brush the cake—every visible inch of it—with the glaze, until the glaze is gone. When the cake is completely cool, the glaze will form a protective crust over the cake, keeping it moist for 5 to 7 days.

Chocolate Chip

Fold 4 oz. very finely chopped semisweet chocolate or ⅔ cup mini semisweet chocolate chips into the completed batter. Then proceed with scraping it into the Bundt pan as directed on the facing page.

If desired, sprinkle the cake with confectioners' sugar before serving. The cake will keep at room temperature for 3 days.

plum coffee cake with brown sugar and cardamom streusel

MAKES ONE 8-INCH-SQUARE
CAKE; SERVES 8 OR 9

FOR THE STREUSEL

- 2¼ oz. (½ cup) unbleached all-purpose flour
- ¼ cup packed dark brown sugar
- ⅛ tsp. kosher salt
- Pinch of ground cardamom
- 1½ oz. (3 Tbs.) unsalted butter, melted; more as needed

FOR THE CAKE

- ¼ lb. (½ cup) cold unsalted butter, cut into small pieces; more softened for the pan
- 6¾ oz. (1½ cups) unbleached all-purpose flour; more for the pan
- 2 large eggs
- ½ cup granulated sugar
- ¼ cup packed dark or light brown sugar
- ¼ cup whole milk
- 1½ tsp. pure vanilla extract
- 1½ tsp. baking powder
- ½ tsp. table salt
- ½ tsp. ground cardamom
- 3 firm-ripe medium plums, pitted and quartered

While this cake is delicious by itself, it's also nice when drizzled with a little crème fraîche. The cake will keep for a day, covered, at room temperature; if you keep it longer, the moisture from the plums will start to soften the streusel.

MAKE THE STREUSEL

Put the flour, brown sugar, kosher salt, and cardamom in a small mixing bowl and stir the ingredients with a fork until thoroughly combined. Drizzle the melted butter over the mixture and stir with the fork until the mixture resembles a clumpy dough. Using your fingers, break the mixture into pistachio-size clumps and large crumbs. (If the streusel is sandy and won't clump, add a little more melted butter, 1 tsp. at a time.) Refrigerate the streusel while you prepare the cake batter.

MAKE THE CAKE

1. Position a rack in the center of the oven and heat the oven to 375°F. Lightly butter and flour an 8x8x2-inch straight-sided cake pan.

2. Beat the eggs lightly in a small mixing bowl. Whisk in the granulated sugar, brown sugar, milk, and vanilla until well blended. Set aside.

3. In a large mixing bowl, whisk the flour, baking powder, table salt, and cardamom until well blended. Add the butter pieces to the bowl and cut them into the flour with a pastry blender or two table knives until the mixture resembles a very coarse meal strewn with pieces of butter the size of small peas and oat flakes.

4. Add the egg mixture to the flour mixture. With a wooden spoon, fold and stir the ingredients together until they form a thick batter speckled with visible lumps of butter, 45 seconds to 1 minute.

5. Scrape the batter into the prepared pan and spread it evenly. Break up the streusel mixture with your fingers and sprinkle half of it evenly over the batter. Arrange the plum quarters skin side down on the batter, with each piece at a 45-degree angle to the sides of the pan. Sprinkle the remaining streusel evenly over the cake.

6. Bake the cake for 20 minutes and then rotate the pan. Continue baking until the top of the cake is golden brown and a toothpick inserted in the center comes out with a few moist crumbs clinging to it, 15 to 20 minutes more.

7. Cool the cake in its pan on a rack for at least an hour before cutting. Serve warm or at room temperature. *–Kim Masibay*

PER SERVING: 350 CALORIES | 5G PROTEIN | 48G CARB | 16G TOTAL FAT | 10G SAT FAT | 4.5G MONO FAT | 1G POLY FAT | 85MG CHOL | 240MG SODIUM | 1G FIBER

Choosing Plums for Baking

Most stores label plums simply red, black, purple, or yellow, but there are actually at least 200 varieties. Once harvested, plums don't store well and must be shipped and sold within 10 days, so growers produce several varieties that ripen on a staggered schedule from mid-May through October to ensure constant supply. What this means is that the red or purple plums you saw on your last market visit are probably not the same varieties you'll find on your next. For most recipes, the variety doesn't matter much. The fruit's ripeness, however, matters quite a bit.

The ideal plum for baking is called firm-ripe; it's neither super-soft nor rock hard but somewhere in between. Take a plum and squeeze it gently in the palm of your hand. It should smell fragrant and feel firm yet springy. These plums are easy to slice, and during baking they become tender without losing their shape or releasing too much juice. If you can find only very firm plums, let them ripen in a paper bag at room temperature for a couple of days.

bourbon-glazed brown sugar pecan pound cake

FOR THE CAKE

- **12 oz. (1½ cups) unsalted butter, at room temperature; more for the pan**
- **½ cup fine, dry, plain breadcrumbs (store-bought are fine)**
- **15¾ oz. (3½ cups) unbleached all-purpose flour**
- **1 tsp. baking powder**
- **¼ tsp. baking soda**
- **¼ tsp. kosher salt**
- **3 cups lightly packed light brown sugar**
- **5 large eggs, at room temperature**
- **2 tsp. pure vanilla extract**
- **¾ cup buttermilk**
- **¼ cup bourbon**
- **2¼ cups toasted, coarsely chopped pecans**

FOR THE GLAZE

- **⅓ cup granulated sugar**
- **⅓ cup bourbon**

Bourbon, brown sugar, and pecans, a traditional Southern combination, make a deeply flavored treat.

MAKE THE CAKE

1. Position a rack in the center of the oven and heat the oven to 350°F. Butter a 10-inch (12-cup) Bundt pan and dust it with the breadcrumbs, shaking out and discarding the excess crumbs.

2. Sift together the flour, baking powder, and baking soda into a medium bowl. Add the salt and mix with a rubber spatula.

3. In a stand mixer fitted with the paddle attachment (or in a large bowl, using a hand-held mixer), beat the butter on medium speed, gradually adding the brown sugar until the mixture is light and fluffy, about 3 minutes. Add the eggs one at a time, mixing just enough to incorporate and pausing to scrape the bowl once or twice. Add the vanilla and mix until just combined.

4. In a measuring cup, combine the buttermilk with the bourbon. With the mixer running on low speed, alternate adding the flour mixture and the buttermilk mixture in five additions, beginning and ending with the dry ingredients, stopping occasionally to scrape the bowl. Mix until just combined. Add the toasted pecan pieces and mix until the nuts are just incorporated.

5. Pour the batter into the prepared pan and smooth the top with a spatula. Bake until the cake is golden brown and a cake tester or skewer comes out clean, 65 to 70 minutes. Transfer the cake to a rack and let cool in the pan for 15 minutes.

MAKE THE GLAZE

Combine the sugar and bourbon in a small saucepan or skillet. Cook over medium-low heat until the mixture comes to a simmer and the sugar dissolves, 3 to 5 minutes. Turn the cake out of the pan onto a cooling rack. With a pastry brush, brush the warm glaze over the entire surface of the cake. Allow to cool completely. This cake can be made up to 2 days ahead. *–Karen Barker*

PER SERVING: 790 CALORIES | 9G PROTEIN | 91G CARB | 42G TOTAL FAT | 17G SAT FAT | 16G MONO FAT | 6G POLY FAT | 150MG CHOL | 170MG SODIUM | 3G FIBER

pineapple crumble snack cake

SERVES 12

FOR THE STREUSEL

6	Tbs. unbleached all-purpose flour
6	Tbs. packed light brown sugar
3	Tbs. unsalted butter, softened
¼	tsp. ground cinnamon

FOR THE CAKE

½	lb. (1 cup) unsalted butter, softened at room temperature; more for the pan
6¾	oz. (1½ cups) unbleached all-purpose flour, unsifted; more for the pan
3	oz. (a generous ½ cup) hazelnuts
1	cup granulated sugar
1	tsp. baking powder
¼	tsp. table salt
3	large eggs, at room temperature
½	tsp. pure vanilla extract
	About ⅓ of a fresh pineapple, peeled, cored, and cut into medium chunks (to yield 1½ cups), set on paper towels to drain
	Confectioners' sugar, for garnish (optional)

This cake freezes well. Cool completely, wrap securely in plastic, and then wrap in foil.

MAKE THE STREUSEL
In a medium bowl, combine the flour, brown sugar, butter, and cinnamon, mixing with your fingertips until the mixture is lumpy and holds together when pinched. Set aside.

MAKE THE CAKE
1. Position a rack in the lower third of the oven and heat the oven to 350°F. Butter and flour a 9-inch springform or round cake pan; set a round of waxed paper or parchment in the bottom of the pan.

2. Process the nuts with 2 Tbs. of the sugar until the nuts are finely ground. Sift the flour, baking powder, and salt onto a sheet of waxed paper; pour the ground nuts on top of the dry ingredients; set aside.

3. In a stand mixer fitted with the paddle attachment, beat the butter on medium until creamy and smooth, about 1 minute. Add the remaining sugar and continue to beat until light and fluffy, about 3 minutes, stopping the mixer to scrape down the sides of the bowl as needed. Add the eggs one at a time, beating well after each addition. Add the vanilla. With the mixer on the lowest speed, gradually add the flour–nut mixture, blending each addition just until incorporated and stopping the mixer to scrape down the sides of the bowl as needed.

4. Spoon half of the batter into the pan and scatter half the pineapple chunks over it, gently pressing them into the batter. Spoon the remaining batter over the pineapple, smooth the surface with a rubber spatula, and scatter the remaining pineapple chunks over the top, gently pressing them into the batter. Sprinkle the streusel over the top.

5. Bake until the cake is golden on top and springs back without leaving an impression when gently pressed in the center and a toothpick comes out clean, not sticky, 45 to 55 minutes.

6. Let cool in its pan on a rack for 10 minutes. Gently tap the pan on the counter to release the sides. Set another rack on top of the cake, invert it, and carefully remove the pan (if using a springform pan, unclasp it and remove the bottom). Invert the cake again so the streusel side is up. Let cool completely. Before serving, put the confectioners' sugar in a fine sieve and dust the cake, if you like. *–Flo Braker*

PER SERVING: 400 CALORIES | 5G PROTEIN | 44G CARB | 24G TOTAL FAT | 12G SAT FAT | 9G MONO FAT | 2G POLY FAT | 100MG CHOL | 110MG SODIUM | 1G FIBER

chocolate banana swirl cake

SERVES 10 TO 12

FOR THE PAN

2 Tbs. granulated sugar

⅓ cup medium-finely chopped walnuts

Softened unsalted butter, for the pan

FOR THE CAKE

9 oz. (2 cups) unbleached all-purpose flour

2 tsp. baking powder

¼ tsp. baking soda

¼ tsp. table salt

6 oz. (¾ cup) unsalted butter, completely softened at room temperature

1¼ cups granulated sugar

3 very ripe medium bananas (unpeeled, about 14 oz. total), peeled

2 tsp. pure vanilla extract

3 large eggs

3 oz. (6 Tbs.) buttermilk

4 oz. bittersweet chocolate, melted and cooled

This cake puts very ripe bananas to good use. Be sure to follow the time guidelines for unmolding the cake. If you wait too long, it will stick to the pan; take it out too early and it might break into chunks.

PREPARE THE PAN

Position a rack in the center of the oven and heat the oven to 350°F. In a small bowl, mix the sugar with the chopped walnuts. Generously butter a large Bundt pan and coat with the nuts and sugar, pressing the nuts with your fingers to help them stick. The pan sides will be coated and some of the nuts will fall to the bottom—that's fine.

MAKE THE CAKE

1. In a medium bowl, whisk the flour, baking powder, baking soda, and salt until well blended. In stand mixer fitted with the paddle attachment (or in a large bowl, using a hand-held mixer), beat the butter, sugar, bananas, and vanilla until well blended and the bananas are almost smooth, scraping down the sides of the bowl as needed. Add the eggs one at a time, beating until just incorporated.

2. Remove the bowl from the mixer. With a rubber spatula, alternately add half the flour mixture, all the buttermilk, and then the rest of the flour mixture, stirring until each addition is just blended.

3. Spoon half the batter into a medium bowl and gently stir in the melted chocolate until just combined. With a large spoon, alternately add a scoopful of each batter to the prepared pan, working around the pan until all the batter is used. Gently run a knife or the tip of a rubber spatula through the batter, once clockwise and once counterclockwise, to slightly swirl the batters. Gently tap the pan on the counter to settle the batter.

4. Bake until a pick inserted in the center comes out with just a few crumbs sticking to it, about 40 minutes. Let the cake cool in the pan on a wire rack for 15 minutes. Gently tap the sides of the pan on the counter to loosen the cake. Invert the pan onto the rack, lift off the pan, and let the cake cool completely. *–Abigail Johnson Dodge*

classic crumb cake

SERVES 12

FOR THE CRUMB TOPPING

12 oz. (1½ cups) unsalted butter; more for the pan

½ cup granulated sugar

¾ cup packed light brown sugar

1½ tsp. ground cinnamon

¼ tsp. ground nutmeg

Pinch of table salt

12 oz. (2⅔ cups) unbleached all-purpose flour

FOR THE CAKE

9 oz. (2 cups) unbleached all-purpose flour

¾ cup granulated sugar

1 tsp. baking powder

½ tsp. table salt

1 large egg

¾ cup milk

Reserved ½ cup melted unsalted butter

1 tsp. pure vanilla extract

1 Tbs. confectioners' sugar, for dusting

This crumb-topped vanilla cake is a nostalgic favorite. Melt all the butter at once and reserve half to help streamline prep.

MAKE THE TOPPING

In a large saucepan, melt all the butter; remove from the heat. Pour ½ cup into a measuring cup and reserve for mixing the cake batter. Add the sugar, brown sugar, cinnamon, nutmeg, and salt to the saucepan. Stir with a fork, pressing when needed, until there are no lumps of sugar. Add the flour and stir gently until well blended and crumbly. Set aside.

MAKE THE CAKE

1. Position a rack in the middle of the oven and heat the oven to 350°F. Lightly butter a 9x13-inch baking pan.

2. In a large bowl, whisk together the flour, sugar, baking powder, and salt. In a medium bowl, whisk the egg, milk, reserved ½ cup melted butter, and vanilla until combined. Pour the liquids over the dry ingredients and gently stir until just blended. Scrape the batter into the prepared pan and spread evenly.

3. Break up the topping mixture with your fingers and sprinkle it evenly and generously over the cake batter. Bake until the top is lightly browned, the cake springs back when lightly pressed in the center, and a pick inserted in the center comes out clean, about 35 minutes. Cool on a rack and dust with the confectioners' sugar. Serve warm or at room temperature. *–Abigail Johnson Dodge*

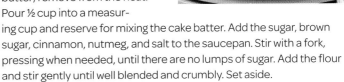

Coffee Cake Basics

• Keep ingredients at room temperature. It's easier to blend them this way, with less risk of overmixing and ending up with a tough cake.

• Make sure the butter is softened so it's easier to beat in air. Along with baking powder, it's air bubbles that help leaven the cake and create a light texture.

• Measure your ingredients carefully, and weigh the dry ingredients. A common reason cake recipes don't turn out is because of imprecise measuring.

• Go easy on the mixing. Follow the recipe directions: "Mix until just incorporated" is meant to ensure a tender crumb.

• Cool all cakes on a rack. This helps air circulate and will keep the cake from getting soggy on the bottom.

steamed coriander–gingerbread cake with eggnog crème anglaise

MAKES TWO 9-INCH CAKES;
EACH SERVES 8 TO 10

Nonstick cooking spray, for the cake pans

17	oz. (3¾ cups) unbleached all-purpose flour
1	Tbs. baking soda
1	Tbs. ground ginger
1½	tsp. ground cinnamon
1½	tsp. ground cloves
1¼	tsp. table salt
6	oz. (generous 1 cup) pitted dates, chopped into ¼-inch pieces
2	Tbs. plus 1 tsp. whole coriander seeds
6	oz. (¾ cup) unsalted butter, at room temperature
¾	cup granulated sugar
1½	cups molasses
3	large eggs, at room temperature
3	oz. (¾ cup) walnut halves, toasted and coarsely chopped

Eggnog Crème Anglaise (recipe on p. 14)

Though the steaming process leaves the cake pleasantly moist straight from the oven, it is also delicious a day or two later, after the spices have had a chance to meld. Spiked with bourbon, rum, and grated nutmeg, the holiday-inspired cream sauce has a velvety consistency; for the most luxurious texture, make it a day ahead.

1. Bring a large kettle of water to a boil—you'll need 1½ cups for the cake batter and about 2 quarts for the steaming pan.

2. Position one rack in the center of the oven and another beneath it in the lowest slot. Set a 10x15x2-inch baking pan or Pyrex® dish on the lower rack and fill the pan halfway with boiling water. Heat the oven to 350°F. Lightly coat two 9x2-inch round cake pans with cooking spray and line the bottoms with parchment. Apply another light coat of cooking spray to the parchment.

3. Sift the flour, baking soda, ginger, cinnamon, cloves, and salt into a large bowl. Stir to combine. Put the chopped dates in a small bowl with 3 Tbs. of the flour mixture. Pull apart any date pieces that may be stuck together and toss to evenly coat with the flour.

4. Crush the coriander seeds with a mortar and pestle or in a spice grinder. Alternatively, seal the seeds in a zip-top plastic bag and use a rolling pin to crush them finely.

5. Put the softened butter in the bowl of a stand mixer fitted with a paddle attachment. Cream the butter on medium speed until very soft and smooth. Gradually add the sugar and continue to beat on medium speed until light and fluffy, about 2 minutes. Stop the mixer and scrape down the sides of the bowl with a spatula. Add the molasses and beat again on medium speed just until evenly incorporated. Add the eggs one at a time, mixing for about 10 seconds after each addition and scraping down the bowl as needed between additions. The batter will look broken.

6. Measure out 1½ cups boiling water. Turn the mixer to very low speed or, if you prefer, do all remaining mixing by hand. Alternate adding the flour mixture and the boiling water in five additions, beginning and ending with the flour. Mix just until each addition is incorporated, as overmixing will lead to a tougher cake—it's fine if the batter looks slightly lumpy. Stir in the reserved date-flour mixture, crushed coriander seeds, and chopped walnuts. The batter will be quite loose.

7. Divide the batter equally between the two prepared cake pans. Set both pans on the center rack and bake until a toothpick inserted in the center of each cake comes out clean, 40 to 55 minutes. Let the cakes cool in their pans for about 10 minutes and then invert them onto cooling racks and peel off the parchment. (Allow the water-filled baking pan to cool in the oven until it can be safely moved without spilling.)

8. Serve the cakes warm or at room temperature. Cut each cake into 8 to 10 slices and serve each piece with 2 to 3 Tbs. of the Eggnog Crème Anglaise. *–Julia Usher*

PER SERVING (BASED ON 20 SERVINGS): 430 CALORIES | 6G PROTEIN | 57G CARB | 20G TOTAL FAT | 11G SAT FAT | 5G MONO FAT | 3G POLY FAT | 1125MG CHOL | 380MG SODIUM | 2G FIBER

continued on p. 14

Make Ahead

If baking ahead, wrap the cakes tightly in plastic while they are still slightly warm to the touch. (Any trapped steam will condense, adding moisture to the cakes.) Store the cakes for up to a week at room temperature.
To reheat, remove the plastic, put the cakes on a cookie sheet, and cover them loosely with foil. Heat them in a 300°F oven until warmed through, 15 to 20 minutes.

eggnog crème anglaise

MAKES ABOUT 2¼ CUPS,
ENOUGH SAUCE FOR
TWO 9-INCH CAKES

- 2 **cups heavy cream**
- ½ **cup granulated sugar**
- 4 **large egg yolks**
- ⅛ **tsp. table salt**
- 1 **Tbs. dark rum**
- 1 **Tbs. bourbon**
- 1 **tsp. freshly grated nutmeg**
- 1 **tsp. pure vanilla extract**

Make Ahead

The sauce can be stored in the refrigerator in a tightly sealed container for 2 to 3 days. Cover the surface of the sauce with plastic wrap to prevent a skin from forming.

1. Set a medium metal bowl in a large bowl of ice water and have a fine sieve at the ready.

2. Combine the cream and sugar in a 3-quart saucepan. Set the pan over medium heat, stirring occasionally to encourage the sugar to dissolve. Heat the mixture through but do not allow it to boil. Remove from the heat.

3. Put the egg yolks and salt in a small heatproof bowl and gently whisk to break up the yolks. Gradually whisk in ½ cup of the warm cream mixture. Pour the yolk mixture into the cream remaining in the saucepan and whisk to combine.

4. Cook over medium-low heat, stirring constantly with a clean wooden or heatproof plastic spoon until the custard thickens slightly, enough to coat the back of the spoon and hold a line drawn through it with a finger, 4 to 8 minutes. An instant-read thermometer should register 170° to 175°F. Do not let the sauce overheat or boil, or it will curdle. Immediately strain the sauce through the sieve into the bowl set in the ice-water bath.

5. Gently whisk in the rum, bourbon, nutmeg, and vanilla extract. Stir the sauce occasionally until cool, 20 to 30 minutes. Transfer it to another container, if you like, and cover the surface of the sauce with plastic to prevent a skin from forming. Wrap the container tightly with more plastic and refrigerate for a minimum of 2 hours, until velvety and slightly thick.

Checking Ground Spices for Freshness

Because the flavor of dried spices fades over time, using a fresh spice can mean the difference between a pleasantly spicy dessert and one that's downright bland. To make sure dried spices are as fresh as possible when you buy them and that they stay fresh, follow these simple steps:

- **Check for freshness.** Choose those with the most distant expiration dates, ideally 6 months away or more.

- **Throw away old spices.** Discard bottled spices if they have been open longer than 6 months.

- **Store spices properly.** Though you might be tempted to store spices (ground or whole) in pretty containers above your stovetop, where they're handy, they will stay fresh longer in a cool, dark cabinet or a corner of your refrigerator.

sour cream coffee cake with toasted pecan filling

SERVES 16

FOR THE STREUSEL TOPPING

- 2 oz. (4 Tbs.) unsalted butter
- 3 oz. (⅔ cup) unbleached all-purpose flour
- ¼ cup toasted pecans, coarsely chopped
- 2 Tbs. granulated sugar
- 2 Tbs. light brown sugar
- ½ tsp. ground cinnamon
- ¼ tsp. baking powder
- ¼ tsp. table salt

FOR THE FILLING

- 1 cup toasted pecans
- 3 Tbs. granulated sugar
- 3 Tbs. light brown sugar
- 1½ tsp. ground cinnamon
- 1 tsp. Dutch-processed or natural cocoa powder

FOR THE CAKE

- 10 oz. (1¼ cups) unsalted butter, slightly softened; more for the pan
- 11¼ oz. (3 cups) sifted cake flour
- 1½ tsp. baking powder
- 1 tsp. baking soda
- ¾ tsp. table salt
- 11½ oz. (1⅔ cups) superfine sugar
- 4 large eggs
- 2 tsp. pure vanilla extract
- 16 oz. (2 cups) sour cream

Every cook needs to know how to make a killer sour cream coffee cake, and this one is it. It bakes up moist and buttery and looks impressive to boot. Superfine sugar has tiny, uniform crystals that help produce a fine crumb. If you can't find it at the market, you can make your own by grinding granulated sugar in a food processor for 30 to 40 seconds.

MAKE THE TOPPING

In a 2-quart saucepan, heat the butter over medium heat until almost melted. Remove from the heat and let cool to tepid. In a medium bowl, combine the flour, pecans, both sugars, cinnamon, baking powder, and salt and stir with a fork. Add the flour mixture to the butter and stir until evenly moistened and crumbly.

MAKE THE FILLING

In a food processor, pulse the pecans, both sugars, cinnamon, and cocoa 4 to 6 times to combine and chop the pecans.

MAKE THE CAKE

1. Position a rack in the center of the oven and heat the oven to 350°F (325°F if using a dark nonstick pan). Generously butter a 10-inch tube pan with a removable bottom.

2. In a medium bowl, whisk the cake flour, baking powder, baking soda, and salt. In a stand mixer fitted with the paddle attachment (or in a large bowl, using a hand-held mixer), beat the butter on medium speed until smooth and creamy, 1 to 2 minutes. Add the superfine sugar slowly, beating until combined. Scrape the bowl. Beat in the eggs one at a time, blending each one completely before adding the next. Scrape the bowl and blend in the vanilla. On low speed, alternate adding flour and the sour cream, adding the flour in four parts and the sour cream in three parts, beginning and ending with the flour, and scraping the bowl as needed.

3. Spoon 2 generous cups of the batter into the prepared pan. Smooth with the back of a soupspoon, spreading the batter to the side of the pan first and then to the center. Sprinkle about ½ cup of the filling evenly over the batter. Cover the filling with about 2 cups of batter, dropping dollops around the pan and smoothing with the spoon. Sprinkle another ½ cup filling evenly over the batter and cover with

continued on p. 16

2 more cups batter. Layer on the remaining filling and then the remaining batter. (You'll have four layers of batter and three layers of filling.)

4. Insert a table knife 1 inch from the side of the pan straight into the batter going almost to the bottom. Run the knife around the pan two times, without lifting up the blade, spacing the circles about 1 inch apart. Smooth the top with the back of the soupspoon.

5. Take a handful of the streusel crumbs and squeeze firmly to form a large mass. Break up the mass into smaller clumps, distributing the streusel evenly over the batter. Repeat with the remaining streusel. Press the streusel lightly into the surface of the cake.

6. Bake until the top of the cake is golden brown, the sides are beginning to pull away from the pan, and a wooden skewer inserted into the center of the cake comes out clean, 70 to 75 minutes. Transfer to a wire rack and let cool for at least an hour before removing from the pan. *–Carole Walter*

PER SERVING: 500 CALORIES | 6G PROTEIN | 51G CARB | 32G TOTAL FAT | 16G SAT FAT | 10G MONO FAT | 3G POLY FAT | 115MG CHOL | 300MG SODIUM | 2G FIBER

techniques for success

Master these three key techniques for impressive results.

LAYER THE BATTER AND FILLING Layers are key to this cake's great flavor and sublime appearance. There are four layers of batter and three of filling. Using a large soupspoon for the batter, start by smoothing it to the sides of the pan and then work toward the center tube. Don't lift the spoon, or you'll disturb the filling.

MARBLE THE BATTER Once the layers are complete, run a table knife through the batter in two circles around the tube, spacing them about an inch apart, without lifting up the blade. This distributes the filling but still keeps it clearly defined.

FORM THE STREUSEL For the topping, form streusel clumps by squeezing the mixture together and breaking the mass into smaller pieces to sprinkle evenly over the top of the batter. Press the streusel lightly into the batter.

buttermilk cake with spiced vanilla icing

SERVES 10 TO 12

FOR THE CAKE

¼	lb. (½ cup) unsalted butter, softened; more for the pan
13½	oz. (3 cups) unbleached all-purpose flour; more for the pan
1½	cups granulated sugar
½	cup canola oil
2	large eggs
1	Tbs. distilled white vinegar
2	tsp. pure vanilla extract
1	tsp. baking soda
1	tsp. table salt
½	tsp. ground ginger
¼	tsp. freshly grated nutmeg
¾	cup buttermilk
2¼	cups peeled and grated butternut squash (about 8 oz.)

FOR THE ICING

9	oz. (2¼ cups) confectioners' sugar
3	Tbs. buttermilk; more as needed
1	tsp. pure vanilla extract
¼	tsp. freshly grated nutmeg
¼	tsp. table salt
¼	cup finely chopped crystallized ginger

The secret to this moist, tender cake is grated butternut squash, which is folded into the batter just before baking. Use the large holes on a box grater to grate the squash.

MAKE THE CAKE

1. Position a rack in the center of the oven and heat the oven to 325°F. Butter and flour a 10-cup Bundt pan; tap out excess flour.

2. In a large bowl using a hand-held mixer or in a stand mixer fitted with the paddle attachment, beat the butter and sugar on medium speed until well combined, about 1 minute. Add the oil and beat until combined, about 15 seconds. Add the eggs one at a time, mixing well on low speed. Add the vinegar and vanilla and mix again until just combined. Add half of the flour and the baking soda, salt, ginger, and nutmeg, mixing on low speed until just combined. Add half of the buttermilk and mix until just combined. Repeat with the remaining flour and buttermilk.

3. Stir the grated squash into the batter and transfer the batter to the prepared pan; smooth the top with a rubber spatula. Bake until a cake tester inserted in the center comes out clean, about 1 hour. Cool on a wire rack for 30 minutes; then carefully invert the cake onto the rack and remove the pan. When the cake is completely cool, transfer it to a serving plate.

MAKE THE ICING

In a medium bowl, whisk the confectioners' sugar, buttermilk, vanilla, nutmeg, and salt until smooth. Add more buttermilk, a few drops at a time, as needed, until the icing is pourable but still quite thick. Pour the icing back and forth in thick ribbons over the cooled cake. Sprinkle the crystallized ginger on top. Let the icing set at room temperature, about 45 minutes, before serving. *–Liz Pearson*

PER SERVING: 510 CALORIES | 5G PROTEIN | 80G CARB | 19G TOTAL FAT | 6G SAT FAT | 8G MONO FAT | 3G POLY FAT | 60MG CHOL | 380MG SODIUM | 2G FIBER

Make Ahead

This cake can be made a day or two in advance. After the icing has set, wrap the cake in plastic and refrigerate. Bring to room temperature before serving.

chocolate nut upside-down cake

SERVES 8 TO 10

FOR THE TOPPING

- ¾ **cup packed dark brown sugar**
- 2½ **oz. (5 Tbs.) unsalted butter**
- 3 **Tbs. water**
- 1¼ **cups toasted assorted unsalted nuts**

FOR THE CAKE

- 6 **oz. (1⅓ cups) unbleached all-purpose flour**
- 1½ **oz. (½ cup) unsweetened natural cocoa powder**
- ¾ **tsp. baking powder**
- ¼ **tsp. baking soda**
- ¼ **tsp. table salt**
- 5 **oz. (10 Tbs.) unsalted butter, at room temperature**
- 1 **cup granulated sugar**
- 1 **tsp. pure vanilla extract**
- 3 **large eggs**
- ½ **cup buttermilk**

For the toasted nuts, use a mixture of whole hazelnuts (roughly chopped after toasting and skinning), slivered almonds, and large walnut pieces. This cake is easiest to cut with a serrated knife at room temperature. It's still delicious a day after baking.

MAKE THE TOPPING

In a small saucepan, combine the brown sugar, butter, and water. Cook over medium heat, stirring often, until the butter is melted and the mixture is smooth. Bring to a boil and pour into the prepared pan, swirling to coat the bottom evenly. Scatter in the nuts evenly and gently press them in.

MAKE THE CAKE

1. Heat the oven to 350°F and lightly butter the sides of a 9x2-inch round cake pan.

2. Sift together the flour, cocoa powder, baking powder, baking soda, and salt. In a medium bowl, beat the butter with an electric mixer until smooth. Gradually add the sugar; continue beating until fluffy. Beat in the vanilla. Add the eggs one at a time, beating briefly after each addition. Sprinkle half of the flour mixture over the butter and mix on low speed just until the flour disappears. Add the buttermilk and mix until just blended. Gently mix in the remaining flour. Scoop spoonfuls of batter onto the nuts and gently spread the batter evenly in the pan. Lightly tap the pan on the counter to settle the ingredients.

3. Bake until a pick inserted in the center comes out clean, about 45 minutes. Immediately run a paring knife around the inside edge of the pan. Set a flat serving plate on top of the pan and invert the cake. Let the inverted pan rest for about 3 minutes to let the topping settle. Gently remove the pan and serve slightly warm or at room temperature. *–Abigail Johnson Dodge*

PER SERVING (BASED ON 10 SERVINGS): 490 CALORIES | 8G PROTEIN | 56G CARB | 28G TOTAL FAT | 12G SAT FAT | 11G MONO FAT | 3G POLY FAT | 110MG CHOL | 150MG SODIUM | 3G FIBER

sour cream pound cake

MAKES 1 LARGE BUNDT CAKE;
SERVES 8 TO 10

Nonsticking cooking spray

11¼ oz. (2½ cups) **unbleached all-purpose flour; more for the pan**

2 tsp. **baking powder**

½ tsp. **table salt**

½ lb. (1 cup) **unsalted butter, slightly softened (70°F)**

2½ cups **granulated sugar**

5 **large eggs, at room temperature**

1 tsp. **pure vanilla extract**

2 tsp. **pure almond extract**

½ tsp. **pure coconut extract**

1 cup **sour cream**

½ cup **golden raisins or currants (optional)**

The three extracts used here create an intriguingly delicious flavor. You can make this cake with only the vanilla, but try the recipe first as written.

1. Position a rack in the center of the oven and heat the oven to 300°F. Spray a large (10- to 12-cup) Bundt pan with a nonstick spray and dust with flour.

2. Whisk together the flour, baking powder, and salt until well blended. In stand mixer fitted with the paddle attachment, beat the butter until it's very pale and little tails have formed. Sprinkle in the sugar and beat well until slightly fluffy. Scrape the sides of the bowl well. Add the eggs one at a time, beating until blended before adding the next. Add the extracts and sour cream; mix well. With the mixer on low, add the flour and mix until it's almost incorporated but not quite. Switch from the mixer to a stiff rubber spatula and fold until the batter is well blended and smooth, taking care to scrape the bowl's bottom and sides. Gently fold in the raisins or currants, if using.

3. Scrape the batter into the prepared pan and bake until the cake is golden brown and a toothpick comes out with just a few crumbs clinging to it when inserted in the center, 60 to 75 minutes. Baking time will vary depending on pan size and depth, so start checking at about 50 minutes. Let the cake cool for about 15 minutes and then invert it onto a large plate or platter, tapping the pan to release the cake. Slide the cake onto a rack and let cool completely before serving. *–Carolyn Weil*

PER SERVING (BASED ON 10 SERVINGS): 560 CALORIES | 7G PROTEIN | 76G CARB | 26G TOTAL FAT | 15G SAT FAT | 8G MONO FAT | 1G POLY FAT | 165MG CHOL | 210MG SODIUM | 1G FIBER

lemon buttermilk pound cake

MAKES ONE 8X5-INCH LOAF;
SERVES 10

Nonstick cooking spray

6¾ oz. (1½ cups) unbleached all-purpose flour

1 tsp. baking powder

½ tsp. table salt

¼ lb. (½ cup) unsalted butter, slightly softened (70°F)

1 cup granulated sugar

2 large eggs, at room temperature

½ cup buttermilk

Zest of 1 lemon, finely chopped or grated

Juice of 1 lemon

3 to 4 Tbs. confectioners' sugar

A little buttermilk improves the flavor and texture of this favorite traditional cake.

1. Position a rack in the center of the oven and heat the oven to 325°F. Spray a loaf pan that's about 8x5x3 inches with nonstick spray.

2. Whisk together the flour, baking powder, and salt until well blended. In a stand mixer fitted with the paddle (or in a large bowl, using a hand-held mixer), beat the butter until it's very pale and little tails have formed. Sprinkle in the sugar and beat well until slightly fluffy. Scrape the sides of the bowl well. Add the eggs one at a time, beating until blended before adding the next. With the mixer on low, add about one-third of the flour and mix until almost combined; then add half the buttermilk and mix until just combined. Repeat with another third of flour, then the last half of the buttermilk, ending with the last third of the flour. Just before all the flour is incorporated, switch from the mixer to a stiff rubber spatula, add the lemon zest, and slowly stir to blend in the flour and zest, taking care to scrape the bowl's bottom and sides.

3. Scrape the batter into the prepared pan and bake until the cake is golden brown and a toothpick comes out with just a few crumbs clinging to it when inserted in the center, 45 to 50 minutes. Let the cake cool for about 10 minutes; as it's cooling, stir together the lemon juice and confectioners' sugar. Carefully invert the loaf pan, tap it to release the cake, and then brush the syrup on the cake while it's still warm. Cool completely on a rack before serving. *–Carolyn Weil*

PER SERVING (BASED ON 10 SERVINGS): 260 CALORIES | 4G PROTEIN | 38G CARB | 11G TOTAL FAT | 6G SAT FAT | 3G MONO FAT | 1G POLY FAT | 70MG CHOL. | 170MG SODIUM | 1G FIBER

cream cheese and wild blueberry pound cake

MAKES ONE 8X5-INCH LOAF; SERVES 10

	Nonsticking cooking spray
6¾	oz. (1½ cups) unbleached all-purpose flour
½	tsp. baking powder
½	tsp. table salt
3	oz. cream cheese, at room temperature
¼	lb. (½ cup) unsalted butter, slightly softened (70°F)
1½	cups granulated sugar
4	large eggs, at room temperature
1	tsp. pure vanilla extract
1	tsp. finely grated lemon zest
1	cup wild blueberries

This cake makes a wonderful breakfast bread, as well as a dessert or tea cake. Its moist texture makes slicing easy. Most grocery stores carry frozen wild blueberries. Don't let them thaw or the juices will streak the batter.

1. Position a rack in the center of the oven and heat the oven to 325°F. Spray a loaf pan that's about 8x5x3 inches with nonstick spray.

2. Whisk together the flour, baking powder, and salt until well blended. In a stand mixer fitted with the paddle attachment (or in a large bowl, using a hand-held mixer), beat the cream cheese and butter until very pale and little tails have formed. Sprinkle in the sugar and beat well until slightly fluffy. Scrape the sides of the bowl well. Add the eggs one at a time, beating until blended before adding the next. With the mixer on low, add the flour, vanilla, and lemon zest and mix until almost incorporated but not quite. Switch from the mixer to a stiff rubber spatula and mix just until the batter is well blended and smooth, taking care to scrape the bowl's bottom and sides. Gently fold in the berries.

3. Scrape the batter into the loaf pan and bake until the cake is golden brown and a toothpick comes out with just a few crumbs clinging to it when inserted in the center, 60 to 65 minutes if using fresh berries, 75 to 90 minutes if using frozen. Let the cake cool for about 15 minutes and then invert the pan and lightly tap it to release the cake. Cool completely on a rack before serving. *–Carolyn Weil*

PER SERVING (BASED ON 10 SERVINGS): 340 CALORIES | 5G PROTEIN | 47G CARB | 14G TOTAL FAT | 8G SAT FAT | 4G MONO FAT | 1G POLY FAT | 120MG CHOL | 180MG SODIUM | 1G FIBER

pumpkin and cornmeal cake
with orange syrup

SERVES 10

FOR THE CAKE

- 8 oz. (1 cup) unsalted butter, at room temperature; more for the pan
- 1 cup granulated sugar
- 1 Tbs. finely grated orange zest
- 1 large egg
- 2 large eggs, separated
- 8 oz. (1 cup) canned pure solid-pack pumpkin (not pumpkin pie filling)
- 1 tsp. pure vanilla extract
- 6¾ oz. (1½ cups) unbleached all-purpose flour
- 2 tsp. baking powder
- ¼ tsp. table salt
- ½ cup (3¼ oz.) fine-ground yellow cornmeal (don't use coarse)
- Sifted confectioners' sugar, for garnish (optional)

FOR THE SYRUP AND FOR SERVING

- ½ cup fresh orange juice (from 1 to 2 medium juice oranges)
- ½ cup granulated sugar
- Vanilla yogurt or vanilla ice cream (optional)

This moist cake is equally good first thing in the morning (with vanilla yogurt) and last thing in the evening (with vanilla ice cream). The syrup can be made up to a week ahead.

MAKE THE CAKE

1. Position a rack in the center of the oven and heat the oven to 350°F. Butter a 9-inch Bundt pan. In a stand mixer fitted with the paddle attachment (or in a large bowl, using a hand-held mixer), beat the butter, sugar, and orange zest until light and fluffy, about 3 minutes. One at a time, add the egg and egg yolks (reserve the whites), beating well and scraping the sides of the bowl after each addition. Beat in the pumpkin and vanilla.

2. Sift together the flour, baking powder, and salt; stir in the cornmeal. Add this mixture to the pumpkin batter in three stages, stirring gently but thoroughly with a rubber spatula after each addition; don't over-work the batter.

3. In a clean bowl with a clean whisk or hand-held mixer, whip the reserved egg whites until they hold soft peaks. Gently fold the whites into the batter with the spatula until you no longer see streaks of white. Scrape the batter into the prepared pan; smooth the surface. Bake until the top of the cake is springy when lightly touched, the sides are beginning to pull away from the pan, and a wooden skewer inserted into the center of the cake comes out clean, 40 to 50 minutes. Let cool in the pan for 10 minutes and then invert the cake onto a wire rack to cool completely. Dust the cake with sifted confectioners' sugar, if you like.

MAKE THE SYRUP AND SERVE

In a small saucepan over low heat, combine the orange juice and sugar, stirring until the sugar has dissolved. Increase the heat to medium high. Boil without stirring for 2 minutes. (If you make the syrup ahead, be sure to warm it gently before serving.) Serve each slice of cake drizzled with syrup and, if you like, accompanied by a scoop of vanilla yogurt or vanilla ice cream. *–Regan Daley*

PER SERVING: 410 CALORIES | 5G PROTEIN | 54G CARB | 20G TOTAL FAT | 12G SAT FAT | 6G MONO FAT | 1G POLY FAT | 115MG CHOL | 180MG SODIUM | 2G FIBER

> At the market, be sure you buy pure solid-pack pumpkin, not pumpkin pie filling, which is sweetened, seasoned, and often contains additives.

espresso gingerbread cake

- **10 oz. (1¼ cups) unsalted butter, softened at room temperature; more for the pan**
- **11 oz. (2½ cups) unbleached all-purpose flour; more for the pan**
- **½ cup dark molasses (not blackstrap)**
- **½ cup very strong brewed coffee or espresso, cooled to just warm**
- **2 tsp. baking powder**
- **½ tsp. table salt**
- **¼ tsp. baking soda**
- **1 Tbs. instant espresso powder**
- **2 tsp. ground ginger**
- **½ tsp. ground cinnamon**
- **⅛ tsp. ground or freshly grated nutmeg**
- **⅛ tsp. ground cloves**
- **1¼ cups packed light brown sugar**
- **3 large eggs plus 2 large egg yolks, at room temperature**
- **Espresso Glaze (optional; recipe below)**

There's no tedious assembly of cake layers or finicky butter-creams required for this gorgeous make-ahead dessert. In fact, this cake is perfectly elegant with a dusting of confectioners' sugar or a simple glaze. It also makes a wonderful hostess gift.

1. Position a rack in the center of the oven and heat the oven to 350°F. Butter and flour a 10- or 12-cup Bundt pan (or four 2-cup mini loaf pans). Tap out any excess flour.

2. In a liquid measuring cup, whisk the molasses with the brewed coffee. Sift the flour with the baking powder, salt, baking soda, espresso powder, ginger, cinnamon, nutmeg, and cloves.

3. In a stand mixer fitted with the paddle attachment (or in a large bowl, using a hand-held mixer), cream the butter in a large bowl on medium speed until smooth, about 1 minute. Add the brown sugar and beat until light and fluffy, about 2 minutes. Beat in the eggs and yolks one at a time, stopping to scrape the bowl after each addition. With the mixer on low speed, alternate adding the flour and coffee mixtures, beginning and ending with the flour. Stop the mixer at least one last time to scrape the bowl and then beat at medium speed until the batter is smooth, about 20 seconds.

4. Spoon the batter into the prepared pan (or pans), spreading it evenly with a rubber spatula. Run a knife through the batter to eliminate any air pockets. Bake until a wooden pick inserted in the center comes out clean, about 40 minutes (about 30 minutes for mini loaves). Set the pan on a rack to cool for 15 minutes. Invert the cake onto the rack, remove the pan, and let cool until just barely warm. Drizzle with the glaze (if using) and then let cool to room temperature before serving. If you're making the cake ahead, wrap it while still barely warm without the glaze. If you plan to freeze the cake, don't glaze it until you're ready to serve. *–Nicole Rees*

espresso glaze

- **1 cup confectioners' sugar**
- **1 tsp. dark rum (optional)**
- **1½ Tbs. brewed espresso (or 1½ tsp. instant espresso powder dissolved in 1½ Tbs. hot water)**

Combine the confectioners' sugar and rum (if using) in a bowl and, adding the espresso gradually, whisk until smooth. If necessary, add more espresso or water to thin the glaze to a drizzling consistency. When the cake is still barely warm, use a fork or spoon to drizzle the glaze over the top.

cranberry streusel pound cake

MAKES ONE 8½-INCH LOAF;
SERVES 10

Nonstick cooking spray
or butter, for the pan

Unbleached all-purpose
flour, for the pan

FOR THE STREUSEL

¼ cup walnut pieces
(about 1 oz.)

2 Tbs. light or dark brown
sugar

¼ tsp. ground cinnamon

FOR THE CAKE

6¾ oz. (1½ cups) unbleached
all-purpose flour

1 tsp. baking powder

¼ tsp. table salt

1 tsp. finely grated
orange zest

¼ lb. (½ cup) unsalted butter,
softened at room
temperature

1 cup granulated sugar

2 large eggs, at room
temperature

1 tsp. pure vanilla extract

½ cup buttermilk

2¾ oz. (½ cup) dried
cranberries, lightly chopped

FOR THE ICING

¼ cup confectioners' sugar

2 tsp. heavy cream;
more if needed

⅛ tsp. ground cinnamon

This tender loaf is perfect for brunch or as a treat with a cup of tea. The loaf can be wrapped well and stored in the refrigerator for up to a week or in the freezer up to a month.

MAKE THE STREUSEL

Position a rack in the center of the oven and heat the oven to 325°F. Grease an 8½x4½-inch loaf pan with the spray and dust with flour, tap out any excess. Put the walnuts, brown sugar, and cinnamon in a food processor. Pulse until the walnuts are chopped into small pieces.

MAKE THE CAKE

1. In a medium bowl, whisk the flour, baking powder, salt, and orange zest until well blended. In a stand mixer fitted with the paddle attachment, beat the butter on medium speed until smooth, about 1 minute. Sprinkle in the sugar and beat well until slightly fluffy, about 2 minutes, scraping the bowl well. Add the eggs one at a time, mixing well after each addition. Beat in the vanilla. With the mixer on low, add about a third of the flour mixture and mix until almost combined; add half of the buttermilk and mix again until just combined. Repeat with another third of the flour, the last half of the buttermilk, and then the remaining flour, mixing each time until just combined. Stir in the dried cranberries with a rubber spatula.

2. With the spatula, spread half of the batter into the loaf pan and sprinkle evenly with the walnut streusel. Spread on the remaining batter. Bake until the loaf is golden brown and a skewer inserted in the center comes out clean, 60 to 75 minutes. Let cool in the pan on a rack for 10 minutes, turn out of the pan, and let cool completely on the rack.

MAKE THE ICING

In a small bowl, mix the confectioners' sugar, cream, and cinnamon with a small spoon until there are no lumps. The icing should drizzle smoothly in a thin line from the tip of the spoon; you may need to add up to another 1 tsp. cream. Drizzle the icing over the cake in thin parallel lines and let set for about 15 minutes before serving. Slice gently with a serrated knife. *–Carolyn Weil*

orange–poppyseed pound cake

12 oz. (1½ cups) **unsalted
butter, softened at room
temperature; more for
the pan**

12 oz. (2⅔ cups) **unbleached
all-purpose flour;
more for the pan**

1½ tsp. **baking powder**

½ tsp. **table salt**

⅓ cup **poppyseeds**

2½ cups **granulated sugar**

4 tsp. **finely grated
orange zest**

8 oz. **cream cheese,
softened at room
temperature**

6 **large eggs plus 2 large egg
yolks, at room temperature**

1 tsp. **pure vanilla extract**

**Orange Glaze (optional)
(recipe on the facing page)**

*The glaze strengthens the citrus flavor of this cake, but if you don't
want to add it, instead lightly sift confectioners' sugar over the cake
right before serving.*

1. Position a rack in the center of the oven and heat the oven to 350°F.
Butter and flour two 9x5x3-inch loaf pans (or eight 5¾x3-inch mini
loaf pans, each with a 2-cup capacity). Tap out any excess flour.

2. In a medium bowl, sift together the flour, baking powder, and salt;
whisk in the poppyseeds. Put the sugar and orange zest in a food processor and pulse for 20 seconds.

3. In a stand mixer fitted with the paddle attachment (or in a large
bowl, using a hand-held mixer), beat the butter and cream cheese
on medium speed until smooth and creamy, about 2 minutes. Add
the sugar and beat until light and fluffy, about 1 minute. Beat in the
whole eggs one at a time, stopping the mixer to scrape the bowl after
each addition. Beat in the egg yolks and vanilla. With the mixer on low
speed, slowly add the flour mixture. Stop the mixer at least one last
time to scrape the bowl and then beat at medium speed until the
batter is smooth, about 10 seconds.

4. Spoon the batter into the prepared pan(s), spreading it evenly with
a rubber spatula. Run a knife through the batter to eliminate any air
pockets or tap the pan lightly against the counter. Bake until a wooden
skewer inserted in the center comes out with only a few moist crumbs
clinging to it, about 50 minutes (25 to 30 minutes for mini loaves). Set
the pan on a rack to cool for 10 minutes. Remove the cake from the
pan; brush while warm with the glaze, if using, following the instructions on the facing page. Serve at room temperature. *–Nicole Rees*

orange glaze

⅔ **cup fresh orange juice**

⅓ **cup granulated sugar**

1 **Tbs. orange liqueur, such as Cointreau®**

Strain the orange juice into a small saucepan and bring to a boil over high heat. Stir in the sugar and continue to cook until the mixture thickens and is reduced to a scant ½ cup, 3 to 4 minutes. Remove from the heat and stir in the liqueur. Brush the tops and sides of the cake while it's still warm. Repeat brushing every few minutes until all the glaze has been used. Let the cake cool before serving.

moist apple crumb cake

SERVES 16

FOR THE TOPPING

- ¼ lb. (½ cup) unsalted butter
- ½ cup firmly packed light brown sugar
- ½ cup granulated sugar
- 1¼ tsp. ground cinnamon
- 4½ oz. (1 cup) unbleached all-purpose flour
- ¼ cup confectioners' sugar
- 4 oz. (1 cup) whole walnuts, coarsely chopped

FOR THE CAKE

- 3 oz. (6 Tbs.) unsalted butter, softened at room temperature; more for the pan
- 9 oz. (2 cups) unbleached all-purpose flour
- 1 tsp. baking powder
- 1 tsp. baking soda
- ¾ tsp. ground cinnamon
- ½ tsp. table salt
- 1¼ cups granulated sugar
- 2 large eggs, at room temperature
- ¾ cup smooth homemade or store-bought applesauce
- 1 cup sour cream

Applesauce makes this cake wonderfully moist, while the walnut crumb topping adds a welcome crunch. Homemade applesauce is best, but store-bought is good, too.

MAKE THE TOPPING

Melt the butter in a medium bowl in the microwave (or in a skillet and pour into a medium bowl). Add the brown sugar, granulated sugar, and cinnamon and stir until blended. Add the flour, confectioners' sugar, and the walnuts, mixing with your fingers until well combined; the mixture should be crumbly but also clump together. Refrigerate until ready to use.

MAKE THE CAKE

1. Position a rack in the center of the oven and heat the oven to 350°F. Butter the bottom and sides of a 9x13-inch baking pan. Line the bottom of the pan with parchment and butter the parchment.

2. In a medium bowl, whisk the flour, baking powder, baking soda, cinnamon, and salt to blend.

3. Combine the butter and sugar in a large bowl. Beat with a hand-held mixer on medium speed until combined (but not fluffy), scraping the bowl as needed, about 30 seconds. Add the eggs, one at a time, beating until combined and scraping the bowl as needed.

4. Add about one-third of the flour mixture, mixing on medium low until combined. Add the applesauce, mixing on medium low until incorporated and scraping the bowl as needed. Mix in another third of the flour mixture, then the sour cream, and then the remaining flour mixture, mixing after each addition until just incorporated. Don't overmix. Scrape the batter into the prepared pan and spread it evenly.

5. Bake until the edges of the cake are slightly set and the rest is very jiggly, about 15 minutes. Scatter the walnut topping evenly over the cake and bake until the crumbs are golden brown, the center of the cake springs back when lightly touched, and a toothpick inserted in the center has a few moist crumbs sticking to it, 30 to 35 minutes; check the cake early and if the crumbs are golden but the cake isn't fully baked, cover loosely with foil. Let cool on a rack for at least 20 minutes. Serve warm. *–Wendy Kalen*

PER SERVING (BASED ON 16 SERVINGS): 380 CALORIES | 5G PROTEIN | 51G CARB | 18G TOTAL FAT | 9G SAT FAT | 4G MONO FAT | 4G POLY FAT | 65MG CHOL | 200MG SODIUM | 2G FIBER

coffee–cocoa snack cake

MAKES ONE 9-INCH-SQUARE
CAKE; SERVES 16

- 5 oz. (10 Tbs.) very soft unsalted butter; more for the pan
- 7¼ oz. (1½ cups plus 2 Tbs.) unbleached all-purpose flour; more for the pan
- 1⅔ cups granulated sugar
- 2 large eggs, at room temperature
- 1 tsp. pure vanilla extract
- ½ tsp. table salt
- 2½ oz. (½ cup plus ⅓ cup) unsweetened natural cocoa powder (not Dutch-processed)
- 1 tsp. baking soda
- 1 tsp. baking powder
- 1½ cups good-quality brewed coffee, cooled to warm

The coffee in the recipe intensifies the chocolate flavor of this super-moist cake. Use a freshly ground, medium-bodied variety, such as Colombian. For a decadent treat, drizzle pieces of the cake with a little warm ganache.

1. Position a rack in the center of the oven and heat the oven to 350°F. Generously butter a 9-inch-square baking pan. Line the bottom of the pan with a square of parchment, butter the parchment, and then flour the bottom and sides of the pan. Tap out any excess flour.

2. If mixing by hand, put the softened butter and sugar in a medium bowl. Using a wooden spoon, cream them until smooth, about 1 minute. Switch to a whisk and blend in the eggs, one at a time. Stir for another 30 seconds, until the batter is smooth and the sugar begins to dissolve. (If using a stand mixer, put the butter and sugar in the bowl and, using the paddle attachment, cream until smooth, about 1 minute. Blend in the eggs one at a time, mixing just until incorporated, about 20 seconds. Then switch to a whisk and blend in the rest of the ingredients by hand.) Mix in the vanilla and salt. Sift the flour, cocoa, baking soda, and baking powder directly onto the batter. Pour in the coffee. Gently whisk the ingredients until the mixture is smooth and mostly free of lumps.

3. Pour the batter into the prepared pan, spreading it evenly with a rubber spatula. Bake until a skewer inserted in the center comes out with only moist crumbs clinging to it, 40 to 43 minutes. Set the pan on a rack to cool for 20 minutes. Carefully run a knife around the edges of the pan, invert the cake onto the rack, and remove the pan. Invert again onto another rack and let cool right side up until just warm. Serve immediately or wrap in plastic and store at room temperature for up to 5 days. *–Nicole Rees*

brown-butter banana cake with chocolate chips

- 8 oz. (1 cup) unsalted butter; more for the pan

- 7½ oz. (1⅔ cups) unbleached all-purpose flour; more for the pan

- 1½ cups granulated sugar

- 3 large eggs

- 1 cup finely mashed ripe bananas (2 medium bananas)

- 1 tsp. pure vanilla extract

- ½ tsp. table salt

- 1¼ tsp. baking soda

- ⅔ cup mini semisweet chocolate chips

*This one-bowl cake is great for brunch, snacking, or dessert.
If you like, dress it up by sifting confectioners' sugar over the top.*

1. Position a rack in the center of the oven and heat the oven to 350°F. Butter and flour a 10-cup decorative tube or bundt pan. Tap out any excess flour.

2. Melt the butter in a medium saucepan over medium-low heat. Once the butter is melted, cook it slowly, letting it bubble, until it smells nutty or like butterscotch and turns a deep golden hue, 5 to 10 minutes. If the butter splatters, reduce the heat to low. Remove the pan from the heat and pour the browned butter through a fine sieve into a medium bowl and discard the bits in the sieve. Let the butter cool until it's very warm rather than boiling hot, 5 to 10 minutes.

3. Using a whisk, stir the sugar and eggs into the butter. (Since the butter is quite warm, you can use cold eggs for this.) Whisk until the mixture is smooth (the sugar may still be somewhat grainy), 30 to 60 seconds. Whisk in the mashed bananas, vanilla, and salt. Sift the flour and baking soda directly onto the batter. Pour the chocolate chips over the flour. Using a rubber spatula, stir just until the batter is uniformly combined. Don't overmix.

4. Spoon the batter into the prepared pan, spreading it evenly with the rubber spatula. Bake until a skewer inserted in the center comes out with only moist crumbs clinging to it, 42 to 45 minutes. Set the pan on a rack to cool for 15 minutes. Invert the cake onto the rack and remove the pan. Let cool until just warm and then serve immediately or wrap well in plastic and store at room temperature for up to 5 days. *–Nicole Rees*

sweet potato spice cake with fresh ginger and pecan streusel topping

This cake is incredibly moist, thanks to the sweet potato, and the fresh ginger adds a vibrancy that other spice cakes can only dream of.

FOR THE TOPPING

- 3 oz. (⅔ cup) unbleached all-purpose flour
- ½ cup very firmly packed light brown sugar
- ½ cup chopped toasted pecans
- ⅛ tsp. table salt
- 2 oz. (¼ cup) unsalted butter, melted; more as needed

FOR THE CAKE

- ¾ cup vegetable oil; more for the pan
- 7½ oz. (1⅔ cups) unbleached all-purpose flour; more for the pan
- 1½ cups very firmly packed light brown sugar
- 3 large eggs, at room temperature
- 1 cup baked, mashed sweet potato, at room temperature or slightly warmer (from about one 15-oz. sweet potato)
- 1 Tbs. molasses
- 1 Tbs. finely grated fresh ginger
- ¾ tsp. table salt
- ¼ tsp. ground cinnamon
- ¼ tsp. ground cardamom
- ⅛ tsp. freshly grated nutmeg or ¼ tsp. ground nutmeg
- 1½ tsp. baking soda

MAKE THE TOPPING

In a small bowl, stir the flour, brown sugar, pecans, and salt. Drizzle the melted butter over the dry ingredients and stir until well combined. The streusel should feel clumpy, not sandy, when gently squeezed between your fingertips. If the streusel seems dry, add more melted butter.

MAKE THE CAKE

1. Position a rack in the center of the oven and heat the oven to 350°F. Lightly oil and flour a 9-inch-square baking pan; tap out excess flour.

2. In a medium bowl, combine the oil, brown sugar, and eggs and, using a whisk, stir until the mixture is smooth and the sugar begins to dissolve, 30 to 60 seconds. If the sugar forms lumps, break them up with your fingers; a few tiny lumps are fine. Whisk in the mashed sweet potato, molasses, grated ginger, salt, cinnamon, cardamom, and nutmeg. Sift the flour and baking soda directly onto the batter. Using a whisk or rubber spatula, combine the ingredients until well blended and almost smooth.

3. Pour the batter into the prepared pan, spreading it evenly with the spatula. Sprinkle the streusel evenly over the batter, creating small clumps as you go by squeezing the streusel between your fingers. Bake until a skewer inserted in the center comes out with only moist crumbs clinging to it, about 45 minutes. Set the pan on a rack to cool for 15 minutes. Run a knife around the edge of the pan. Let cool until just warm and then cut into squares and serve from the pan, or wrap well in plastic. Store at room temperature for up to a week.

–Nicole Rees

Baking a Sweet Potato

Baking and mashing a sweet potato is easy. Heat the oven to 450°F. Prick the skin of the sweet potato several times with a fork, set the potato directly on the oven rack, and bake until very tender, about 1 hour. (If you're in a hurry, prick a large sweet potato with a fork, set on a paper towel, and microwave on high until tender, about 5 minutes.) When the potato is cool enough to handle, peel off the skin and smash the flesh in a bowl with a masher, or whisk until smooth.

vanilla and sour cream pound cake with vanilla glaze

Vanilla beans and their tiny seeds lend an especially intense flavor and heavenly aroma to any dessert. Here, we've got double the vanilla; the seeds are incorporated in both the cake and the glaze, creating not only delicious flavor, but also a beautifully speckled thick glaze.

SERVES 12

FOR THE CAKE

- ½ lb. (1 cup) unsalted butter, softened at room temperature; more for the pan
- 13½ oz. (3 cups) unbleached all-purpose flour; more for the pan
- 2½ tsp. baking powder
- ¼ tsp. baking soda
- ½ tsp. table salt
- 1½ cups granulated sugar
- Seeds scraped from ¾ vanilla bean, or 2½ tsp. pure vanilla extract
- 6 large eggs
- 1 cup sour cream

FOR THE GLAZE

- 4 oz. (1 cup) confectioners' sugar, sifted if lumpy
- 3 Tbs. heavy cream; more as needed
- 1 Tbs. light corn syrup
- Seeds scraped from ¼ vanilla bean, or ½ tsp. pure vanilla extract

MAKE THE CAKE

1. Position a rack in the center of the oven and heat the oven to 325°F. Butter and lightly flour the bottom and sides of a 10-cup fluted tube pan.

2. In a medium bowl, combine the flour, baking powder, baking soda, and salt; whisk until well blended. In a stand mixer fitted with a paddle attachment (or using a large bowl and a hand-held mixer), beat the butter on medium-high speed until smooth, 1 minute. Add the sugar and vanilla bean seeds or extract and continue beating until well combined and fluffy, 2 minutes. Stop to scrape the bowl as needed. Add the eggs, one at a time, beating well for 30 seconds and then stopping to scrape the bowl after each addition. Add half of the flour mixture and mix on low speed until just blended. Add the sour cream and mix until just blended. Add the remaining flour mixture and beat on low speed until just blended.

3. Scrape the batter into the prepared pan and spread evenly with a rubber spatula. Bake until the top of the cake is light brown and a cake tester or toothpick inserted in the center comes out with just a few small crumbs attached, 50 to 55 minutes.

4. Transfer the cake pan to a rack and let cool for about 15 minutes. If necessary, run a knife between the cake and the pan to loosen the cake. Invert the cake onto the rack and lift off the pan. Set the rack over a large sheet of waxed paper or foil (to catch the glaze later) and let the cake cool completely.

GLAZE THE CAKE

In a small bowl, combine the confectioners' sugar, heavy cream, corn syrup, and vanilla bean seeds or extract. Stir until well blended, smooth, and shiny. The glaze should be thick but fluid enough to fall from a spoon. If it isn't, add more cream, 1 tsp. at a time, until the glaze thins to the right consistency. Spoon the glaze evenly over the top of the cake. The glaze should form thick ribbons that drip down the sides of the cake. If the glaze resists dripping on its own, use the back of the spoon to encourage it. Let the glaze set for at least 1 hour before serving. Store loosely covered at room temperature for up to 3 days. (The cake can also be frozen unglazed.) *–Abigail Johnson Dodge*

PER SERVING (BASED ON 12 SERVINGS): 490 CALORIES | 7G PROTEIN | 62G CARB | 24G TOTAL FAT | 14G SAT FAT | 7G MONO FAT | 1G POLY FAT | 160MG CHOL | 290MG SODIUM | 1G FIBER

pumpkin–pecan cake with brown sugar and bourbon glaze

SERVES 10 TO 12

FOR THE CAKE

- ¼ lb. (½ cup) unsalted butter, softened; more for the pan
- 13½ oz. (3 cups) unbleached all-purpose flour; more for the pan
- 2 tsp. baking powder
- 2 tsp. ground ginger
- 2 tsp. ground cinnamon
- 1¼ tsp. kosher salt
- 1 tsp. baking soda
- ½ tsp. freshly grated nutmeg
- ⅛ tsp. ground cloves
- ¾ cup buttermilk
- 3 Tbs. bourbon or Cognac
- 1½ tsp. pure vanilla extract
- ½ cup vegetable oil
- 2½ cups packed dark brown sugar
- 4 large eggs, at room temperature
- 1 15-oz. can pure solid-pack pumpkin purée
- 4 oz. (1 cup) pecan halves, toasted and chopped

This cake's warm spices are complemented by bourbon or Cognac and the crunch of sweet candied pecans. Bake the cake at least a day ahead to let the flavors deepen.

MAKE THE CAKE

1. Position a rack in the center of the oven and heat the oven to 350°F. Generously butter and flour a 10- to 12-cup tube pan.

2. In a medium bowl, sift together the flour, baking powder, ginger, cinnamon, salt, baking soda, nutmeg, and cloves. In a measuring cup, combine the buttermilk, bourbon, and vanilla.

3. In a stand mixer fitted with the paddle attachment, beat the butter on medium speed until creamy. Gradually add the oil, beating until combined. Add the brown sugar. Increase the mixer speed to high and beat, scraping down the sides of the bowl as needed, until light and fluffy, about 4 minutes. Add the eggs one at a time, beating well on medium-high speed after each addition. Beat in the pumpkin.

4. Reduce the speed to low, slowly pour in the buttermilk mixture, and mix until combined. Gradually add the dry ingredients to the batter, mixing just until combined. Use a rubber spatula to fold in the pecans. Scrape the batter into the prepared pan, smooth the top, and tap the pan on the counter once or twice to settle the batter.

5. Bake until a wooden skewer inserted into the center of the cake comes out with just a few moist crumbs clinging to it, 45 to 55 minutes. Leave the oven on. Cool the cake in the pan on a rack for 10 to 15 minutes and then invert the cake onto the rack, remove the pan, and let cool completely, at least 3 hours.

Make Ahead

For the best flavor and texture, make the cake at least 1 day before serving. To store at room temperature, set the completely cooled unglazed cake on a plate, wrap tightly in 2 layers of plastic wrap, and store for up to 2 days. Up to 10 hours before serving, unwrap and glaze the cake. Serve at room temperature. To freeze, set the completely cooled unglazed cake on a 10-inch cardboard cake round. Wrap tightly in 2 layers of plastic wrap and then in foil. Freeze for up to 1 week. Up to 10 hours before serving, remove the foil but not the plastic wrap from the cake. When completely thawed, unwrap and glaze the cake. Make the candied pecans up to 1 week ahead and store in an airtight container.

FOR THE CANDIED PECANS

- **2 Tbs. packed dark brown sugar**
- **1½ tsp. mild honey, such as clover**
- **3 oz. (¾ cup) pecan halves**
- **Vegetable oil, for the pan**

FOR THE GLAZE

- **¾ cup packed light or dark brown sugar**
- **¼ lb. (½ cup) unsalted butter**
- **2 Tbs. light corn syrup**
- **1½ Tbs. bourbon**
- **⅛ tsp. kosher salt**
- **⅓ cup heavy cream**
- **4 oz. sifted confectioners' sugar (1¼ cups)**
- **⅛ tsp. pure vanilla extract**

MAKE THE CANDIED PECANS

Heat the brown sugar, honey, and 1 Tbs. water in a 1-quart saucepan over medium heat, stirring until the sugar is dissolved. Add the pecans and stir until coated. Spread the pecans curved side up on an oiled rimmed baking sheet and bake in the 350°F oven until fragrant and shiny, 7 to 10 minutes. Transfer the pecans with a metal spatula to parchment to crisp and cool completely, about 20 minutes.

GLAZE THE CAKE

1. Set the cake on a rack over a rimmed baking sheet.

2. In a 3-quart saucepan, combine the brown sugar, butter, corn syrup, bourbon, and salt. Cook over medium heat, stirring, until the butter melts and the sugar dissolves, about 2 minutes. Add the cream, raise the heat to high, and bring to a boil, stirring occasionally. Continue to boil, stirring occasionally, for exactly 1 minute. Remove from the heat. Gently whisk in the confectioners' sugar and the vanilla until completely smooth. Let stand until the glaze is thick enough to coat the back of a spoon but still warm and pourable, 3 to 8 minutes. If a skin forms, gently stir it back into the glaze with a spatula; don't overstir or the glaze may crystallize.

3. Pour the glaze slowly and evenly over the cake. Decorate with the candied pecans while the glaze is warm. When the glaze is set, after about 15 minutes, transfer the cake to a serving plate. *–Jill O'Connor*

PER SERVING: 820 CALORIES | 8G PROTEIN | 105G CARB | 42G TOTAL FAT | 14G SAT FAT | 16G MONO FAT | 9G POLY FAT | 115MG CHOL | 370MG SODIUM | 4G FIBER

blueberry–lemon cornmeal cake

SERVES 8 TO 10

- 3 oz. (6 Tbs.) unsalted butter, at room temperature; more for the pan
- 6 oz. (1⅓ cups) unbleached all-purpose flour; more for the pan
- ¼ cup (1½ oz.) finely ground yellow cornmeal
- 1 tsp. baking powder
- ¼ tsp. baking soda
- ¼ tsp. table salt
- 1 cup granulated sugar
- 1 tsp. finely grated lemon zest
- 2 large eggs
- 1 Tbs. fresh lemon juice
- ½ cup buttermilk

FOR THE TOPPING

- 1 cup (about 5 oz.) fresh blueberries, rinsed and well dried
- 1 Tbs. granulated sugar
- 1 Tbs. unbleached all-purpose flour

The combination of cornmeal and buttermilk offers both texture and tang.

1. Position a rack in the center of the oven and heat the oven to 350°F. Lightly butter a 9x2-inch round cake pan. Line the bottom with a parchment round cut to fit the pan, lightly flour the sides, and tap out the excess.

2. In a medium bowl, whisk the flour, cornmeal, baking powder, baking soda, and salt until well blended. In a stand mixer fitted with the paddle attachment (or in a large bowl, using a hand-held mixer), beat the butter, sugar, and lemon zest on medium high until well blended and fluffy, about 3 minutes. Add the eggs, one at a time, beating on medium speed until just blended and adding the lemon juice with the second egg (the batter will appear curdled; don't worry). Using a wide rubber spatula, fold in half the dry ingredients, then the buttermilk, and then the remaining dry ingredients. Scrape the batter into the prepared pan and spread evenly. Bake for 15 minutes.

3. Meanwhile, make the topping. Combine the blueberries, sugar, and flour in a small bowl. Using a table fork, mix the ingredients, lightly crushing the blueberries and evenly coating them with the flour and sugar. After the cake has baked for 15 minutes, slide the oven rack out and quickly scatter the blueberries evenly over the top of the cake (discard any flour and sugar that doesn't adhere to the berries). Continue baking until a toothpick inserted in the center of the cake comes out clean, another 23 to 25 minutes.

4. Let the cake cool on a rack for 15 minutes. Run a knife around the inside edge of the pan. Using a dry dishtowel to protect your hands, lay a rack on top of the cake pan and, holding onto both rack and pan, and invert the cake. Lift the pan from the cake. Peel away the parchment. Lay a flat serving plate on the bottom of the cake and flip the cake one more time so that the blueberries are on top. Serve warm or at room temperature. *–Abigail Johnson Dodge*

PER SERVING (BASED ON 10 SERVINGS): 240 CALORIES | 4G PROTEIN | 39G CARB | 8G TOTAL FAT | 5G SAT FAT | 2G MONO FAT | 0G POLY FAT | 60MG CHOL | 160MG SODIUM | 1G FIBER

glazed orange pound cake

SERVES 8

- 6 oz. (¾ cup) unsalted butter, softened; more for the pan
- 4 medium navel oranges (about 2 lb.)
- 9 oz. (2 cups) unbleached all-purpose flour
- 1½ tsp. baking powder
- ½ tsp. plus 1 pinch table salt
- 1¼ cups granulated sugar
- 3 large eggs
- 1 tsp. pure vanilla extract
- 5 oz. (1¼ cups) confectioners' sugar

This super-tender cake is packed with bright citrus flavor, thanks to orange zest and juice in the batter and a sweet orange glaze.

1. Position a rack in the center of the oven and heat the oven to 350°F. Butter a 9x5-inch loaf pan. Line the bottom of the pan with parchment and then butter the parchment.

2. Finely grate enough zest from the oranges to yield 2 Tbs., and then squeeze the oranges to yield 1 cup strained juice. Set aside ¼ cup juice for the glaze.

3. In a medium bowl, whisk the flour, baking powder, and ½ tsp. salt.

4. In a stand mixer fitted with the paddle attachment (or in a large bowl, using a hand-held mixer), beat the butter and sugar on medium-high speed until light and fluffy, about 2 minutes. Add the eggs one at a time, beating on medium speed until incorporated and scraping down the bowl as necessary. Add the vanilla and orange zest and beat until incorporated (the mixture may look curdled). With the mixer on low, alternately add the flour mixture in 3 additions, and the remaining ¾ cup orange juice in 2 additions, beginning and ending with the flour.

5. Scrape the batter into the prepared pan, smooth the top, then tap the pan on the counter a couple of times to pop any air pockets. Bake until a tester inserted in the center of the cake comes out clean, 45 minutes to 1 hour. Let the cake cool in its pan on a rack for 10 minutes, run a knife around the sides, then invert it onto the rack. Remove the parchment and invert again.

6. In a medium bowl, whisk the reserved ¼ cup orange juice with the confectioners' sugar and the pinch of salt until smooth. Set the warm cake on its rack over a rimmed baking sheet (or a sheet of parchment). Using a toothpick, poke holes at ¾-inch intervals in the top of the cake, stopping about three-quarters of the way down the cake.

7. Repeatedly brush the glaze evenly over the top and sides of the cake until you've used it all. Let the cake cool completely, about 2 hours, before slicing and serving. (Store the cake at room temperature, wrapped in plastic, for up to 3 days.) *–Shelley Wiseman*

PER SERVING: 510 CALORIES | 6G PROTEIN | 77G CARB | 20G TOTAL FAT | 12G SAT FAT | 5G MONO FAT | 1G POLY FAT | 120MG CHOL | 270MG SODIUM | 1G FIBER

cinnamon-caramel-ganache layer cake
(recipe on p. 60)

layer cakes, cupcakes & other party cakes

vanilla layer cake with chocolate buttercream frosting and raspberry jam

SERVES 12

Nonstick cooking spray for the pans

10½ oz. (2¾ cups) cake flour

1½ cups granulated sugar

3¾ tsp. baking powder

¾ tsp. table salt

6 oz.(12 Tbs.) unsalted butter, cut into tablespoon-size pieces, at room temperature

¾ cup whole or low-fat milk, at room temperature

1½ tsp. pure vanilla extract

4 large eggs, at room temperature

¾ cup seedless raspberry jam or marmalade

3 Tbs. Chambord or other liqueur

1 recipe Chocolate Buttercream Frosting (recipe on the facing page)

Making stunning four-layer cakes isn't that difficult. Start with this reliable and versatile vanilla base cake and add the other components—fruity jam and smooth buttercream—to create an impressive and delicious dessert.

MAKE THE CAKE

1. Position a rack in the center of the oven and heat the oven to 350°F. Lightly coat two 9x2-inch round cake pans with nonstick cooking spray and line the bottoms with parchment.

2. Sift the cake flour, sugar, baking powder, and salt into the bowl of a stand mixer fitted with the paddle attachment. Mix on low speed until the ingredients are well combined.

3. Add the softened butter pieces and mix on low speed for 20 to 30 seconds to mix the butter into the dry ingredients—the mixture should look a little lumpy, with the largest lumps being about the size of a hazelnut. Add the milk and vanilla extract. Mix on medium speed for 1 minute to thoroughly blend the ingredients and aerate the batter. Scrape the sides of the bowl with a spatula.

4. Add the eggs one at a time, mixing on medium speed for about 15 seconds after each addition. Scrape down the bowl after the second egg.

5. Divide the batter equally between the two prepared pans. Use a small offset spatula or spoon to spread the batter evenly in each pan. Bake until the cakes are golden brown and the tops feel firm but spring back a little when tapped lightly with a finger, and a pick inserted in the center of the cake comes out clean, 30 to 35 minutes. Set the pans on a rack, run a table knife around the edge of each cake, and let them cool in the pans for 30 minutes. Invert the cakes onto the rack, lift the pans, peel off the parchment, and let the cakes cool completely before filling and frosting.

ASSEMBLE THE CAKE LAYERS

1. Level the cakes, if necessary, and slice each cake into two layers, making a total of four layers of cake.

2. In a small bowl, stir together the jam and liqueur. Place the bottom layer on a flat serving platter or a cake stand lined with strips of waxed paper to keep it clean while assembling the cake. Top the layer with a scant 1½ cups buttercream, spreading it evenly with a metal cake spatula almost to the cake's edge. Spread a third of the jam on the next cake layer, then lay it, jam side down, over the buttercream filling. Repeat with the next two layers.

FROST THE CAKE

1. Apply a light coat of frosting (called crumb coating) to seal the cake crumbs in: Spoon about ½ cup buttercream into a small bowl. Spread it in a very thin layer over the entire cake with a small metal cake spatula. You should be able to see the cake layers through the icing. Chill the cake for about 20 minutes or until the icing is firm.

2. Spread the icing thickly and evenly over the entire cake with a large metal cake spatula. Don't worry about getting a smooth, perfect finish; just make sure the cake is completely covered and the frosting is spread uniformly. You shouldn't be able to see the layers underneath the buttercream.

3. With the back of a teaspoon, smear the icing and pull it upward to form curls and swirls over the entire cake. *–Katherine Eastman Seeley*

PER SERVING: 800 CALORIES | 7G PROTEIN | 80G CARB | 52G TOTAL FAT | 32G SAT FAT | 14G MONO FAT | 2G POLY FAT | 205MG CHOL | 350MG SODIUM | 0G FIBER

chocolate buttercream frosting

MAKES 7½ TO 8 CUPS, ENOUGH TO FILL AND FROST A 9-INCH FOUR-LAYER CAKE

5	large egg whites
1¼	cups granulated sugar
½	cup plus 2 Tbs. light corn syrup
1	lb. 4 oz. (2½ cups) unsalted butter, at room temperature
12	oz. bittersweet chocolate, melted

1. Place the egg whites in the clean bowl of a stand mixer fitted with the whisk attachment and whisk on medium-high speed until foamy. Sprinkle in 6 Tbs. of the sugar and beat on high speed to medium peaks (the whites should be smooth, full, and shiny, and the peaks should curl a little). Turn off the mixer.

2. Combine the remaining ¾ cup plus 2 Tbs. sugar and the corn syrup in a medium (3-quart) saucepan over medium-high heat, stirring briefly to dissolve the sugar. Continue to cook just until the mixture comes to a rolling boil.

3. Immediately remove the syrup from the heat, turn the mixer onto medium-high speed, and slowly pour the syrup down the side of the bowl in a steady stream, being very careful not to let the syrup hit the whisk.

4. Reduce the speed to medium and continue whisking until the whites are barely warm, 5 to 7 minutes. Add the butter 1 Tbs. at a time. Add the melted chocolate and continue beating until the frosting is smooth and creamy.

mocha chip cupcakes with chocolate–sour cream frosting

3 oz. unsweetened chocolate, chopped

4½ oz. (1 cup) unbleached all-purpose flour

½ tsp. baking soda

¼ tsp. table salt

¼ lb. (½ cup) unsalted butter, at room temperature

1 cup granulated sugar

2 large eggs

1½ tsp. pure vanilla extract

2 tsp. instant espresso powder, dissolved in ½ cup cool water

4 oz. (⅔ cup) semisweet chocolate chips

Chocolate–Sour Cream Frosting (recipe on the facing page)

The popular flavor combination of coffee and chocolate inspired these cupcakes.

1. Position a rack in the lower third of the oven and heat the oven to 350°F. Line 12 standard-size muffin cups with paper liners.

2. Put the unsweetened chocolate in the top of a double boiler or in a metal bowl set over a small saucepan of barely simmering water. Stir occasionally until the chocolate is melted and smooth. Set aside to cool slightly.

3. Sift the flour, baking soda, and salt into a small bowl. In a stand mixer fitted with the paddle attachment (or in a large bowl, using a hand-held mixer) beat the butter on medium speed until the butter is smooth, 30 to 60 seconds. With the mixer running, slowly pour in the sugar. Stop the mixer, scrape the bowl and beaters, and then beat on medium-high speed until the mixture is light and fluffy, 2 to 3 minutes. Beat in the eggs, one at a time, on medium speed, beating until the batter is smooth after each addition (about 30 seconds). Scrape the bowl after each addition. Add the vanilla and melted chocolate (which may be slightly warm) and beat until smooth and blended. On low speed, add the dry ingredients in three installments, alternating with the espresso in two additions, mixing after each addition only until the batter is smooth. Stir in the chocolate chips by hand.

4. Portion the batter evenly among the prepared muffin cups. (Use two rounded soupspoons: one to pick up the batter, one to push it off.) Don't smooth the batter. Bake until the cupcakes spring back when gently pressed in the center, 20 to 22 minutes. Let them cool in the tin for 5 minutes on a wire rack. Carefully remove the cupcakes from the tin, set them on the rack, and let cool completely.

5. Put a generous spoonful of the frosting on top of each cupcake and use the back of the spoon to spread and swirl it. Let the frosting set for about 30 minutes before serving. *–Greg Patent*

PER CUPCAKE: 280 CALORIES | 4G PROTEIN | 34G CARB | 15G TOTAL FAT | 9G SAT FAT | 4G MONO FAT | 1G POLY FAT | 55MG CHOL | 135MG SODIUM | 2G FIBER

tips for tender cupcakes

• When mixing cupcake batter, it's important to beat the butter and sugar thoroughly. This creates tiny air bubbles that will expand and help the batter rise. When adding dry ingredients, beat only enough to incorporate them; overbeating may toughen the cupcakes.

• Line muffin tins with cupcake liners, which make it easier to remove the cupcakes from the pan and also give the cupcakes a portable casing.

• To prevent overbaking, test the cupcakes for doneness at the minimum baking time. If you're not sure of your oven's temperature, check it with an oven thermometer.

chocolate–sour cream frosting

MAKES ABOUT 1¼ CUPS

- 2 oz. unsweetened chocolate, chopped
- 1 Tbs. unsalted butter
- ⅓ cup sour cream (not low-fat)
- ¾ tsp. pure vanilla extract
- Pinch of salt
- 6 oz. confectioners' sugar (1½ cups, spooned and leveled)
- Milk, if necessary

1. Put the chocolate and butter in the top of a double boiler or in a metal bowl set over a small saucepan of barely simmering water. Stir occasionally until the chocolate mixture is melted and smooth. Set aside to cool until barely warm.

2. In a medium bowl, whisk the sour cream, vanilla, and salt to blend. Gradually whisk in the confectioners' sugar until smooth. Add the chocolate mixture and beat it in with the whisk until the frosting is smooth and creamy. The frosting must be thick and spreadable. If it's too thick, thin it with droplets of milk. If it's too thin, chill it briefly, stirring occasionally, until adequately thickened.

bite-size ginger cupcakes with lemon–cream cheese frosting

4 oz. (1 cup plus 3 Tbs.) sifted cake flour

1 tsp. ground ginger

¼ tsp. freshly grated nutmeg

¼ tsp. table salt

¼ tsp. baking soda

⅛ tsp. baking powder

3 oz. (6 Tbs.) unsalted butter, at room temperature

⅔ cup granulated sugar

½ tsp. pure vanilla extract

1 1-inch cube (¾-oz. peeled piece) fresh ginger, finely grated (plus any juice)

4 tsp. lightly packed, finely grated lemon zest

1 large egg, at room temperature

½ cup sour cream (not low-fat), at room temperature

¼ cup (about 1 oz.) finely chopped crystallized ginger

Lemon–Cream Cheese Frosting (recipe on the facing page)

Candied lemon peel, for garnish (optional)

Ginger is available in many forms—fresh, ground, and crystallized—and this cupcake combines them all. The lemon–cream cheese frosting helps to balance the intense flavor of the ginger.

1. Position a rack in the center of the oven and heat the oven to 350°F. Line three miniature muffin pans (with 12 cups each) with miniature paper cupcake liners.

2. Sift the cake flour with the ground ginger, nutmeg, salt, baking soda, and baking powder. Whisk to ensure thorough mixing. In a stand mixer fitted with the paddle attachment (or in a large bowl, using a hand-held mixer), beat the butter on medium speed until smooth, about 1 minute. Add 3 Tbs. of the sugar, the vanilla, grated ginger, and lemon zest; beat on medium speed for 1 minute. Add the remaining sugar, about 2 Tbs. at a time, beating for a few seconds after each addition. Scrape the bowl and beat for another 2 minutes. Scrape the bowl again. Add the egg and beat on medium high until very smooth, about 1 minute.

3. Add about one-third of the flour mixture and stir gently with a rubber spatula only until incorporated. Add half the sour cream and stir until incorporated. Repeat with half of the remaining flour mixture, the rest of the sour cream, and ending with the last of the flour mixture. Stir in the crystallized ginger.

4. Portion the batter evenly among the prepared muffin cups, filling each cup about three-quarters full. (Use two regular teaspoons: one to pick up the batter and one to push it off.) Don't smooth the batter.

5. Arrange the pans in the oven so that there's a bit of space between them and bake until the cupcakes are pale golden and spring back when gently pressed in the center, 17 to 20 minutes. Let the cupcakes cool in the tins on wire racks for 5 minutes and then invert the pans onto the racks to remove the cupcakes. Immediately turn the cupcakes right side up on the racks and let cool completely.

6. Spoon a heaping teaspoonful of the frosting onto the center of each cupcake and spread and swirl it with the back of the teaspoon. Garnish with small slices of candied lemon peel, if desired.
–Greg Patent

PER CUPCAKE: 56 CALORIES | 0.5G PROTEIN | 7G CARB | 2.5G TOTAL FAT | 1.5G SAT FAT | 1G MONO FAT | 0G POLY FAT | 15MG CHOL | 30MG SODIUM | 0G FIBER

lemon–cream cheese frosting

MAKES 1¼ CUPS

- **5 oz. cream cheese (not low-fat or whipped), at room temperature**
- **2 Tbs. unsalted butter, at room temperature**
- **2 Tbs. lightly packed, finely grated lemon zest**
- **4 tsp. fresh lemon juice**
- **½ tsp. pure vanilla extract**
- **5 oz. confectioners' sugar (1¼ cups)**

In a medium bowl, beat the cream cheese with a hand-held electric mixer on medium speed until very smooth, about 30 seconds. Add the butter and beat until smooth, about 30 seconds. Beat in the lemon zest, lemon juice, and vanilla. On low speed, gradually add the confectioners' sugar, beating until smooth. Increase the speed to high and beat for just a few seconds, until the frosting is smooth and fluffy. Don't overbeat or you may thin the frosting.

chocolate-honey ganache layer cake

SERVES 16

FOR THE CAKE

Nonstick cooking spray

2¼ oz. (¾ cup) unsweetened natural cocoa powder

1½ oz. (½ cup) unsweetened Dutch-processed cocoa powder

1½ cups hot, strong brewed coffee

1 cup mild honey, such as clover

13½ oz. (3 cups) unbleached all-purpose flour

1½ tsp. baking powder

1½ tsp. baking soda

1 tsp. kosher salt

6 oz. (¾ cup) unsalted butter, softened

¾ cup vegetable oil

1 cup packed dark brown sugar

1 cup granulated sugar

4 large eggs, at room temperature

¾ cup sour cream, at room temperature

2 tsp. pure vanilla extract

The combination of natural and Dutch-processed cocoa powder, coffee, and mild honey gives this cake an incredibly moist texture and an intense, complex, and very grown-up chocolate flavor. Making the cake layers ahead allows the flavors to develop, and making the ganache ahead gives it time to firm up to the perfect texture for spreading.

MAKE THE CAKE

1. Position a rack in the center of the oven and heat the oven to 350°F.

2. Spray two 10-inch round cake pans (with at least 2-inch sides) with cooking spray and line the bottom of each with parchment.

3. Sift both cocoa powders into a medium bowl. Whisk in the coffee and then the honey. Let cool completely.

4. Sift the flour, baking powder, baking soda, and salt into a medium bowl.

5. In a stand mixer fitted with the paddle attachment, beat the butter on medium speed. Gradually add the oil, beating until combined. Add the brown sugar and granulated sugar. Raise the mixer speed to high and beat until light and fluffy, about 3 minutes. Add the eggs one at a time, beating well on medium-high speed after each addition. Add the sour cream and vanilla, beating just until combined.

6. With the mixer on low, alternately add the flour mixture in three additions and the cocoa mixture in two additions, beginning and ending with the flour (scrape down the sides of the bowl as necessary). Beat just until combined. Divide the batter between the two pans, using an offset spatula to spread it evenly. Tap the pans once or twice on the counter to settle the batter.

7. Bake, rotating the pans halfway through, until a wooden skewer inserted in the center of each cake comes out with only a few moist crumbs clinging to it, 40 to 50 minutes. Cool the cakes in their pans on a rack for 10 to 15 minutes. Run a knife along the sides of the pans, invert the cakes onto the rack, and remove the pans and the parchment. Let cool completely.

FOR THE CHOCOLATE-HONEY GANACHE

- **1 lb. semisweet chocolate (60% cacao), finely chopped**
- **2 cups heavy cream**
- **¼ cup mild honey, such as clover**
- **2 oz. (4 Tbs.) cold unsalted butter, cut into 4 pieces**
- **3 Tbs. dark rum (optional)**
- **1 tsp. pure vanilla extract**

FOR THE CHOCOLATE CURLS (OPTIONAL)

- **1 thick block semisweet chocolate**

MAKE THE GANACHE

1. Put the chocolate in a large heatproof bowl.

2. Combine the heavy cream and honey in a 2-quart saucepan. Stir with a silicone spatula over medium-high heat until the honey dissolves into the cream, about 30 seconds. Just as the cream comes to a simmer, remove it from the heat and pour it over the chocolate. Let stand for about 1 minute, then whisk until smooth. Whisk in the butter, rum (if using), and vanilla until the butter is melted and the mixture is glossy. Cool the ganache at room temperature for at least 8 hours. It will thicken as it cools. (The ganache can sit, covered, at room temperature for up to 24 hours.)

FROST THE CAKE

Set one of the cake layers on a serving plate. Spread about 1 cup ganache over the surface of the cake. Top with the second cake layer and spread a very thin layer of ganache over the top and sides of the cake to seal in any crumbs. Refrigerate for 5 to 10 minutes to allow the crumb coat to set. Spread the remaining ganache evenly over the top and sides of the cake.

MAKE THE CHOCOLATE CURLS

To decorate the cake with chocolate curls, if using, soften the chocolate in the microwave on high power for 30 to 50 seconds. Scrape a vegetable peeler firmly down one side of the chocolate block to form thick curls. Put the curls on a plate and refrigerate until they're firm enough to handle. Scatter over the top of the frosted cake.
–*Jill O'Connor*

PER SERVING: 760 CALORIES | 8G PROTEIN | 89G CARB | 46G TOTAL FAT | 22G SAT FAT | 15G MONO FAT | 6G POLY FAT | 125MG CHOL | 270MG SODIUM | 4G FIBER

Make ahead

For the best spreading texture, make the ganache 8 to 24 hours ahead. Keep covered at room temperature.

For the best flavor and texture, make the cake at least 1 day before serving. To store at room temperature, wrap each completely cooled layer tightly in two layers of plastic wrap and store for up to 2 days. Once filled and frosted, keep the cake at room temperature, covered with a dome, until ready to serve.

classic carrot cake with vanilla cream cheese frosting

FOR THE CAKE

- 1 cup canola, corn, or vegetable oil; more for the pans
- 2 cups (9 oz.) unbleached all-purpose flour; more for the pans
- 2 tsp. ground cinnamon
- 1¾ tsp. baking soda
- ¾ tsp. ground nutmeg
- ¾ tsp. ground ginger
- ¾ tsp. table salt
- 4 large eggs
- 2½ cups (8¾ oz.) lightly packed, finely grated carrots
- 2 cups packed light brown sugar
- ¾ cup chopped walnuts, toasted
- ½ cup raisins
- 1½ tsp. pure vanilla extract

FOR THE FROSTING

- 1 lb. cream cheese, softened
- 12 oz. (1½ cups) unsalted butter, softened
- 1 lb. (4 cups) confectioners' sugar
- 4 tsp. pure vanilla extract
- ¾ tsp. table salt

The flavors of this moist cake only improve with time, so feel free to bake and frost the cake up to a few days ahead.

MAKE THE CAKE

1. Position a rack in the center of the oven and heat the oven to 350°F. Lightly oil and flour the sides of two 9x2-inch round cake pans, tapping out any excess flour. Line the bottoms of the pans with parchment.

2. In a medium bowl, whisk the flour, cinnamon, baking soda, nutmeg, ginger, and salt. In a large bowl with a hand-held mixer or in a stand mixer fitted with the paddle attachment, mix the oil, eggs, carrots, brown sugar, walnuts, raisins, and vanilla on medium speed until well blended, about 1 minute. Add the dry ingredients and mix on low speed until just blended, about 30 seconds. Divide the batter evenly between the prepared pans.

3. Bake until the tops of the cakes spring back when lightly pressed and a cake tester inserted into the centers comes out clean, 28 to 30 minutes.

4. Let cool in the pans on a rack for 15 minutes. Run a knife around the inside edge of the pans to loosen the cakes, invert them onto the rack, remove the pans, and carefully peel away the parchment. Set the cakes aside to cool completely before frosting.

MAKE THE FROSTING

In a large bowl, beat the cream cheese and butter with the mixer on medium speed until very smooth and creamy, about 1 minute. Add the confectioners' sugar, vanilla, and salt and beat on medium high until blended and fluffy, about 2 minutes. Cover the frosting and set aside at room temperature until the layers are completely cool.

ASSEMBLE THE CAKE

1. Carefully set one cake layer upside down on a large, flat serving plate. Using a metal spatula, evenly spread about 1½ cups of the frosting over the top of the cake. Top with the remaining cake layer, upside down. Spread a thin layer (about ⅓ cup) of frosting over the entire cake to seal in any crumbs and fill in any gaps between layers. Refrigerate until the frosting is cold and firm, about 20 minutes. Spread the entire cake with the remaining frosting. For more tips on how to frost a layer cake, see the sidebar on p. 52.

2. Refrigerate the cake for at least 4 hours or up to 2 days. The cake is best served slightly chilled or at room temperature.
–Abigail Johnson Dodge

PER SERVING: 840 CALORIES | 8G PROTEIN | 86G CARB | 54G TOTAL FAT | 22G SAT FAT | 20G MONO FAT | 9G POLY FAT | 150MG CHOL | 550MG SODIUM | 2G FIBER

continued on p. 52

how to frost a cake

Knowing how to frost a layer cake can be both a blessing and a curse. On the one hand, it's not hard, and your friends will be impressed. On the other hand, everyone will want you to make them a birthday cake!

POSITION AND LEVEL YOUR CAKE Set a cake plate on a rotating cake stand or lazy Susan. Position your first layer of cake upside down on the plate. If necessary, level the cake layer with a long serrated knife. Slide strips of parchment or waxed paper under the edge of the cake to keep the plate clean as you frost.

FILL THE LAYERS Gently brush any crumbs from the cake. Using an offset spatula, spread the recommended amount of frosting across the surface of the cake in an even layer (don't worry about getting the surface perfectly smooth).

Place the second cake layer on the frosting, aligning the layers in a perfectly vertical column. If using split layers that were cut unevenly, match up the layers so the cake stays flat. If the cake is three or more layers, continue to fill between the layers, ending with the top layer unfrosted.

SEAL IN THE CRUMBS Frosting the cake is easier if you first seal the crumbs in a thin layer of frosting, called a crumb coat. With an offset spatula, spread about ½ cup of frosting in a thin, even layer all over the cake. Smooth any frosting protruding between the layers and use that extra frosting as part of the crumb coat. It's fine if the cake is still visible through the thin crumb coat. Refrigerate the cake to firm up the crumb coat, about 20 minutes.

FINISH WITH STYLE Spread the remaining frosting evenly over the chilled crumb coat. Once the cake is frosted, you can decorate the surface in a variety of ways, using a spoon or offset spatula to create swoops or stripes. If you prefer a smooth look, dip the spatula in hot water, wipe it dry, and hold it against the surface as you rotate the cake. Keep dipping the spatula in water and wiping it dry.

southern devil's food cake

FOR THE GANACHE

- 1 lb. semisweet chocolate (preferably 58% cacao), finely chopped
- 2 cups heavy cream
- 1 oz. (2 Tbs.) unsalted butter, softened

FOR THE CAKE

- 6 oz. (¾ cup) unsalted butter, softened; more for the pans
- 8 oz. (1¾ cups) unbleached all-purpose flour; more for the pans
- 2 cups packed dark brown sugar
- 2 tsp. pure vanilla extract
- 3 large eggs, at room temperature
- 2¼ oz. (¾ cup) unsweetened Dutch-processed cocoa powder
- 1¼ tsp. baking soda
- 1 tsp. baking powder
- 1 tsp. kosher salt
- 1½ cups buttermilk, preferably low fat, at room temperature
- ¼ cup mayonnaise

This four-layer Southern classic is made with cocoa powder, not chocolate, with a generous spoonful of mayonnaise in the batter to keep the cake moist and rich. A simple, luscious ganache of semisweet chocolate, cream, and butter does double duty as filling and frosting.

MAKE THE GANACHE

Put the chopped chocolate in a medium bowl. Bring the cream to a boil in a 2-quart saucepan over medium-high heat. Pour the hot cream directly over the chocolate and let it sit without stirring for 5 minutes. Using a whisk, stir in the center of the mixture in a small, tight circular motion until fully combined. Add the butter and stir until it is fully incorporated. Put a piece of plastic wrap directly onto the surface of the ganache and set aside at room temperature for at least 8 hours or overnight.

MAKE THE CAKE

1. Position a rack in the center of the oven and heat the oven to 350°F.

2. Butter two 8x2-inch round cake pans and line each with a parchment round. Butter the parchment, dust with flour, and tap out any excess.

3. In a stand mixer fitted with the paddle attachment, beat the butter, brown sugar, and vanilla on medium-high speed until lighter in color and slightly increased in volume, 3 to 5 minutes. Lower the speed to medium and add the eggs, one at a time, mixing until each is fully incorporated before adding the next.

4. Sift the flour, cocoa powder, baking soda, and baking powder onto a piece of parchment. Add the salt to the dry ingredients after sifting.

continued on p. 54

5. Using the parchment as a chute, add one-quarter of the dry ingredients to the batter and mix on low speed until incorporated. Add about ½ cup of the buttermilk and mix on low speed until incorporated. Continue to alternate dry ingredients and buttermilk, mixing until incorporated after each addition and stopping to scrape the bowl and beater as necessary. Using a whisk, fold the mayonnaise into the batter.

6. Divide the batter evenly between the prepared pans and bake until a toothpick inserted in the center of the cakes comes out clean and the sides of the cake have begun to pull away from the pan slightly, 40 to 45 minutes. Remove the pans from the oven and cool on a rack for 15 minutes. Invert the cakes onto the rack and remove the pans and parchment. Cool the cakes completely. (The cakes may be made 1 day ahead; wrap well and store at room temperature.)

ASSEMBLE THE CAKE

With a serrated knife, cut each cake in half horizontally. Put one of the base layers on a cake plate and tuck strips of waxed paper under the cake to keep the plate clean while icing the cake. Top the cake with about ⅓ cup of the ganache, spreading it evenly over the top. Add another cake layer, top with ganache, and repeat until the last layer is in place. Spread a thin layer of ganache over the top and sides of the cake and refrigerate for 15 minutes to seal in any crumbs. Spread the remaining ganache over the top and sides. Remove the waxed paper. The cake may be refrigerated, covered, for up to 2 days. Return to room temperature 2 hours before serving. *–David Guas*

PER SERVING: 890 CALORIES | 11G PROTEIN | 98G CARB, 53G TOTAL FAT | 30G SAT FAT | 15G MONO FAT | 4.5G POLY FAT | 175MG CHOL | 440MG SODIUM | 6G FIBER

What Is Dutch-processed Cocoa Powder?

In the mid-nineteenth century, a Dutch chocolate manufacturer came up with a process by which he could better control and standardize the color and flavor of cocoa. The process, which involves washing the cocoa (before or after grinding) in an alkaline solution, became known as Dutch-processing.

The resulting cocoa is consistently darker in color, mellower in flavor, and less acidic than the natural (non-alkalized) powder. In cakes and brownies, the Dutch-processed cocoas tend to produce moister and deeper colored baked goods—an advantage that makes it a favorite of many pastry chefs.

You can substitute natural cocoa powder for Dutch in most recipes (though not vice versa). Flavor and texture can be affected, but generally only in recipes calling for ¾ cup or more. Stored in a cool, dry place, cocoa powder will keep almost indefinitely.

caramel cupcakes with butterscotch frosting

MAKES 12 CUPCAKES

⅓ cup plus ¾ cup granulated sugar

6 oz. (1⅓ cups) unbleached all-purpose flour

½ tsp. baking powder

¼ tsp. table salt

¼ lb. (½ cup) unsalted butter, at room temperature

2 large eggs

1 tsp. pure vanilla extract

Butterscotch Frosting (recipe on p. 56)

1 cup finely chopped toasted pecans, or 12 toasted pecan halves (optional)

The burnt-sugar flavor of caramel pairs well with the mellow notes of the frosting. If you like, top the cupcakes with toasted chopped pecans (or pecan halves) to balance the sweetness.

1. Position a rack in the lower third of the oven and heat the oven to 350°F. Line 12 standard-size muffin cups with paper liners.

2. Bring ⅓ cup water to a boil in a small saucepan; keep very hot. Put the ⅓ cup sugar in a heavy-based 8-inch skillet or shallow saucepan. Set the pan over medium heat. Shake the pan to level the sugar and leave it alone until it's about half melted. Shake and swirl the pan to help the sugar melt completely. Cook the melted sugar, constantly swirling or stirring with a wooden spoon, until it bubbles and turns a deep reddish caramel color.

3. Immediately take the pan off the heat and carefully drizzle the boiling water over the caramel. The mixture will sputter. Return the pan to medium heat; stir constantly with the wooden spoon just until the caramel is completely dissolved. Pour the caramel into a heatproof liquid measuring cup. Pour about ⅓ cup water into the empty caramel pan and return to medium heat until very hot, stirring to dissolve any remaining caramel. Spoon enough of this liquid into the measuring cup with the caramel to bring the level up to ½ cup. Let cool until warm. (You can make the caramel hours or even a day ahead. When cool, cover and leave at room temperature.)

4. Sift the flour, baking powder, and salt into a small bowl. In a stand mixer fitted with the paddle attachment (or in a large bowl, using a hand-held mixer), beat the butter on medium speed until smooth, 30 to 60 seconds. With the mixer running, slowly pour in the remaining ¾ cup sugar, stop the mixer, and scrape the bowl and beaters. Beat on medium-high speed until light and fluffy, about 2 minutes. Beat in the eggs, one at a time, on medium speed until the batter is smooth, 30 to 60 seconds after each addition; scrape the bowl each time. Beat in the vanilla. On low speed, add the dry ingredients in three installments, alternating with the caramel. Mix only until the batter is smooth.

continued on p. 56

5. Portion the batter evenly among the prepared muffin cups. (Use two rounded soupspoons: one to pick up the batter, one to push it off.) Don't smooth the batter. Bake until the cupcakes are golden brown and spring back when gently pressed in the center, 18 to 20 minutes. Let the cupcakes cool in the tin for 5 minutes on a wire rack. Carefully remove the cupcakes from the tin, set them on the rack, and let cool completely.

6. Spoon a slightly heaping tablespoon of the frosting on top of each cupcake and use the back of the spoon to spread and swirl the frosting. If the frosting starts to stiffen, rewarm it briefly over medium-low heat until it's spreadable.

7. Holding a cupcake by its liner, dip it into the chopped pecans, if using, and turn it gently all around to coat the frosting thoroughly with the pecans. Alternatively, top with pecan halves, if using. Repeat with the remaining cupcakes. (Save any leftover pecans for another use.) Let the frosting set for about 30 minutes before serving.
–Greg Patent

PER CUPCAKE: 210 CALORIES | 2G PROTEIN | 30G CARB | 9G TOTAL FAT | 5G SAT FAT | 3G MONO FAT | 1G POLY FAT | 60MG CHOL | 75MG SODIUM | 0G FIBER

butterscotch frosting

MAKES ABOUT 1 CUP

- ¼ **cup unsalted butter**
- ⅓ **cup firmly packed dark brown sugar**
- ¼ **cup heavy cream; more as needed**
- 6 **oz. confectioners' sugar (1½ cups, spooned and leveled)**
- ½ **tsp. pure vanilla extract**

Melt the butter in a heavy 2- or 3-quart saucepan over medium-low heat. Add the brown sugar and stir almost constantly with a wooden spoon. After 2 to 3 minutes, the sugar will melt and smooth out, and the mixture will begin to bubble (it's all right if it still looks separated at this point). Once this happens, stir constantly for 2 minutes (less if the sugar smells like it's burning). Carefully add the ¼ cup cream and stir constantly for another 2 minutes. The mixture will thicken slightly and look smooth and glossy. Remove the pan from the heat and let cool for 5 minutes, stirring frequently. Beat in the confectioners' sugar and vanilla with the wooden spoon. If the frosting seems a little dry, beat in more cream, ½ Tbs. at a time, until it's thick, smooth, and spreadable.

brown butter pumpkin layer cake

SERVES 12

FOR THE CAKE

- 6 oz. (¾ cup) unsalted butter; more for the pans
- 9 oz. (2 cups) unbleached all-purpose flour; more for the pans
- 1½ tsp. baking soda
- 1½ tsp. ground cinnamon
- 1 tsp. ground ginger
- ¾ tsp. table salt
- ¼ tsp. ground cloves
- 1½ cups canned solid-pack pumpkin purée (not pumpkin pie filling)
- 1½ cups granulated sugar
- ⅔ cup firmly packed light brown sugar
- 2 large eggs
- ⅓ cup buttermilk

FOR THE TOPPING

- 1½ Tbs. unsalted butter
- ⅔ cup pecans
- ½ cup unsalted, raw, hulled pepitas
- 2 Tbs. firmly packed light brown sugar
- ¼ tsp. table salt
- 1½ Tbs. chopped crystallized ginger

continued on p. 58

A gingery glazed nut topping and brown-butter–spiked cream cheese frosting are the finishing touches for this spectacular spiced pumpkin cake. Double the topping if you want to pile on the nuts.

MAKE THE CAKE

1. Position a rack in the center of the oven and heat the oven to 350°F.

2. Butter and flour two 9-inch round cake pans with removable bottoms (or butter two 9-inch round cake pans, line the bottoms with parchment, butter the parchment, and flour the pans).

3. Melt the butter in a heavy-duty 1-quart saucepan over medium heat. Cook, swirling the pan occasionally until the butter turns a nutty golden brown, about 4 minutes. Pour into a small bowl and let stand until cool but not set, about 15 minutes.

4. In a medium bowl, whisk the flour, baking soda, cinnamon, ginger, salt, and cloves. In a large bowl, whisk the pumpkin purée with the granulated sugar, brown sugar, eggs, and buttermilk until very well blended. With a rubber spatula, stir in the flour mixture until just combined. Gently whisk in the brown butter until completely incorporated. Divide the batter evenly between the prepared pans.

5. Bake the cakes until a tester inserted in the center comes out clean, about 28 minutes. Let the cakes cool in the pans for 10 minutes. Turn the cakes out onto racks, remove the pan bottoms or parchment, and cool completely.

continued on p. 58

FOR THE FROSTING

- ¼ lb. (½ cup) unsalted butter
- 8 oz. cream cheese, at room temperature
- ¼ cup firmly packed light brown sugar
- 5 oz. (1¼ cups) confectioners' sugar

Make Ahead

The assembled, frosted cake can be covered with a cake dome and refrigerated for up to 2 days. Serve at room temperature.

MAKE THE TOPPING

Melt the butter in a heavy-duty 12-inch nonstick skillet over medium heat. Add the pecans and pepitas and cook until the pecans brown slightly and the pepitas begin to pop, about 2 minutes. Sprinkle in the brown sugar and salt and stir until the sugar melts and the nuts are glazed, about 2 minutes. Stir in the ginger. Remove from the heat and let the mixture cool in the skillet.

MAKE THE FROSTING AND ASSEMBLE THE CAKE

1. Melt the butter in a heavy-duty 1-quart saucepan over medium heat. Cook, swirling the pan occasionally, until the butter turns a nutty golden brown, about 4 minutes. Pour into a small bowl and let stand until the solids settle at the bottom of the bowl, about 5 minutes. Carefully transfer the bowl to the freezer and chill until just firm, about 18 minutes. Using a spoon, carefully scrape the butter from bowl, leaving the browned solids at the bottom; discard the solids.

2. Using an electric mixer, beat the butter, cream cheese, and brown sugar on medium-high speed until light in color and the brown sugar has dissolved, 2 minutes. Gradually beat in the confectioners' sugar and continue beating until fluffy, 1 to 2 minutes.

3. Put one cake layer on a cake plate. Spread ½ cup of the frosting on the layer. Sprinkle ½ cup of the nut mixture over the frosting and top with the second layer. Frost the top and sides of the cake with the remaining frosting. Arrange the remaining topping in a ring 1½ inches in from the edge of the cake.

4. Serve immediately or cover with a cake dome and refrigerate for up to 2 days. Serve at room temperature. *–Jeanne Kelley*

PER SERVING: 660 CALORIES | 7G PROTEIN | 80G CARB | 36G TOTAL FAT | 18G SAT FAT | 11G MONO FAT | 4G POLY FAT | 115MG CHOL | 440MG SODIUM | 2G FIBER

More about Pumpkins

Save the hefty, perfectly shaped jack-o'-lantern varieties like Connecticut Field and Spirit for Halloween; their flesh is thin and stringy, with little flavor. Instead, look for heirloom varieties, which are great for cooking, at farmers' markets and pumpkin patches.

Local pumpkins will vary by region, but here are three relatively common types that make delicious eating.

Sugar Pie (and the similar Baby Pam and New England Pie)

These small, volley-ball size, thin-skinned, burnt-orange pump-kins are probably the most commonly found baking pump-kins. They have sweet, smooth flesh that tends to be firm and dry, so they're espe-cially good for pie. If you find one with stringy flesh, don't bake or cook with it, because it will spoil the texture of the finished dish.

Casper

Casper pumpkins are white on the outside and dark orange inside. They resemble the traditional jack-o'-lantern pumpkin in shape and tend to be heavy, at 10 to 20 pounds.

Marina di Chioggia (aka Chioggia Sea Pumpkin)

This Italian heirloom pumpkin originally comes from Chioggia, near Venice. It's a large (about 10 pounds), blue-green, bumpy, ridged pumpkin, with dense, meaty, yellow-orange flesh.

Buying

Look for pumpkins that are free of cracks and soft spots. Be sure to inspect both the stem and bottom ends. If you're at a farmers' market or pumpkin patch, ask the farmer if the pumpkins have been exposed to frost. If they have, they will spoil quickly.

Storing

Most pumpkins can be stored, or cellared, in a cool, dark place for 2 to 6 months, depending on the variety. Arrange them in a single layer on top of a breathable surface such as cardboard or wood. Check on them every 2 weeks and immediately use (or discard) any that are starting to soften.

cinnamon-caramel-ganache layer cake

SERVES 16

FOR THE FILLING

2	cups heavy cream
1	3-inch cinnamon stick, lightly crushed
¼	tsp. table salt
4½	oz. semisweet chocolate (up to 62% cacao), coarsely chopped
½	cup granulated sugar

FOR THE FROSTING

6	oz. bittersweet chocolate (70% or 72% cacao), chopped medium fine
2	oz. (4 Tbs.) unsalted butter, cut into 4 pieces
1	Tbs. light corn syrup
	Pinch of table salt

FOR THE CAKE

1½	oz. (½ cup) unsweetened natural cocoa powder
½	cup buttermilk, at room temperature
6	oz. (1½ cups) cake flour
¾	tsp. baking soda
¼	tsp. table salt
¼	lb. (½ cup) slightly softened unsalted butter, cut into 4 pieces
1	cup granulated sugar
½	cup packed light brown sugar
2	large eggs, lightly beaten and at room temperature
	Bittersweet chocolate shards, for garnish (optional; see the sidebar on p. 63)

This intensely flavored cake requires some time to make, but it's worth the effort, and some elements can be made ahead. Make the filling and the frosting first, letting the former chill and the latter thicken slightly for a few hours at room temperature while the cake is baking and cooling.

MAKE THE FILLING

1. In a medium saucepan, bring the cream, cinnamon, salt, and 2 Tbs. water to a simmer over medium-high heat. Remove from the heat, cover, and steep for 15 minutes. Meanwhile, put the chocolate in a medium bowl and set a fine strainer over it.

2. Pour ¼ cup water into a heavy-duty 3-quart saucepan. Pour the sugar in the center of the pan and pat it down until evenly moistened (there should be clear water all around the sugar). Cover the pan and cook over medium-high heat until the sugar dissolves, 2 to 4 minutes. Uncover and cook without stirring until the syrup begins to color slightly, about 1 minute. Reduce the heat to medium and continue to cook, swirling the pot gently if the syrup colors unevenly.

3. When the caramel turns reddish amber, 1 to 2 minutes longer, take the pan off the heat and immediately stir in the cream mixture. Simmer over low heat, stirring constantly, until the caramel is completely dissolved, 1 to 3 minutes.

4. Pour the caramel cream through the strainer onto the chocolate; discard the cinnamon stick. Whisk until the chocolate melts and the mixture is smooth. Scrape into a wide, shallow bowl, cover loosely, and refrigerate until thoroughly chilled, at least 4 hours and up to 3 days.

MAKE THE FROSTING

Put the chocolate, butter, corn syrup, and salt in a heatproof bowl set in a skillet of barely simmering water. Stir gently until the chocolate melts and the mixture is perfectly smooth. Off the heat, stir in 6 Tbs. cool water. Let cool and thicken at room temperature without stirring for at least 3 hours. The consistency should be like chocolate pudding.

MAKE THE CAKE

1. Line the bottoms of three 9x2-inch round cake pans with parchment.

2. Position a rack in the lower third of the oven if the three pans will fit on it. Otherwise, position racks in the upper and lower thirds of the oven. Heat the oven to 350°F.

3. In a small bowl, whisk the cocoa and ½ cup lukewarm water. In a liquid measuring cup, mix the buttermilk with ½ cup cool water.

4. In a medium bowl, whisk the flour, baking soda, and salt and sift them three times onto a sheet of parchment.

5. In a stand mixer fitted with the paddle attachment, beat the butter on medium speed until creamy, about 15 seconds. Add the sugars gradually, beating until the mixture lightens in color and appears sandy but fluffy, about 5 minutes total. Dribble the eggs in a little at a time, taking a full minute to add them. Continue to beat for a few seconds until the mixture is smooth and fluffy.

6. Stop the mixer and add the cocoa mixture. Beat on medium speed just until combined. Stop the mixer and, using the parchment as a chute, add about one-quarter of the flour. Mix on low speed just until incorporated. Stop the mixer and add one-third of the buttermilk. Mix just until blended. Repeat, stopping the mixer between additions and scraping the bowl as necessary, until the remaining flour and butter-milk are mixed in.

continued on p. 62

7. Portion the batter evenly among the pans. Bake until a toothpick inserted in the center of each cake comes out clean, 17 to 20 minutes (if baking on two levels, rotate the upper and lower pans halfway through baking). Cool the cakes on racks for 5 minutes and then turn onto the racks, remove the parchment, and cool completely.

ASSEMBLE AND FROST THE CAKE

1. Beat the chilled filling in a stand mixer fitted with the paddle attachment at medium speed until it's very thick and stiff enough to hold a shape but still spreadable, 1 to 2 minutes. Don't overbeat.

2. Put a cake layer upside down on a cardboard cake round or tart pan bottom. Spread half of the filling evenly all the way to the edge of the layer. Top with a second upside-down layer and gently press in place. Spread with the remaining filling. Top with the third layer, again upside down. Smooth any filling protruding from the sides.

3. With an offset spatula, spread a very thin layer (about ½ cup) of frosting evenly over the top and sides of the assembled cake to smooth the surface, glue on crumbs, and fill cracks. Spread the remaining frosting all over the top and sides of the cake, swirling the surface with the spatula if desired. Top with the chocolate shards (if using) and serve at room temperature. *–Alice Medrich*

PER SERVING: 430 CALORIES | 4G PROTEIN | 49G CARB | 26G TOTAL FAT | 16G SAT FAT | 8G MONO FAT | 1G POLY FAT | 90MG CHOL | 190MG SODIUM | 3G FIBER

Why Every Baker Needs a Kitchen Scale

Baking is just as much a science as an art. A delicate, fluffy cake is the result of many chemical reactions, and when one element is off, the result can fall flat—literally. A small digital kitchen scale truly is a baker's best friend. Here's why:

Depending on what scooping method you use, a leveled cup measure can hold anywhere from 3.5 to 5.5 oz. of flour. A fluffy ingredient like confectioners' sugar or cocoa can be even more variable. Weighing these ingredients eliminates the inconsistencies. It's also much faster and makes for less dishwashing; rather than measuring one cup at a time in a cup measure, you can weigh your ingredients right in the mixing bowl.

A scale is also helpful if you need to divide batter between two or more baking pans, as in this recipe. Weighing the batter ensures that each layer is uniform, both in quantity and in baking time.

Even if you don't do a lot of baking, a scale is a worthwhile investment. You'll find yourself pulling it out again and again to weigh all sorts of things, like 12 oz. of pasta, a pound of potatoes, or even a letter that seems a little heavy for regular postage.

how to make bittersweet chocolate shards

Delicate chocolate shards decorating the cake are easy to make.

Start by melting 4 oz. chopped bittersweet chocolate in a clean, dry heatproof bowl set in a wide pan of nearly simmering water, stirring frequently with a dry spatula until smooth. Remove the bowl from the water and wipe the bottom dry.

Tear off two 16-inch-long sheets of waxed paper. Scrape the melted chocolate onto one sheet and spread with an offset metal spatula in a thin, even layer to within about ⅓ inch from each edge. Cover the chocolate with the second sheet of waxed paper.

Starting at one short edge, roll the paper and chocolate into a narrow tube about 1 inch in diameter. Refrigerate the tube seam side down on a baking sheet for at least 2 hours.

Remove the tube from the fridge and quickly unroll it while the chocolate is still cold and brittle; this will crack the chocolate it into long curved shards. Peel back the top sheet of waxed paper.

Immediately slide a metal spatula under the chocolate to release it from the waxed paper, and then slide the shards onto a rimmed baking sheet. Refrigerate until ready to use. Warm fingers will melt the shards, so handle them with a spatula or tongs.

chocolate–beet layer cake

FOR THE CAKE

2	medium beets, trimmed
½	Tbs. vegetable oil
6	oz. (¾ cup) unsalted butter, softened; more for the pans
9	oz. (2 cups) unbleached all-purpose flour; more for the pans
2	oz. (⅔ cup) unsweetened, natural cocoa powder, such as Scharffen Berger®
1	tsp. baking soda
1	tsp. kosher salt
1¾	cups granulated sugar
2	large eggs, at room temperature
1	tsp. pure vanilla extract

FOR THE FROSTING

5	oz. (10 Tbs.) unsalted butter
1	cup granulated sugar
2¼	oz. (¾ cup) unsweetened, natural cocoa powder, such as Scharffen Berger
¾	cup heavy cream
1	tsp. instant espresso powder
1	tsp. pure vanilla extract
½	tsp. kosher salt

The roasted beets in this cake make it moist, dense, and rich. You can't taste them—there's no earthy, beety flavor—but without them, this cake is nowhere near as delicious.

PREPARE THE BEETS

Position a rack in the center of the oven and heat the oven to 375°F. Put the beets on a piece of foil large enough to wrap them. Drizzle with the vegetable oil and turn to coat well. Enclose the beets in the foil and roast until tender when pierced with a paring knife, about 1 hour. Let cool.

MAKE THE CAKE

1. Reduce the oven temperature to 350°F. Coat two 9-inch round cake pans generously with softened butter. Line the bottom of the pans with parchment and coat the parchment with butter. Dust the pans with flour, tapping out any excess.

2. Peel and finely grate enough of the beets to yield ¾ cup. Sift the flour, cocoa powder, baking soda, and salt into a medium bowl.

3. Using a stand mixer fitted with the paddle attachment or an electric hand mixer, beat the butter and sugar on medium-low speed until fluffy, about 3 minutes. Beat in the eggs, one at a time. Mix in the grated beets and the vanilla. Reduce the speed to low and carefully add half of the flour mixture; mix until fully incorporated. Add 1¼ cups hot water and the remaining flour mixture, return to medium-low speed and mix until smooth, about 2 minutes. Divide the batter evenly between the prepared pans, smoothing the tops.

4. Bake the cakes, rotating the pans halfway through baking, until a toothpick inserted in the center of the cakes comes out clean, about 25 minutes. Cool the cakes in their pans on a rack for 10 minutes and then turn them out onto racks and peel off the parchment. Let the cakes cool completely.

MAKE THE FROSTING

Melt the butter in a 3-quart saucepan over medium heat. Add the sugar and cocoa powder and mix until combined. Stir in the cream, espresso powder, vanilla, and salt. Bring the mixture to a simmer and cook, stirring constantly, until smooth. Pour the mixture into a bowl and cool slightly. Refrigerate, stirring every 10 minutes, until soft peaks form and the frosting is completely cool, about 1 hour.

ASSEMBLE THE CAKE

Place one of the cake layers on a cake plate and spread a generous ½ cup frosting evenly over the top. Top with the second layer and spread a generous ½ cup frosting over it. Frost the sides with the remaining frosting. *–Jeanne Kelley*

PER SERVING: 690 CALORIES | 7G PROTEIN | 82G CARB | 37G TOTAL FAT | 22G SAT FAT | 9G MONO FAT | 2G POLY FAT | 130MG CHOL | 330MG SODIUM | 3G FIBER

Make Ahead

The beets can be roasted up to 3 days ahead and refrigerated. The cake can be assembled up to 2 days ahead. Cover with a cake dome and store at room temperature.

german chocolate cake

FOR THE CAKE

- ¼ lb. (½ cup) unsalted butter, softened; more for the pans
- 4 oz. semisweet or bitter-sweet chocolate (up to 70% cacao), coarsely chopped (about 1 cup)
- ½ cup boiling water
- 9 oz. (2 cups) unbleached all-purpose flour
- 1 tsp. baking soda
- ½ tsp. table salt
- 4 large eggs, at room temperature
- 2 cups granulated sugar
- 1 tsp. pure vanilla extract
- 1 cup buttermilk, at room temperature

FOR THE COCONUT–PECAN FILLING

- 7 oz. (about 2 cups) sweetened, shredded dried coconut
- 4 large egg yolks
- 1 12-oz. can evaporated milk
- 1½ cups granulated sugar
- 2 tsp. pure vanilla extract
- ¾ tsp. table salt
- 6 oz. (¾ cup) unsalted butter, cut into chunks
- 1½ cups pecan halves, toasted and coarsely chopped

This ultimate version combines a sweet, gooey, coconut-and-pecan studded filling with three layers of light, chocolate cake.

MAKE THE CAKES

1. Position racks in the upper and lower thirds of the oven and heat the oven to 350°F. Butter the sides of three 9x2-inch round cake pans and line the bottoms with parchment rounds.

2. Put the chocolate in a small bowl and pour the boiling water over it. Let stand for several seconds and then whisk until the chocolate is dissolved. Set aside until cool to the touch before mixing the batter.

3. Sift the flour, baking soda, and salt onto a sheet of waxed paper. Whisk the eggs in a small measuring cup.

4. In a stand mixer fitted with the paddle attachment, beat the butter on medium-low speed for a few seconds. Add the sugar in a steady stream and then beat on medium speed, scraping the bowl as necessary, until the mixture is lightened in color and fluffy, 4 to 5 minutes. Still on medium speed, add the eggs a little at a time, taking a full 1½ minutes to add them all. Add the melted chocolate and vanilla and beat just until blended. With the mixer turned off, add a quarter of the flour mixture. Mix on medium-low speed just until incorporated. Add a third of the buttermilk and mix until blended. Repeat, each time adding another quarter of the flour, then a third of the buttermilk, until the

last of the flour is added. Scrape the bowl as necessary and mix each addition only until it is incorporated.

5. Portion the batter among the pans and spread it evenly. Bake, rotating the pans and swapping their positions, until the cakes just start to pull away from the sides of the pans and spring back when very gently pressed with a finger, 20 to 25 minutes. Let the cakes cool in their pans on a rack for 10 minutes.

6. Run a knife or small spatula around the edges to separate the cakes from the pans. Turn the cakes out onto the rack and peel off the parchment. Cool completely.

MAKE THE FILLING
1. Spread the coconut on a rimmed baking sheet. Bake at 350°F, stirring every 2 minutes, until golden brown , about 10 minutes. Scrape the toasted coconut onto a sheet of waxed paper and let cool completely.

2. Whisk the egg yolks with the evaporated milk, sugar, vanilla, and salt in a heavy-duty, nonreactive, 4-quart saucepan. Add the butter. Set over medium heat and stir constantly with a heatproof spatula, scraping the bottom and corners of the pot. When the mixture starts to boil, adjust the heat so that it boils actively but not furiously, and cook, stirring constantly, until golden and thickened, 3 to 4 minutes. Off the heat, stir in the coconut and pecans. Let cool completely.

ASSEMBLE THE CAKE
Put one cake layer on a cake plate. Spread a third of the filling over the top, leaving a ¼-inch border. Top with a second cake layer. Spread with half of the remaining filling. Put the third cake layer on top and cover it with the remaining filling. Leave the sides of the cake exposed. Serve at room temperature. –*Alice Medrich*

PER SERVING: 590 CALORIES | 8G PROTEIN | 72G CARB | 31G TOTAL FAT | 16G SAT FAT | 10G MONO FAT | 3.5G POLY FAT | 170MG CHOL | 360MG SODIUM | 3G FIBER

Make Ahead

The cake will keep in the refrigerator for up to 2 days. Let it come back to cool room temperature before serving.

triple-lemon layer cake

SERVES 10

FOR THE CAKE

- 6 oz. (¾ cup) unsalted butter, completely softened at room temperature; more for the pans
- 9¼ oz. (2⅓ cups) cake flour; more for the pans
- 2¾ tsp. baking powder
- ¼ tsp. table salt
- 1¾ cups granulated sugar
- 2 Tbs. lightly packed finely grated lemon zest
- 1 cup whole milk, at room temperature
- 5 large egg whites, at room temperature
- ¼ tsp. cream of tartar

    Lemon Curd (recipe on the facing page), chilled

FOR THE FROSTING

- ½ lb. (1 cup) unsalted butter, completely softened at room temperature
- 2 Tbs. lightly packed finely grated lemon zest
- 3½ cups sifted confectioners' sugar
- 3 Tbs. fresh lemon juice

FOR GARNISH

- 2 lemons, zested with a channel zester and silver dragées (optional)

This light and tender cake is flavored with lemon, layered with tangy lemon curd, and coated with a voluptuous lemony butter frosting.

MAKE THE CAKE

1. Position a rack in the center of the oven; heat the oven to 350°F. Generously butter and flour two 8x2-inch round cake pans.

2. Sift the cake flour, baking powder, and salt together into a medium bowl.

3. Pulse ¼ cup of the sugar with the zest in a food processor until well combined.

4. In a large bowl, beat the butter and lemon sugar with an electric mixer on medium speed until light and fluffy (about 1½ minutes). Add the remaining 1½ cups sugar and beat until smooth (about 1½ minutes). Beat in a quarter of the milk just until blended. On low speed, add the flour mixture alternately with the milk in three batches, scraping the bowl with a rubber spatula; beat just until blended.

5. In another large bowl, beat the egg whites with an electric mixer (with clean beaters or the whip attachment) on medium speed just until foamy. Add the cream of tartar, increase the speed to medium high, and beat just until the whites form stiff peaks when the beaters are lifted. Add a quarter of the whites to the batter and gently fold them in with a whisk or a rubber spatula; continue to gently fold in the whites, a quarter at a time, being careful not to deflate the mixture.

6. Divide the batter evenly between the prepared pans. Smooth the tops with the spatula. Bake until a pick inserted in the centers comes out clean, 35 to 40 minutes. Let cool in the pans on a rack for 10 minutes. Run a table knife around the inside of the pans and carefully invert each cake out onto the rack. Flip them right side up and let cool completely.

7. With the palm of one hand pressed on top of a cake layer, cut each in half horizontally, using a long serrated knife. Put one of the four cake layers on a serving plate, cut side up. With an offset spatula or a table knife, spread a generous ⅓ cup chilled lemon curd on top of the cake layer. Lay another cake layer on top, spread it with another generous ⅓ cup lemon curd, and repeat with the third cake layer, using the last ⅓ cup lemon curd. Top with the fourth cake layer.

MAKE THE FROSTING

In a medium bowl, beat the butter and lemon zest with an electric mixer on medium speed until light and fluffy. Add the confectioners' sugar in batches and beat until light and fluffy. Add the lemon juice and beat for 1 minute. (You can make the frosting a couple of hours ahead and keep it, covered, at cool room temperature.)

FROST THE CAKE

Up to a few hours before serving, spread a thin layer of frosting on the cake, filling in any gaps as you go. Chill until the frosting firms a bit, about ½ hour. Spread the remaining frosting decoratively over the top and sides of the cake. Scatter with bits of lemon zest and dragées (if desired), or garnish as you like.   *–Lori Longbotham*

PER SERVING: 870 CALORIES | 6G PROTEIN | 115G CARB | 44G TOTAL FAT | 27G SAT FAT | 11G MONO FAT | 2G POLY FAT | 240MG CHOL | 240MG SODIUM | 1G FIBER

lemon curd

MAKES ABOUT 1¼ CUPS

¼	**lb. (½ cup) unsalted butter**
¾	**cup granulated sugar**
½	**cup fresh lemon juice**
3	**Tbs. lightly packed finely grated lemon zest**
	Pinch of table salt
6	**large egg yolks**

Melt the butter in a heavy medium saucepan over medium heat. Remove the pan from the heat and whisk in the sugar, lemon juice, zest, and salt. Whisk in the yolks until smooth. Return the pan to medium-low heat and cook, whisking constantly, until the mixture thickens, 5 to 6 minutes. To check if the curd is thick enough, dip a wooden spoon into it and draw your finger across the back of the spoon; your finger should leave a path. Don't let the mixture boil. Immediately force the curd through a fine-mesh sieve into a bowl, using a rubber spatula. Let cool to room temperature, whisking occasionally. Refrigerate, covered, until ready to use.

curling zest

To create curls of zest, strip the zest from two lemons with a channel zester. Cover the strands loosely with a damp paper towel; they'll curl as they begin to dry.

sweet potato cupcakes with maple cream cheese frosting

MAKES 24 CUPCAKES

FOR THE CUPCAKES

1¾	lb. orange or red sweet potatoes
11	oz. (2½ cups) unbleached all-purpose flour
2	tsp. baking powder
½	tsp. baking soda
1	tsp. kosher salt
1	tsp. ground cinnamon
1	tsp. ground ginger
¼	tsp. ground cloves
3	large eggs
1¾	cups granulated sugar
5	oz. (10 Tbs.) unsalted butter, softened
1	tsp. pure vanilla extract
¼	cup sour cream
¼	cup whole milk

FOR THE FROSTING

5	oz. crème fraîche or sour cream
¼	lb. (½ cup) unsalted butter, softened
2	8-oz. packages cream cheese, softened, each cut into 3 chunks
¼	cup pure maple syrup
1	tsp. pure vanilla extract
	Kosher salt
6¾	oz. (1½ cups) confectioners' sugar
	Ground cinnamon, for garnish (optional)

Sweet potatoes lend moisture and complexity to these tender, lightly spiced, and utterly addictive cupcakes. A tangy maple-syrup–infused frosting serves as both the topping and filling.

MAKE THE CUPCAKES

1. Position a rack in the center of the oven and heat the oven to 400°F. Line a heavy-duty rimmed baking sheet with foil or parchment. Poke the sweet potatoes with a sharp knife and put them on the baking sheet. Bake until completely tender, 35 to 60 minutes, depending on the shape and moisture content of the potato; remove and set aside to cool.

2. Reduce the oven temperature to 350°F. Line two 12-cup cupcake tins with paper liners. When cool enough to handle, peel the sweet potatoes and purée the flesh in a food processor. Measure out 2 cups and set aside. Save the remaining potatoes for another use.

3. In a medium bowl, whisk the flour, baking powder, baking soda, salt, cinnamon, ginger, and cloves until well blended.

4. Separate the eggs. In another medium bowl, beat the egg whites with an electric hand mixer on high speed until very foamy and white, about 1 minute. With the mixer running, sprinkle in ¼ cup of the sugar and continue to beat until very fluffy and glossy, about 3 minutes; set aside.

5. In a stand mixer fitted with the paddle attachment (or in a large bowl, using a hand-held mixer), beat the butter and remaining 1½ cups sugar on medium speed until very light and fluffy, scraping down the sides of the bowl as needed, 3 to 4 minutes. Beat in the egg yolks one at a time, and then add the vanilla and continue to beat 1 minute more to combine. Slowly beat in the sweet potato purée, followed by the sour cream and milk. The mixture should look smooth.

6. With the mixer on low, or using a rubber spatula, gently and gradually mix in the dry ingredients, mixing until each addition is just blended.

continued on p. 72

7. Scoop out about one-quarter of the egg whites and use a spatula to fold it into the batter; gently fold in the rest of the meringue. Portion the batter among the prepared cupcake tins (about ¼ cup for each cupcake). Lightly tap the tins on the counter to settle the batter. Bake, rotating the pans halfway through baking, until the cupcakes are puffed, lightly browned, and the center is springy when pressed lightly with a finger, 25 to 30 minutes. Be careful not to underbake the cupcakes, or they will be gummy.

8. Let the cupcakes sit in the pans until cool enough to handle. Carefully transfer them to a rack and let cool completely.

MAKE THE FROSTING

1. In a stand mixer fitted with the whisk attachment (or in a large bowl, using a hand-held mixer), whip the crème fraîche on medium speed until thick, about 1 minute (if using sour cream, skip this step). Scrape it into a medium bowl and set aside.

2. Switch to the paddle attachment if using a stand mixer, and put the butter in the mixing bowl. Beat until light and fluffy, about 2 minutes. With the mixer running, add the cream cheese, one chunk at a time, and beat until smooth, about 2 minutes. Slowly beat in the maple syrup, vanilla, and ¼ tsp. salt until incorporated. Gradually sprinkle in the confectioners' sugar and beat until very smooth, about 3 minutes.

3. Fold one-quarter of the cream cheese mixture into the crème fraîche. Then fold the mixture back into the cream cheese frosting just until thoroughly blended.

FILL AND FROST THE CUPCAKES

1. Using a ¼-inch plain pastry tip (Ateco® #801), punch a hole into the top of each cupcake, pushing the tip in at least ½ inch.

2. Fit the tip onto a pastry bag and fill the bag with 1½ cups of frosting. Insert the tip into the hole in the top of one of the cupcakes and squeeze the bag lightly to fill with about 1 Tbs. filling. As you fill the cupcake, pull the bag upwards. Don't worry if some of the frosting comes out of the hole. Repeat with the remaining cupcakes.

3. Dollop 2 Tbs. of the remaining frosting on top of each cupcake. Using a small offset spatula or butter knife, spread the frosting over the tops. Lightly sprinkle with ground cinnamon (if using) and serve.
–Martha Holmberg

chocolate cupcakes
with dark chocolate frosting

MAKES 16 CUPCAKES

FOR THE FROSTING

4   oz. unsweetened chocolate, coarsely chopped

¾   cup evaporated milk

1   cup granulated sugar

    Pinch of salt

FOR THE CUPCAKES

½   cup vegetable oil; more for the pan

4   oz. unsweetened chocolate, coarsely chopped

6   oz. (1½ cups) unbleached all-purpose flour

¾   tsp. baking soda

½   tsp. table salt

2   cups granulated sugar

1   cup strong, hot coffee

½   cup sour cream

2   large eggs

These cupcakes become even more moist and fudgy the day after you make them.

MAKE THE FROSTING

In a double boiler or in a bowl set over simmering water, melt the chocolate carefully. In a blender, blend the evaporated milk, sugar, and salt until the sugar is dissolved. Add the chocolate and blend until the mixture is thick and glossy, about 3 minutes. Store the frosting at room temperature, covered for up to 2 days.

MAKE THE CUPCAKES

1. Position a rack in the center of the oven and heat the oven to 350°F. Grease 16 standard muffin tins. Melt the chocolate carefully in a double boiler or in a bowl set over simmering water; set aside to cool.

2. Sift the flour, baking soda, salt, and sugar into a medium bowl. In a large bowl, whisk together the coffee, sour cream, oil, and eggs; whisk in the chocolate. Add the dry ingredients, whisking until there are no lumps.

3. Pour the batter into the prepared muffin tins, portioning it evenly. Bake until a toothpick inserted into the middle of a cupcake comes out clean, 19 to 20 minutes. Cool for 15 minutes in the pan; then remove from the pan and cool completely before frosting.
—David Page and Barbara Shinn

PER CUPCAKE: 360 CALORIES | 5G PROTEIN | 52G CARB | 18G TOTAL FAT | 7G SAT FAT | 5G MONO FAT | 4G POLY FAT | 35MG CHOL | 170MG SODIUM | 3G FIBER

Make Ahead

The frosting can be made up to 2 days ahead and kept covered at room temperature.

chocolate stout cake

MAKES 1 LARGE BUNDT CAKE
OR 12 MINIATURE BUNDT
CAKES

2¼ oz. (¾ cup) unsweetened natural cocoa powder (not Dutch-processed); more for the pan

10 oz. (1¼ cups) unsalted butter, softened at room temperature; more for the pan

1¼ cups stout, such as Guinness® (don't include the foam when measuring)

⅓ cup dark molasses (not blackstrap)

7½ oz. (1⅔ cups) unbleached all-purpose flour

1½ tsp. baking powder

½ tsp. baking soda

½ tsp. table salt

1½ cups packed light brown sugar

3 large eggs, at room temperature

6 oz. semisweet chocolate, very finely chopped

Chocolate Glaze (optional; recipe on the facing page)

Rich, dark, and toasty stout beer plus deeply flavored molasses give the chocolate flavor of this cake some wonderful nuance. With this recipe, you can bake one big beautiful cake, perfect for entertaining, or a dozen irresistible miniature Bundt cakes.

1. Position a rack in the center of the oven and heat the oven to 350°F. Butter a 10- or 12-cup Bundt pan (or twelve 1-cup mini Bundt pans) and then lightly coat with sifted cocoa powder. Tap out any excess cocoa.

2. In a small saucepan over high heat, bring the stout and molasses to a simmer. Remove the pan from the heat and let stand while preparing the cake batter.

3. Sift together the flour, cocoa powder, baking powder, baking soda, and salt. With a stand mixer (using the paddle attachment) or a hand-held mixer, cream the butter in a large bowl on medium speed until smooth, about 1 minute. Add the brown sugar and beat on medium speed until light and fluffy, about 3 minutes. Stop to scrape the sides of the bowl as needed. Beat in the eggs one at a time, stopping to scrape the bowl after each addition. With the mixer on low speed, alternate adding the flour and stout mixtures, beginning and ending with the flour. Stop the mixer at least one last time to scrape the bowl and then beat at medium speed until the batter is smooth, about 20 seconds. Stir in the chopped chocolate.

4. Spoon the batter into the prepared pan (or pans), spreading it evenly with a rubber spatula. Run a knife through the batter to eliminate any air pockets. Bake until a wooden pick inserted in the center comes out with only a few moist crumbs clinging to it, 45 to 50 minutes (about 35 minutes for mini cakes). Set the pan on a rack to cool for 20 minutes. Invert the cake onto the rack and remove the pan. Let cool until just barely warm. Drizzle with the glaze (if using) and then let cool to room temperature before serving. If you're making the cake ahead, wrap it while still barely warm without the glaze. If you plan to freeze the cake, don't glaze it until you're ready to serve it or give it away. *–Nicole Rees*

chocolate glaze

¾ cup heavy cream

6 oz. semisweet chocolate, chopped

Bring the cream to a boil in a small saucepan over high heat. Remove the pan from the heat and add the chocolate. Let stand for 1 minute and then whisk until the chocolate is melted and smooth. Let cool for 5 minutes before drizzling over the barely warm cake.

classic vanilla layer cake with vanilla mascarpone frosting and raspberries

MAKES ONE 9-INCH CAKE;
SERVES 12

FOR THE CAKE LAYERS

- ½ lb. (1 cup) unsalted butter, softened at room temperature; more for the pan
- Unbleached all-purpose flour, for the pan
- 12 oz. (3 cups) cake flour
- 1 Tbs. plus 1 tsp. baking powder
- ¾ tsp. table salt
- 1¾ cups granulated sugar
- Seeds scraped from ¾ vanilla bean, or 2 tsp. pure vanilla extract
- 1 cup whole milk
- 6 large egg whites, at room temperature

FOR THE FROSTING

- 1 lb. mascarpone cheese, at room temperature
- 2 cups heavy cream
- ⅔ cup granulated sugar
- Seeds scraped from 1 vanilla bean, or 2 tsp. pure vanilla extract
- Pinch of table salt

FOR GARNISH

- 2 pints fresh raspberries, rinsed and patted dry

Whoever says vanilla is boring has not tried this cake with luxurious frosting that's rich but not too sweet.

MAKE THE CAKE

1. Position a rack in the center of the oven and heat the oven to 350°F. Grease the bottom and sides of two 9-inch round cake pans. Line the bottoms with parchment and lightly flour the sides of the pans, tapping out any excess.

2. Sift the cake flour, baking powder, and salt onto a paper plate or into a medium bowl. In a stand mixer fitted with the paddle attachment (or using a hand-held mixer), beat the butter on medium speed until smooth, 1 minute. Add 1½ cups of the sugar and the vanilla bean seeds or extract. Continue beating until well combined and fluffy, 2 minutes. Stop to scrape the bowl as needed. On low speed, add the one-third of the dry ingredients at a time, alternating with ½ cup of the milk at a time, beginning and ending with the flour. After the last addition, scrape the bowl and mix for about 30 seconds to mix the batter fully.

3. In a medium bowl, beat the egg whites with a hand-held mixer (or in a stand mixer fitted with the whisk attachment) on medium-high speed until soft peaks form. Increase the speed to high and gradually add the remaining ¼ cup sugar. Continue beating until the whites form medium-firm peaks. Using a rubber spatula, scoop up about one-quarter of the whites and stir them gently into the cake batter to lighten it. Gently fold in the remaining whites until just blended.

4. Scrape the batter evenly into the prepared pans. Bake until the tops are light brown and a toothpick or cake tester inserted in the center of the cake comes out clean, about 30 minutes. Set the pans on a rack and let cool for about 15 minutes. Run a knife between the cake and the pan to loosen each cake. Invert the layers onto a rack, lift off the pans, and peel away the parchment. Let cool completely.

MAKE THE FROSTING

In a medium bowl, combine the mascarpone, cream, sugar, vanilla seeds or extract, and salt. Using an electric mixer, beat on low speed until almost smooth, 30 to 60 seconds. Increase the speed to medium high and beat until the mixture is thick and holds firm peaks, another 30 to 60 seconds. Don't overbeat or the frosting will look grainy.

ASSEMBLE THE CAKE

1. Gently brush away any excess crumbs from the layers. Set one cake layer, top side down, on a flat serving plate. To protect the plate from smears, slide small strips of foil or parchment under the bottom of the cake to cover the plate.

2. Using a metal spatula or the back edge of a table knife, spread about 2 cups of the frosting evenly over the layer. Arrange about half the berries in a single layer on the frosting but leave a half-inch ring of space around the edge of the cake uncovered. Place the second cake layer, top side down, on top of the frosting. Be sure the sides are aligned and then press gently on the layer. Apply a very thin layer of frosting over the entire cake to seal in any stray crumbs. Chill in the refrigerator for 5 minutes.

3. Spread the remaining frosting over the top and sides of the cake, leaving lots of swirls and peaks on the top. Garnish the top with the remaining berries. Carefully remove the foil or parchment strips from under the cake. Refrigerate the cake for 4 hours or up to 2 days. To keep the fruit looking fresh, cover the cake loosely with plastic after it has chilled for 1 hour. *–Abigail Johnson Dodge*

PER SERVING (BASED ON 12 SERVINGS): 750 CALORIES | 9G PROTEIN | 73G CARB | 49G TOTAL FAT | 29G SAT FAT | 13G MONO FAT | 3G POLY FAT | 145MG CHOL | 420MG SODIUM | 3G FIBER

fastest fudge cake

SERVES 10

- ¼ lb. (½ cup) unsalted butter, melted and warm; more for the cake pan
- 4½ oz. (1 cup) unbleached all-purpose flour
- 1 oz. (¼ cup plus 2 Tbs.) unsweetened natural cocoa powder (not Dutch-processed)
- ½ tsp. baking soda
- ¼ tsp. table salt
- 1¼ cups packed light brown sugar
- 2 large eggs
- 1 tsp. pure vanilla extract
- ½ cup hot water
- 1 cup Ganache, warmed (optional; recipe below)

This cake is delicious on its own but even better topped with ganache.

1. Position a rack in the lower third of the oven and heat the oven to 350°F. Grease the bottom of an 8x2- or 9x2-inch round cake pan or line it with parchment.

2. In a small bowl, whisk the flour, cocoa powder, baking soda, and salt. Sift only if the cocoa remains lumpy after whisking. In a large bowl, combine the melted butter and brown sugar with a wooden spoon or rubber spatula. Add the eggs and vanilla; stir until well blended. Add the flour mixture all at once and stir just until all the flour is moistened. Pour the hot water over the batter; stir just until it's incorporated and the batter is smooth.

3. Scrape the batter into the prepared pan. Bake until a toothpick inserted in the center comes out clean, about 30 minutes for a 9-inch pan or 35 to 40 minutes for an 8-inch pan. Let cool in the pan on a rack for 10 minutes. Run a thin knife around the edge and invert the cake (peel off the parchment if necessary). Invert it again onto the rack and let cool completely.

4. Once cool, set the rack over a baking sheet or foil. Pour some of the warm ganache over the cake and use an icing spatula to spread it over the top of the cake and down the sides. Let set for about an hour before serving. You'll have a bit of ganache left over after icing the cake; use it as a sauce for ice cream or another dessert. It keeps for a week in the refrigerator. Rewarm gently. *–Alice Medrich*

PER SERVING: 270 CALORIES | 4G PROTEIN | 40G CARB | 11G TOTAL FAT | 7G SAT FAT | 2G MONO FAT | 0G POLY FAT | 70MG CHOL | 150MG SODIUM | 1G FIBER

ganache

MAKES 1½ CUPS

- 8 oz. bittersweet or semisweet chocolate, finely chopped
- 1 cup heavy cream; more as needed
- Granulated sugar (optional)

Put the chocolate in a medium heatproof bowl. In a small saucepan, bring the cream to a boil. Pour the hot cream over the chocolate and whisk gently until the chocolate is completely melted and smooth. (If using a 70% bittersweet chocolate, the ganache might be a bit thick; add more cream, a tablespoon at a time, to thin it. You might also want to add a couple of teaspoons of sugar when you add the hot cream.)

sour cream chocolate cake with coconut frosting

SERVES 12 TO 16

FOR THE CAKE

¾	cup unsweetened cocoa powder
1½	cups boiling water
6	oz. (¾ cup) unsalted butter, cut into 6 pieces
¾	cup sour cream
3	large eggs
1	tsp. pure vanilla extract
12	oz. (3 cups) cake flour
3	cups granulated sugar
2¼	tsp. baking soda
1½	tsp. table salt

FOR THE BUTTERCREAM FROSTING

6	large egg yolks
1	cup granulated sugar
½	cup pure coconut milk
1	to 2 tsp. coconut extract (or to taste)
1	lb. unsalted butter, cut into tablespoons, softened
4	cups large-shaved coconut (fresh or desiccated), toasted

Make Ahead

The buttercream can be made in advance and refrigerated until ready to use. Bring chilled buttercream to room temperature before using, beating briefly to smooth it, if necessary.

Baking the layers at 300°F keeps the cake moist. Serve it at room temperature; the coconut softens when refrigerated.

MAKE THE CAKE

1. Heat the oven to 300°F. Line the bottoms of two 9-inch cake pans with parchment.

2. Put the cocoa powder in the bowl of an electric mixer fitted with the whisk attachment. Pour the boiling water over the cocoa and whisk until smooth. Add the butter and sour cream and blend on low speed until the butter melts. Let the mixture cool for a minute if very hot, then add the eggs and vanilla; whisk until smooth. Let cool for 10 minutes.

3. Meanwhile, sift together the cake flour, sugar, baking soda, and salt. With the mixer on low speed, add the dry ingredients a little at a time to the butter mixture, scraping down the sides once or twice. Increase the speed to medium and blend for another 3 minutes.

4. Pour the batter into the prepared pans and bake until the center of the cake feels firm and the cake just barely begins to pull away from the sides of the pan, 50 to 60 minutes (begin checking after 45 minutes). Remove the cakes from the oven and let cool completely before frosting.

MAKE THE FROSTING

1. Put the yolks in the bowl of an electric mixer fitted with a whisk attachment. In a small saucepan, combine the sugar and coconut milk. Stir to combine, then bring to a boil. As the mixture heats, begin whipping the eggs on high speed. Boil the coconut milk and sugar until the mixture reaches the soft-ball stage (238°F on a candy thermometer). Remove from the heat. Stop the mixer and pour a small amount of the syrup into the yolks. Quickly beat on high again. Repeat twice more until all the syrup is incorporated. (You can also add the sugar syrup in a steady stream with the mixer on, but be careful not to let it hit the beater or the syrup will be flung to the sides of the bowl, where it will harden.) Continue beating until the mixture is cool.

2. Add the coconut extract. With the mixer on medium speed, beat in the butter 1 or 2 Tbs. at a time. When it is completely incorporated, scrape down the sides of the bowl and beat for another 1 minute.

4. Fill and frost the cooled cake, then pat on a generous coating of the shaved toasted coconut over the sides and top. *–Kay Cabrera*

PER SERVING (BASED ON 16 SERVINGS): 660 CALORIES | 5G PROTEIN | 63G CARB | 46G TOTAL FAT | 30G SAT FAT | 11G MONO FAT | 2G POLY FAT | 210MG CHOL | 430MG SODIUM | 3G FIBER

vanilla layer cake with whipped rum–ganache icing

FOR THE CAKE

6	oz. (¾ cup) unsalted butter, at room temperature; more for the cake pans
10¼	oz. (2¼ cups) unbleached all-purpose flour; more for the pans
2	tsp. baking powder
¾	tsp. table salt
3	large eggs, at room temperature
4	large egg yolks, at room temperature
3	Tbs. vegetable oil
2	tsp. pure vanilla extract
2	cups granulated sugar
¾	cup buttermilk, at room temperature

FOR THE WHIPPED GANACHE

12	oz. semisweet chocolate (55 to 60% cacao), coarsely chopped or broken into pieces (2 slightly heaping cups)
2	cups heavy cream
2	to 3 Tbs. dark rum or brandy

The flavors of this gorgeous cake are best experienced at room temperature. Store the cake in the refrigerator, but take it out about 30 minutes before you intend to serve it.

MAKE THE CAKE

1. Position a rack in the center of the oven and heat the oven to 350°F. Butter and flour two 9x2-inch round cake pans and line the bottoms with parchment.

2. In a medium bowl, whisk the flour, baking powder, and salt. In another medium bowl, whisk the eggs, yolks, oil, and vanilla.

3. In a stand mixer fitted with the paddle attachment, mix the butter on medium-high speed until smooth and light in color, about 2 minutes. Scrape the sides of the bowl with a rubber spatula. Add the sugar and mix on medium-high speed until very well blended, about 2 minutes longer. Scrape the bowl again.

4. With the mixer running on medium-high speed, add the egg mixture to the butter mixture in a steady stream. Beat until light and fluffy, about 2 minutes. Reduce the mixer speed to low. Add half the dry ingredients to the butter mixture and mix until combined. Add half the buttermilk and mix until combined. Repeat with remaining flour and buttermilk.

5. Scrape the sides of the bowl and divide the batter evenly between the prepared pans. The batter will be thick; spread it in the pans as smoothly as possible.

6. Bake until the tops are golden brown on top and a toothpick inserted into the center of each cake comes out clean, 30 to 35 minutes. Cool them in the pan for 15 to 20 minutes on a rack and then turn them out onto a rack and cool completely.

MAKE THE WHIPPED GANACHE

1. Grind the chocolate in a food processor until it reaches the consistency of coarse meal, about 30 seconds. Bring the cream to a boil in a small saucepan over medium heat. Add the cream and rum to the food processor and process until smooth, 10 to 20 seconds. Transfer to the cleaned stand mixer bowl and refrigerate, stirring occasionally, until the ganache reaches 55° to 65°F, about 1½ hours.

2. In the stand mixer fitted with the whisk attachment, whip the chilled ganache on medium-high speed until lightened in color and fluffy, about 1 minute. Don't overwhip, or the ganache may seize. Scrape the sides of the bowl with a rubber spatula and mix gently.

ASSEMBLE THE CAKE

1. Put one cake layer on a cake plate and tuck strips of waxed paper under the cake to keep the plate clean. Using an offset spatula, spread about 2 cups of the whipped ganache over the top in an even layer right to the edges of the cake. Top with the second cake layer.

2. Brush any large, loose crumbs off the cake and quickly ice the top and sides with a thin layer of the whipped ganache to seal the cake. Spread most or all of the remaining ganache over the sides and top of the cake, using the spatula to decoratively dimple and swirl the icing. Carefully pull the waxed paper from under the cake and discard. Store the cake in the refrigerator, but let it sit at room temperature for 20 to 30 minutes before serving. *–Greg Case*

frozen lemon cream cakes with
toasted meringue and caramel
sauce (recipe on p. 108)

cool & creamy cakes

triple-chocolate cheesecake

MAKES ONE 9-INCH CAKE;
SERVES 16

An intense creamy filling and three layers of chocolate flavor will satisfy both cheesecake and chocolate fans alike.

FOR THE CRUST

- 1½ **cups very finely crushed chocolate cookie crumbs (such as Nabisco® FAMOUS® Chocolate Wafers)**
- 3 **Tbs. granulated sugar**
- ⅛ **tsp. ground cinnamon (optional)**
- ¼ **cup unsalted butter, melted**

FOR THE FILLING

- ½ **cup sour cream**
- 2 **tsp. pure vanilla extract**
- 1 **tsp. instant coffee granules or espresso powder**
- 8 **oz. bittersweet chocolate, finely chopped**
- 3 **8 oz. packages cream cheese, at room temperature**
- 3 **Tbs. unsweetened natural cocoa powder, sifted if lumpy**
- ¼ **tsp. table salt**
- 1¼ **cups granulated sugar**
- 3 **large eggs, at room temperature**

MAKE THE CRUST

Position a rack in the center of the oven and heat the oven to 400°F. In a medium bowl, stir together the cookie crumbs, sugar, and cinnamon (if using) until blended. Drizzle with the melted butter and mix until well blended and the crumbs are evenly moist. Dump the mixture into a 9-inch springform pan and press evenly onto the bottom and about 1 inch up the sides of the pan (to press, use plastic wrap, a straight-sided, flat-based coffee mug, or a tart tamper). Bake for 10 minutes and set on a wire rack to cool. Reduce the oven temperature to 300°F.

MAKE THE FILLING AND BAKE

1. Mix the sour cream, vanilla, and coffee granules in a small bowl. Set aside and stir occasionally until the coffee dissolves.

2. Melt the chocolate in a double boiler over medium heat (or in a microwave; see the sidebar below). Stir until smooth. Set aside to cool slightly.

3. In a stand mixer fitted with the paddle attachment, beat the cream cheese, cocoa powder, and salt until very smooth and fluffy, scraping the sides of the bowl and paddle frequently (and with each subsequent addition). Add the sugar and continue beating until well blended and smooth. Scrape the cooled chocolate into the bowl; beat until blended. Beat in the sour cream mixture until well blended. Add the eggs, one at a time, and beat until just blended. (Don't overbeat the filling once the eggs have been added or the cheesecake will puff too much.) Pour the filling over the cooled crust, spread evenly, and

Melting Chocolate in the Microwave

This shortcut is a great alternative to the traditional method of melting chocolate in a double boiler. Microwaves vary greatly, so you may need to adjust the timing to suit your appliance.

Put the finely chopped chocolate in a wide, shallow bowl and heat it in the microwave on high or medium high until it just starts to melt, about a minute. Give the chocolate a good stir and microwave it again until it's almost completely melted, another 15 to 30 seconds. Remove the bowl and continue stirring until the chocolate is completely melted.

smooth the top. Bake at 300°F until the center barely jiggles when nudged, 50 to 60 minutes. The cake will be slightly puffed, with a few little cracks around the edge. Let cool to room temperature on a rack and then refrigerate until well chilled, at least a few hours, or overnight for the best texture and flavor. (This cake freezes well, too: Put the unmolded cake in the freezer, uncovered, until the top is cold and firm, and then wrap it in two layers of plastic and one layer of foil.)

TO SERVE

Unclasp the pan's ring, remove it, and run a long, thin metal spatula under the bottom crust. Carefully slide the cake onto a flat serving plate. Run a thin knife under hot water, wipe it dry, and cut the cake into slices, heating and wiping the knife as needed.

–Abigail Johnson Dodge

PER SERVING (BASED ON 16 SERVINGS): 390 CALORIES | 7G PROTEIN | 35G CARB | 27G TOTAL FAT | 16G SAT FAT | 8G MONO FAT | 3G POLY FAT | 100MG CHOL | 240MG SODIUM | 1G FIBER

new york style cheesecake
with cranberry–cointreau sauce

MAKES ONE 9-INCH
CHEESECAKE; SERVES
12 TO 16

FOR THE CRUST

5¾ oz. finely ground graham
cracker crumbs (about
10 cracker rectangles
ground to yield 1½ packed
cups)

¼ cup granulated sugar

2½ oz. (5 Tbs.) unsalted butter,
melted; plus 1 tsp. melted
butter for the pan

FOR THE FILLING

4 8-oz. packages cream
cheese, at room
temperature

1⅓ cups granulated sugar

1 Tbs. unbleached
all-purpose flour

4 large eggs, at room
temperature

¾ cup sour cream, at room
temperature

2 Tbs. fresh lemon juice

1 tsp. pure vanilla extract

FOR SERVING

Cranberry–Cointreau Sauce
(recipe on p. 88)

Cheesecakes can be prone to cracking on top. But this recipe has several safeguards against it including getting baked in a water bath. Of course, the festive cranberry topping will also hide any imperfections.

MAKE THE CRUST

1. Position a rack in the center of the oven and heat the oven to 350°F.

2. In a medium bowl, combine the graham cracker crumbs and sugar. Stir in the 5 Tbs. melted butter until the crumbs are evenly moistened. Dump the crumbs into a 9-inch springform pan that's about 2½ inches deep and press them firmly into the bottom and about halfway up the sides. Bake until the crust is fragrant and warm to the touch, 5 to 7 minutes; it's fine if the crust starts to look golden, but it shouldn't brown too much. Let the pan cool on a rack while you prepare the cheesecake batter. Leave the oven on.

FILL AND BAKE THE CAKE

1. In a stand mixer fitted with the paddle attachment, beat the cream cheese with the sugar at medium-low speed until the mixture is smooth and somewhat fluffy, about 2 minutes. Scrape the bowl. On low speed, beat in the flour. One at a time, beat in the eggs on low speed, mixing the batter for only 15 to 20 seconds after each egg is added, just until it's incorporated, and scraping the bowl each time. Don't overbeat. Add the sour cream, lemon juice, and vanilla. Beat at low speed until well combined, about 30 seconds. The batter should be smooth and have the consistency of a thick milkshake.

2. Wrap the outside of the pan tightly with two sheets of extra-wide (18-inch) heavy-duty aluminum foil to make the pan waterproof. Brush the inside rim of the pan with a light coating of the remaining 1 tsp. melted butter, taking care not to disturb the crust.

3. Pour the batter into the prepared crust; it should cover the crust completely and come to within about ½ inch of the pan's rim. Put the springform pan in a roasting pan and carefully pour hot water into the roasting pan until the water reaches halfway up the sides of the springform pan. Bake at 350°F, without opening the oven door for the first hour, until the top of the cake is golden brown and doesn't wobble in the center when the pan is nudged (a little jiggle is fine), about 1 hour 10 minutes to 1 hour 15 minutes. (The cheesecake will be gooey in the center; don't worry, it will set as it cools.)

4. Remove the springform pan from the water bath, remove the foil wrapping (you may need an extra set of hands for this), and set the pan on a wire rack. Run a thin-bladed knife around the inside rim of the pan to free the cheesecake from the sides of the pan. Let the

cake cool on the rack until barely warm, and then refrigerate uncovered for at least 8 hours or overnight. The cheesecake will firm up during chilling.

TO SERVE THE CHEESECAKE

1. Run a thin-bladed knife around the inside rim of the pan again, taking care not to disturb the crust, to loosen the chilled cheesecake. Unclasp and remove the side of the springform pan, and then use a wide spatula to transfer the cake to a serving plate.

continued on p. 88

2. Right before serving, use a slotted spoon to scoop the cranberries out of the Cranberry–Cointreau Sauce and let them drain briefly before spooning them onto the top of the cake. (Save the leftover syrup for pouring onto vanilla ice cream or mixing with seltzer to make cranberry spritzers.)

3. Before slicing, rinse a long, thin-bladed knife under hot water. Wipe the blade between slices and rinse it under hot water again as needed.

4. Wrapped and refrigerated, the topped cheesecake will keep for a week. *–Nicole Rees*

PER SERVING (BASED ON 16 SERVINGS): 500 CALORIES | 7G PROTEIN | 58G CARB | 28G TOTAL FAT | 17G SAT FAT | 8G MONO FAT | 1.5G POLY FAT | 130MG CHOL | 250MG SODIUM | 1G FIBER

cranberry–cointreau sauce

MAKES ABOUT 3½ CUPS

- 1¼ **cups granulated sugar**
- ½ **cup honey**
- 1 **12-oz. package fresh cranberries, rinsed, dried, and picked over**
- 2 **Tbs. Cointreau**

In a medium saucepan, bring the sugar, honey, and ¾ cup water to a boil over high heat, stirring until the sugar dissolves. Reduce the heat to medium and stir in the cranberries. Cook, stirring occasionally, until the foam has turned fuchsia and many of the berries have popped, about 5 minutes. Remove the saucepan from the heat and stir in the Cointreau. Pour into a heatproof bowl and refrigerate until cold, about 3 hours, but preferably overnight. The sauce can be made 2 days in advance and stored in an airtight container in the refrigerator.

spiced pumpkin cheesecake with gingersnap crust

MAKES ONE 9-INCH
CHEESECAKE; SERVES 16

FOR THE GINGERSNAP CRUST

> **About 40 gingersnap wafers (to yield 2 cups cookie crumbs)**

¼ **cup packed light brown sugar**

2½ **oz. (5 Tbs) unsalted butter, melted and cooled**

FOR THE FILLING

4 **8 oz. packages cream cheese, at room temperature**

1⅓ **cups packed light brown sugar**

1 **tsp. ground cinnamon**

½ **tsp. ground ginger**

¼ **tsp. ground allspice**

¼ **tsp. freshly grated nutmeg**

¼ **tsp. table salt**

4 **large eggs**

2 **large egg yolks**

1 **Tbs. pure vanilla extract**

1 **15-oz. can pure solid-pack pumpkin purée (not pumpkin pie filling)**

This cheesecake is a luxurious twist on the traditional Thanksgiving pumpkin pie.

MAKE THE CRUST

1. Position a rack in the center of the oven and heat the oven to 350°F.

2. Pulse the cookies and brown sugar in a food processor until well combined and the crumbs are uniform. Transfer to a medium bowl; add the melted butter. Combine thoroughly, first with a spoon and then with your fingers, until the mixture is evenly moist, crumbly, and holds together when you squeeze a handful. Press the mixture evenly over the bottom and partway up the sides of a 9-inch springform pan. Chill for 5 minutes and then bake for 10 minutes. Let cool. Leave the oven on.

MAKE THE FILLING

1. Heat a kettle of water. With an electric mixer or a wooden spoon, beat the cream cheese until smooth. In a separate bowl, whisk together the brown sugar, cinnamon, ginger, allspice, nutmeg, and salt. Add this mixture to the cream cheese. Beat until well blended, scraping the bowl as needed. Add the eggs and yolks one at a time, making sure each is thoroughly incorporated before adding the next and scraping the bowl after each. Blend in the vanilla and pumpkin.

2. Wrap the outside of the pan tightly with two sheets of heavy-duty aluminum foil. Scrape the batter into the cooled crust. The batter will come up past the crust and will fill the pan to the rim. Tap the pan gently once or twice on the counter to release any air bubbles. Set the springform pan in a roasting pan, and add enough hot water from the kettle to come about halfway up the sides of the springform pan. Bake until the top of the cake looks deep golden and burnished and the center is set (the cake may just barely begin to crack), 1 hour 35 minutes to 1 hour 45 minutes. The cake will jiggle a little bit when tapped. The top may rise a bit but will settle as it cools.

3. Remove the cheesecake from the oven and run a thin-bladed knife between the crust and the pan sides (this will prevent the cake from breaking as it cools). Let the cheesecake cool to room temperature in the pan on a wire rack. Cover and chill overnight. Unclasp and remove the side of the springform pan before slicing and serving.
—*Regan Daley*

PER SERVING (BASED ON 16 SERVINGS): 410 CALORIES | 7G PROTEIN | 36G CARB |
27G TOTAL FAT | 16G SAT FAT | 8G MONO FAT | 1G POLY FAT | 155MG CHOL |
320MG SODIUM | 1G FIBER

ginger–molasses cheesecake

MAKES ONE 10-INCH
CHEESECAKE; SERVES
16 TO 20

This creamy cake tastes like gingerbread. Serve it with a dollop of whipped cream and a few candied nuts, if you'd like.

FOR THE CRUST

2	cups finely crushed ginger-snap cookies (about 8½ oz.; crush in a food processor or in a zip-top bag with a rolling pin)
2	Tbs. granulated sugar
2½	oz. (5 Tbs.) unsalted butter, melted; plus 1 tsp. melted butter for the pan

FOR THE FILLING

5	8-oz. packages cream cheese, at room temperature
1¾	cups granulated sugar
1	Tbs. unbleached all-purpose flour
1	Tbs. ground ginger
1½	tsp. ground cinnamon
½	tsp. ground cloves
¼	tsp. table salt
4	large eggs, at room temperature
3	large egg yolks, at room temperature
¼	cup molasses
2	Tbs. heavy cream, at room temperature
1	tsp. pure vanilla extract

MAKE THE CRUST

1. Position one rack in the center of the oven and another directly beneath it. Heat the oven to 350°F.

2. Mix the crushed gingersnaps and sugar in a small bowl. Using a fork or your hands, gradually work in the melted butter, mixing until all the crumbs are moistened. Use your fingers and the bottom of a straight-sided, flat-bottomed metal measuring cup or drinking glass to press the mixture firmly into a 10x3-inch springform pan to create a uniform ⅛- to ¼-inch-thick crust that covers the bottom and goes 1 to 1½ inches up the sides. Bake the crust on the center oven rack until it's fragrant and warm to the touch, 5 to 7 minutes. Let the pan cool on a rack while you prepare the filling. Leave the oven on.

MAKE THE FILLING

1. Put the softened cream cheese in the bowl of a stand mixer fitted with a paddle attachment. Beat on medium speed until very smooth and entirely free of lumps. Gradually add the sugar. Scrape the sides of the bowl and continue mixing until the sugar has dissolved, 1 to 2 minutes. (Smear a small amount of the mixture between your finger-tips; there should be no grittiness if the sugar has dissolved.)

2. In a small bowl, mix the flour, ginger, cinnamon, cloves, and salt. Sprinkle the mixture evenly over the cream cheese and mix on low speed until blended.

3. Add the eggs and yolks, one at a time, beating on medium speed until just combined. Scrape the bowl after every other addition. (Beat no more than necessary to mix in each egg or you'll incorporate too much air, making the cheesecake dry and porous as opposed to dense and creamy.) Add the molasses, cream, and vanilla and mix until well combined.

ASSEMBLE AND BAKE THE CHEESECAKE

1. Brush the inside rim of the pan above the crust with the remaining 1 tsp. melted butter, without disturbing the crust. Pour the batter into the pan—it should fill the pan to a little above the crust. Put the pan on the center rack and position a foil-lined baking sheet directly beneath it to catch any batter drips. Bake until the top of the cake is golden brown and the center just barely jiggles when the side of the pan is gently tapped, 1 hour 10 minutes to 1 hour 20 minutes. It's fine if the cake develops a few cracks on the surface. Turn off the oven, open the door, and let the cheesecake cool in the oven for 15 minutes.

2. Set the cake on a rack until completely cool, at least 4 hours. Cover the cake loosely with plastic, cut a few air vents in the plastic, and refrigerate it overnight in the pan. When ready to serve, slowly

release the pan sides. If any of the cake edge appears stuck, gently loosen it with a sharp paring knife before continuing.

3. For the cleanest servings, use a sharp chef's knife and wipe it clean with a warm, damp cloth between slices. To store, cover the cake loosely with plastic and refrigerate. It's best if eaten within a day or two, as the crust will soften. *–Julia Usher*

PER SERVING (BASED ON 20 SERVINGS): 390 CALORIES I 7G PROTEIN I 33G CARB I
26G TOTAL FAT I 16G SAT FAT I 8G MONO FAT I 1.5G POLY FAT I 145MG CHOL I
290MG SODIUM I 0G FIBER

flourless chocolate and vanilla marble cake

SERVES 16

FOR THE VANILLA BATTER

8	oz. cream cheese, softened to room temperature
⅔	cup granulated sugar
1	large egg
1	tsp. pure vanilla extract

FOR THE CHOCOLATE BATTER

10	oz. bittersweet chocolate, finely chopped
5	oz. (10 Tbs.) unsalted butter, cut into 6 pieces; more for the pan
3	large eggs
⅓	cup granulated sugar
1	Tbs. dark rum or espresso
1	tsp. pure vanilla extract
	Pinch of table salt
	Cocoa powder for dusting

This dense, luscious cake has a texture a little like fudge and a little like cheesecake. A small slice goes a long way.

1. Position a rack in the center of the oven and heat the oven to 300°F. Lightly grease a 9x2-inch round cake pan and line the bottom with parchment.

2. Make the vanilla batter: In a medium bowl, beat the softened cream cheese with an electric mixer until smooth. Add the sugar and continue beating until well blended and no lumps remain. Add the egg and vanilla and beat just until blended. Set aside.

3. Make the chocolate batter: In a medium bowl, melt the chocolate and butter in a large metal bowl over a pan of simmering water or in the microwave. Whisk until smooth and set aside to cool slightly. In a stand mixer fitted with the whip attachment (or in a large bowl, using a hand-held mixer), beat the eggs, sugar, rum or espresso, vanilla, and salt on medium high until the mixture is pale and thick, 3 to 4 minutes. With the mixer on low, gradually pour in the chocolate mixture and continue beating until well blended.

4. Assemble and bake: Spread about half of the chocolate batter in the bottom of the pan. Alternately add large scoopfuls of each of the remaining batters to the cake pan. Using a knife or the tip of a rubber spatula, gently swirl the two batters together so they're mixed but not completely blended. Rap the pan against the countertop several times to settle the batters.

make slicing easier

Sprinkle cocoa on the bottom of the cake before inverting it onto another plate; the cocoa will keep the cake from sticking when you slice and serve it.

5. Bake until a pick inserted about 2 inches from the edge comes out gooey but not liquid, 40 to 42 minutes; don't overbake. The top will be puffed and slightly cracked, especially around the edges. It will sink down as it cools. Let cool on a rack until just slightly warm, about 1½ hours.

6. Loosen the cake from the pan by holding the pan almost perpendicular to the counter; tap the pan on the counter while rotating it clockwise. Invert onto a large flat plate or board. Remove the pan and carefully peel off the parchment. Sift some cocoa powder over the cake (this will make it easier to remove the slices when serving). Invert again onto a similar plate so that the top side is up. Let cool completely. Cover and refrigerate until very cold, at least 4 hours or overnight, or freeze. *–Abigail Johnson Dodge*

Make Ahead

Wrap the cooled cake (unmolded as directed in the recipe) in plastic and refrigerate until firm and well chilled. Slide the cake from the plate and wrap it again in plastic. Freeze for up to a month. To serve, unwrap the cake and set it on a flat serving plate. Cover with plastic wrap and thaw in the refrigerator overnight, or at room temperature for an hour or two.

mini pumpkin swirl cheesecakes

MAKES 12 MINI CHEESECAKES

Nonstick cooking spray

2 8 oz. packages cream cheese, at room temperature

⅔ cup granulated sugar

1½ tsp. pure vanilla extract

Pinch of table salt

2 large eggs

⅓ cup pure solid-pack canned pumpkin purée (not pumpkin pie filling)

2¼ tsp. unbleached all-purpose flour

½ tsp. ground cinnamon

¼ tsp. ground ginger

⅛ tsp. ground nutmeg

These quick-to-make crust-less cheesecakes are delicious and look beautiful. The baked cheesecakes can be refrigerated, covered, for 3 days or frozen for 1 month. Freeze the cooled cheesecakes in the tins in heavy-duty zip-top plastic bags, or remove them from the tins and arrange in airtight containers.

1. Position a rack in the center of the oven and heat the oven to 300°F. Line 12 standard muffin tins with foil liners and coat lightly with cooking spray.

2. In a stand mixer fitted with the paddle attachment (or in a large mixing bowl, using a hand-held mixer), beat the cream cheese on medium-high speed until very smooth and fluffy, stopping to scrape the bowl as necessary, about 4 minutes. Add the sugar, vanilla, and salt, and continue beating until well blended and smooth, scraping the bowl frequently, about 1 minute; there should be no lumps. Add the eggs, one at a time, beating on medium speed until just blended. (Don't overbeat once the eggs are added or the cheesecakes will puff and crack during baking.)

3. Transfer ⅔ cup of the batter to a small bowl. Add the pumpkin, flour, cinnamon, ginger, and nutmeg to the small bowl and stir with a wooden spoon until well blended.

4. Divide the plain batter among the muffin cups (about 2 generous Tbs. in each). Then divide the pumpkin batter evenly among the cups (about 1 generous Tbs. in each). Drag the tip of a wooden skewer, toothpick, or paring knife through the two batters in a random, swirly pattern to create a marbled look.

5. Bake until the centers of the cheesecakes barely jiggle when nudged, 15 to 18 minutes. Set the muffin tins on a rack and let cool completely. Cover and refrigerate until very cold, at least 6 hours or up to 3 days. *–Abigail Johnson Dodge*

PER CHEESECAKE: 190 CALORIES | 4G PROTEIN | 13G CARB | 14G TOTAL FAT | 9G SAT FAT | 4G MONO FAT | 0.5G POLY FAT | 75MG CHOL | 150MG SODIUM | 0G FIBER

butter–rum pudding cakes

MAKES 8 INDIVIDUAL CAKES

Softened butter, for the ramekins

2 oz. (¼ cup) unsalted butter, melted and cooled slightly

⅔ cup packed dark brown sugar

3 large eggs, separated, at room temperature

1⅛ oz. (¼ cup) unbleached all-purpose flour

¼ plus ⅛ tsp. table salt

1⅓ cups plus 1 Tbs. whole milk, at room temperature

3 Tbs. good-quality light rum (this is an adult amount; reduce the rum to 2 Tbs. and increase the milk by 1 Tbs. for a kid-friendly version)

1 tsp. pure vanilla extract

¼ cup granulated sugar

Lightly sweetened whipped cream, for serving (optional)

removing ramekins from a water bath

Wrap rubber bands around the ends of your tongs to get a better grip when lifting ramekins out of a water bath.

With a tender cake on top and a creamy custard on the bottom, a pudding cake is two desserts in one. Chilling the cakes for a few hours or overnight allows the flavors to intensify, the custard to thicken— and, most important, the cake and pudding layers to be more distinct.

1. Position a rack in the center of the oven and heat the oven to 350°F. Butter eight 6-oz. ceramic ovenproof ramekins or Pyrex custard cups and arrange them in a baking dish or roasting pan (a 10x15-inch or two 8x8-inch Pyrex dishes work well).

2. In a large bowl, whisk the melted butter with the brown sugar and egg yolks until smooth, about 1 minute. Add the flour and salt and pour in just enough milk to whisk the flour smoothly into the egg yolk mixture. Then whisk in the remaining milk, along with the rum and vanilla, until smooth. The mixture will be very fluid.

3. Put the egg whites in a large bowl. Beat with an electric mixer on medium speed until the egg whites begin to foam, 30 to 60 seconds. Increase the speed to high and beat just until the egg whites hold soft peaks when the beater is pulled away from the whites, another 1 to 2 minutes. Reduce the mixer speed to medium. With the mixer running, very slowly sprinkle in the granulated sugar; this should take about a minute. Stop the mixer and scrape the bowl. Beat on high speed until the whites hold medium-firm peaks when the beater is pulled away, about another 30 seconds.

4. Scrape one-third of the egg whites onto the egg yolk mixture and whisk until the batter is combined. Gently incorporate the remaining egg whites evenly into the batter, using the whisk in a folding/stirring motion. The batter will still be thin.

5. Portion the mixture evenly among the ramekins; the cakes don't rise much, so you can fill the ramekins to within ⅛ inch of the top. Pull out the oven rack and put the baking dish full of ramekins on the rack. Pour warm water into the dish to reach halfway up the sides of the ramekins. Bake until the tops of the cakes are light golden and slightly puffed and, when touched with a finger, feel spongy and spring back a bit but hold a shallow indentation, 25 to 30 minutes. Using tongs, carefully transfer the ramekins from the water bath to a rack. Let cool to room temperature and then refrigerate for at least 2 hours and up to 24 hours before serving, with whipped cream if you like. —*Nicole Rees*

PER CAKE: 230 CALORIES | 4G PROTEIN | 29G CARB | 10G TOTAL FAT | 5G SAT FAT | 3G MONO FAT | 1G POLY FAT | 100MG CHOL | 160MG SODIUM | 0G FIBER

lemon pudding cakes

Softened butter, for the ramekins

2 oz. (¼ cup) **unsalted butter, melted and cooled slightly**

1 cup **granulated sugar**

3 **large eggs, separated, at room temperature**

1⅛ oz. (¼ cup) **unbleached all-purpose flour**

¼ **plus ⅛ tsp. table salt**

1¼ cups **whole milk, at room temperature**

⅓ cup **fresh lemon juice, at room temperature**

1 Tbs. **finely grated lemon zest**

Lightly sweetened whipped cream, for serving (optional)

This dessert is elegant enough for guests but can be made ahead and refrigerated (they're best chilled!) until ready to serve.

1. Position a rack in the center of the oven and heat the oven to 350°F. Butter eight 6-oz. ceramic ovenproof ramekins or Pyrex custard cups and arrange them in a baking dish or roasting pan (one 10x15-inch or two 8x8-inch Pyrex dishes work well).

2. In a large bowl, whisk the melted butter with ⅔ cup of the sugar and the egg yolks until smooth and light, about 1 minute. Add the flour and salt and pour in just enough milk to whisk the flour smoothly into the egg yolk mixture. Then whisk in the remaining milk and the lemon juice until smooth. The mixture will be very fluid.

3. Put the egg whites in a large bowl. Beat with an electric mixer (a hand-held or a stand mixer fitted with the whisk attachment) on medium speed until the whites begin to foam, 30 to 60 seconds. Increase the speed to high and beat just until the whites hold soft peaks when the beater is pulled away, another 1 to 2 minutes. Reduce the mixer speed to medium. With the mixer running, very slowly sprinkle in the remaining ⅓ cup sugar; this should take about a minute. Stop the mixer and scrape the bowl. Beat on high speed until the whites hold medium-firm peaks when the beater is pulled away, about another 30 seconds.

4. Scrape one-third of the egg whites onto the egg yolk mixture, sprinkle the lemon zest on top, and whisk until the batter is combined. Gently incorporate the remaining whites into the batter, using the whisk in a folding/stirring motion. The batter will still be thin.

5. Portion the mixture evenly among the ramekins; the cakes don't rise much, so you can fill the ramekins to within ⅛ inch of the top. Pull out the oven rack and put the baking dish full of ramekins on the rack. Pour warm water into the dish to reach halfway up the sides of the ramekins. Bake until the tops of the cakes are light golden and slightly puffed, and when touched with a finger, feel spongy and spring back a bit but hold a shallow indentation, 25 to 30 minutes. Using tongs, carefully transfer the ramekins to a rack. Let cool to room temperature and then refrigerate for at least 2 hours and up to 24 hours before serving, with whipped cream if you like.   *–Nicole Rees*

PER CAKE: 220 CALORIES | 4G PROTEIN | 31G CARB | 9G TOTAL FAT | 5G SAT FAT | 3G MONO FAT | 1G POLY FAT | 100MG CHOL | 150MG SODIUM | 1G FIBER

how to make perfect pudding cakes

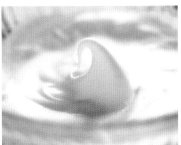

MAKE A THIN BATTER. After you mix the melted butter, sugar, egg yolks, flour, milk, and flavorings, you'll have a very thin batter that flows off a spoon like liquid. A liquid batter lets pudding cakes separate into two layers as they bake.

WHIP THE EGG WHITES TO MEDIUM-FIRM PEAKS. The peaks should curl over slightly and then hold their shape when the whip is pulled away from the whites.

WHISK THE WHIPPED WHITES INTO THE BATTER. Use a stirring motion to incorporate one-third of the whites. Then, still using the whisk, quickly but gently fold in the rest. The batter will still be thin.

ginger–mascarpone icebox cake

SERVES 12

- **12 oz. gingersnap crumbs,** about 2¼ cups
- **2½ oz. (5 Tbs.) unsalted butter,** melted
- **8 oz. cream cheese,** at room temperature
- **½ cup plain low-fat yogurt**
- **⅔ cup granulated sugar;** more for the pan
- **½ tsp. pure vanilla extract**
- **½ cup minced crystallized ginger**
- **1 lb. mascarpone cheese**
- **⅓ cup heavy cream**

Although delicious on its own, this cake is also lovely paired with some bright-flavored fruit, such as blueberries or slices of mango or peach.

1. Spray a 9-inch springform pan with nonstick cooking spray or grease it lightly. Dust the pan with a little sugar and knock out any excess. In a bowl, combine the gingersnap crumbs and butter, rubbing them together with your fingertips to combine thoroughly. Sprinkle half of the crumbs over the bottom of the pan and pat down evenly; reserve the rest.

2. With an electric mixer, whip together the cream cheese, yogurt, sugar, vanilla, and candied ginger until smooth, scraping down the sides. Add the mascarpone and cream and whip until the mixture is thoroughly combined and just holds peaks. Don't overwhip or the mixture may separate. Carefully spoon half of the mascarpone cream over the gingersnap crust, spreading it evenly to the edges of the pan. Sprinkle half of the remaining crumbs over the mascarpone cream in the pan. Top with remaining mascarpone cream and finish with the remaining crumbs. Gently tap the pan on the counter to eliminate any air bubbles. Cover with plastic wrap and refrigerate overnight.

3. To serve, warm a sharp knife under hot water and dry it off. Cut one slice, clean the knife, and warm it again before cutting the next slice.
–Heather Ho

PER SERVING: 500 CALORIES | 6G PROTEIN | 43G CARB | 34G TOTAL FAT | 19G SAT FAT | 12G MONO FAT | 2G POLY FAT | 90MG CHOL | 280MG SODIUM | 1G FIBER

mocha pudding cakes

Softened butter, for the ramekins

2 oz. (¼ cup) unsalted butter, melted and cooled slightly

1 cup granulated sugar

3 large eggs, separated, at room temperature

⅓ cup unsweetened Dutch-processed cocoa

2 Tbs. unbleached all-purpose flour

¼ plus ⅛ tsp. table salt

1¼ cups strong brewed coffee, at room temperature

⅓ cup whole milk, at room temperature

1 tsp. pure vanilla extract

Lightly sweetened whipped cream, for serving (optional)

You can make pudding cakes in large ramekins and serve them family style, but serving a small individual dish to each guest adds a special touch.

1. Position a rack in the center of the oven and heat the oven to 350°F. Butter eight 6-oz. ovenproof ceramic ramekins or Pyrex custard cups and arrange them in a baking dish or roasting pan (a 10x15-inch or two 8x8-inch Pyrex dishes work well).

2. In a large bowl, whisk the melted butter with ⅔ cup of the sugar and the egg yolks until smooth and light, about 1 minute. Add the cocoa, flour, and salt and pour in just enough coffee to whisk the flour smoothly into the egg yolk mixture. Then whisk in the remaining coffee, along with the milk and vanilla, until smooth. The mixture will be very fluid.

3. Put the egg whites in a large bowl. Beat with an electric mixer (a hand-held or a stand mixer fitted with the whisk attachment) set at medium speed until the whites begin to foam, 30 to 60 seconds. Increase the speed to high and beat just until the egg whites hold soft peaks when the beater is pulled away from the whites, another 1 to 2 minutes. Reduce the mixer speed to medium. With the mixer running, very slowly sprinkle in the remaining ⅓ cup sugar; this should take about a minute. Stop the mixer and scrape the bowl. Beat on high speed until the whites hold medium-firm peaks when the beater is pulled away, about another 30 seconds.

4. Scrape one-third of the egg whites onto the egg yolk mixture and whisk until the batter is combined. Gently incorporate the remaining egg whites evenly into the batter, using the whisk in a folding/stirring motion. The batter will still be thin.

5. Portion the mixture evenly among the ramekins; the cakes don't rise much, so you can fill the ramekins to within ⅛ inch of the top. Pull out the oven rack and put the baking dish full of ramekins on the rack. Pour warm water into the dish to reach halfway up the sides of the ramekins. Bake until the tops of the cakes are slightly puffed and, when touched with a finger, they feel spongy and spring back a bit but hold a very shallow indentation, 25 to 30 minutes. Using tongs, carefully transfer the ramekins to a rack. Let cool to room temperature and then refrigerate for at least 2 hours and up to 24 hours before serving, with whipped cream if you like. *–Nicole Rees*

PER CAKE: 200 CALORIES | 4G PROTEIN | 29G CARB | 5G TOTAL FAT | 5G SAT FAT | 3G MONO FAT | 1G POLY FAT | 95MG CHOL | 140MG SODIUM | 1G FIBER

classic vanilla tres leches cake

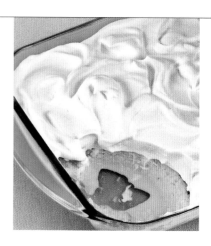

SERVES 12 TO 16

FOR THE CAKE

	Unsalted butter, softened, for the pan
4½	oz. (1 cup) unbleached all-purpose flour
1½	tsp. baking powder
¼	tsp. kosher salt
5	large eggs, at room temperature
1	cup granulated sugar
⅓	cup whole milk
¾	tsp. pure vanilla extract

FOR THE SOAKING LIQUID

1	14-oz. can sweetened condensed milk
1	12-oz. can evaporated milk
½	cup heavy cream
	Pinch of kosher salt

FOR THE TOPPING

2½	cups heavy cream
2	Tbs. confectioners' sugar
½	tsp. pure vanilla extract

Soaked in sweet milk and topped with billowy whipped cream, this Latin American dessert is positively addictive— and makes a great summer party cake. You can soak the cake in the milk mixture up to a day ahead and top it up to 2 hours ahead.

BAKE THE CAKE

1. Position a rack in the center of the oven and heat the oven to 350°F.

2. Butter the bottom and sides of a 9x13-inch Pyrex baking dish or a nonreactive metal pan. Line the bottom of the baking dish or pan with parchment and lightly butter the parchment.

3. Sift the flour, baking powder, and salt into a medium bowl and set aside.

4. Separate the eggs, putting the whites in a medium bowl and the yolks in a large bowl. With an electric mixer, beat the yolks with ¾ cup of the sugar on medium speed until the mixture is pale and creamy, about 2 minutes. Add the milk and vanilla and beat until combined, 1 minute more.

5. Clean and dry the beaters and then beat the egg whites, gradually increasing the speed to high, until they reach soft peaks, 2 to 3 minutes. Add the remaining ¼ cup sugar in a stream, continuing to beat on high, until you reach firm but not dry peaks, 1 to 2 minutes more.

6. Whisk a third of the dry ingredients into the yolk mixture until thoroughly combined. Gently fold in a third of the egg whites with a rubber spatula. Fold in the remaining dry ingredients and egg whites, alternately, in two more batches each, until fully incorporated.

7. Pour the batter into the prepared dish or pan and bake until a toothpick inserted in the center comes out clean, 20 to 25 minutes. Let the cake cool in the pan on a rack for 10 minutes, then invert the cake onto the rack, remove the parchment, and let cool completely. Return the cake to the baking dish or pan (the cake will soak up more of the liquid if returned to the pan it was baked in), or invert it onto a rimmed platter.

SOAK THE CAKE

1. In a 2-quart saucepan, stir together the condensed milk, evaporated milk, heavy cream, and salt until the condensed milk is well blended. Cook over medium-low heat, stirring to avoid scorching, until it begins to bubble around the edges, 3 to 5 minutes. Remove from the heat and pour into a heatproof 4-cup measuring cup.

2. With a toothpick, prick the cake to the bottom in ½-inch intervals. Pour the soaking liquid slowly over the cake, starting at the edges and pausing to let it soak in before adding more. Cover loosely with plastic wrap and refrigerate until the cake is well chilled, at least 2 hours and up to 24 hours.

TOP THE CAKE

1. In a large bowl, beat the heavy cream with an electric mixer on medium speed. When it begins to thicken, slowly add the sugar and vanilla and continue to beat just until it holds firm peaks, 3 to 4 minutes (be careful not to overbeat).

2. Spread the whipped cream over the top of the cake and serve.
–Fanny Gerson

PER SERVING (BASED ON 16 SERVINGS): 370 CALORIES | 7G PROTEIN | 37G CARB | 22G TOTAL FAT | 13G SAT FAT | 7G MONO FAT | 1G POLY FAT | 135MG CHOL | 160MG SODIUM | 0G FIBER

Variations

To make a chocolate version of the classic or of any of the following variations, replace ⅓ cup of the flour with unsweetened cocoa powder.

Toasted coconut

In the soaking liquid, substitute one 13½-oz can unsweetened coconut milk for the cream. Beat 3 Tbs. dark rum into the whipped cream topping with the sugar and vanilla. Scatter 1 cup lightly toasted flaked coconut over the topping.

Boozy berry

Beat 3 Tbs. gin or tequila into the whipped cream topping with the sugar and vanilla. Combine 2 cups each raspberries and sliced strawberries with 1 tsp. finely grated lemon or lime zest. Spoon over the topping.

Café con leche

In the soaking liquid, substitute strong brewed coffee for ½ cup of the evaporated milk. For the topping, stir 1 tsp. instant coffee into 2 Tbs. of the cream until dissolved. Add the remaining cream and beat as directed. Sprinkle the topping with toasted slivered almonds or chocolate curls.

lemon–caramel icebox cake

FOR THE LEMON CURD

4   **large eggs**

4   **large egg yolks
(reserve the whites from
2 of the eggs for the
meringue topping)**

3   **Tbs. finely grated lemon
zest (from about 3 lemons)**

½   **cup granulated sugar**

⅔   **cup fresh lemon juice**

5   **oz. (10 Tbs.) unsalted
butter, cut in pieces**

FOR THE CARAMEL

¾   **cup granulated sugar**

2   **Tbs. light corn syrup**

¼   **cup water**

¼   **cup plus 2 Tbs. heavy cream**

¼   **tsp. pure vanilla extract**

FOR ASSEMBLY

5   **Tbs. granulated sugar;
more for the pan**

5   **oz. (about 1½ cups)
graham cracker crumbs
(from about 10 crackers),
lightly toasted in a 350°F
oven until they just take on
some color, about 7 minutes**

2   **oz. (¼ cup) unsalted butter,
melted**

1½   **cups heavy cream**

2   **egg whites**

*The caramel and the lemon curd can be made ahead and
refrigerated for up to 5 days. The caramel needs to be warmed
to a pourable consistency before using.*

MAKE THE LEMON CURD

Bring a medium pot filled halfway with water to a simmer. In a medium
stainless-steel bowl that will fit over the pot without touching the
water, whisk the eggs, yolks, zest, sugar, and lemon juice. Put the bowl
over (not touching) the simmering water and whisk until the mixture
thickens and becomes smooth and custard-like, about 10 minutes;
remove from the heat. Whisk in the butter a piece at a time. Strain the
curd through a fine-mesh sieve into a bowl. Put plastic wrap directly
on its surface and refrigerate.

MAKE THE CARAMEL

In a medium, heavy-based saucepan, combine the sugar, corn syrup,
and water; stir until the sugar dissolves. Cook over high heat until
the mixture turns dark amber. Don't stir the caramel while it cooks;
instead, swirl the pan gently to get an even color. Remove from the
heat and whisk in the cream (be careful: it will splatter). Return the
mixture to the heat, whisk until smooth, and then whisk in the vanilla.
Let cool to room temperature.

ASSEMBLE THE CAKE

1. Spray a 9-inch springform pan with nonstick cooking spray or grease
it lightly. Dust the pan with sugar and knock out any excess. Combine
the toasted graham cracker crumbs and butter, rubbing them together
with your fingertips to combine thoroughly. Sprinkle half of the
crumbs over the bottom of the pan and pat down; reserve the rest.

2. In a large bowl, whisk the cream to firm peaks. Fold in the cooled
lemon curd. Spoon half of the lemon cream over the cracker crust
and spread it evenly to the edges of the pan. Sprinkle the remaining
crumbs over the lemon cream. Spread the remaining lemon cream
over the crumbs. Pour a little more than half of the caramel over the
lemon cream, reserving the rest in the refrigerator. Put the cake in the
freezer while you make the meringue topping.

3. Whisk the egg whites and sugar in a double boiler over medium-
high heat (as you did with the lemon curd) and cook until the mixture
is warm and the sugar is dissolved, about 2 minutes. With an electric
mixer, whisk the whites to stiff peaks. Spread the meringue on the top
of the cake. Freeze the cake, unwrapped, overnight. (For longer storage, wrap it in plastic once the meringue has firmed up; unwrap before
defrosting.)

4. About an hour before serving, transfer the cake to the refrigerator.
Just before serving, reheat the remaining caramel sauce if you want
to drizzle some on the plate. Brown the meringue by running it under a
hot broiler, rotating the cake if necessary, until evenly browned

(or brown it with a kitchen torch). Run a thin knife around the sides of the cake and remove the springform. Cut the cake into slices with a warm knife. If the cake seems very frozen, let the slices soften somewhat before serving. Serve with a drizzle of warm caramel sauce.
–Heather Ho

PER SERVING: 460 CALORIES | 5G PROTEIN | 41G CARB | 32G TOTAL FAT | 18G SAT FAT | 10G MONO FAT | 2G POLY FAT V 230MG CHOL | 125MG SODIUM | 1G FIBER

coffee and cream icebox cake

SERVES 8

- 1¾ cups heavy cream
- 1 Tbs. instant espresso powder
- 1 Tbs. granulated sugar
- 44 Nabisco FAMOUS Chocolate Wafers
- ¼ cup finely chopped, toasted hazelnuts, for garnish
- ¼ cup crushed chocolate wafer cookie crumbs, for garnish

Coffee and hazelnuts give this cake—a variation on Nabisco's Famous Wafer Roll recipe— a more sophisticated flavor. To be safe, buy two boxes of cookies, as some may break. This cake slices best after 2 days in the refrigerator.

1. Lightly grease a 6-cup loaf pan. Line the pan with two pieces of overlapping plastic wrap, allowing the excess to hang over the edges of the pan.

2. In a bowl, combine the cream, espresso powder, and sugar. Whisk until the cream holds firm peaks. Spoon about two-thirds of the whipped cream into the prepared pan. Tap the pan firmly on the counter to even out the cream and eliminate any air bubbles.

3. Starting at a short side of the pan, arrange 11 cookies in the cream, standing them on their edge in a row like dominoes. Gently squeeze the cookies together as you go. Do the same with a second row of cookies, slightly overlapping the cookies from the second row with the cookies in the first row. Continue with two more rows for a total of four rows.

4. Press down on the cookies gently. Cover them with the remaining cream. Smooth the cream with a spatula, gently pressing to make sure any gaps between the cookies are filled. Tap the pan on the counter several times to eliminate any air pockets.

5. Cover the cake with the excess plastic wrap and refrigerate for at least 24 hours, preferably 2 days. When ready to serve, peel the plastic wrap from the top and gently tug on the plastic to loosen the cake from the sides of the pan. Set a cutting board on top of the pan and invert the cake onto the board. Lift the pan off and gently peel away the plastic wrap. Mix the hazelnuts with the cookie crumbs and sprinkle over the top of the cake. Slice carefully with a warm knife.
–Heather Ho

PER SERVING: 380 CALORIES | 4G PROTEIN | 33G CARB | 26G TOTAL FAT | 14G SAT FAT | 9G MONO FAT | 2G POLY FAT | 75MG CHOL | 300MG SODIUM | 1G FIBER

lemon icebox cake

FOR THE LEMON FILLING

1½   Tbs. firmly packed finely grated lemon zest (from 2 lemons)

¾   cup egg yolks (from 11 to 12 large eggs)

6   Tbs. granulated sugar

⅔   cup fresh lemon juice (from about 2 lemons)

3   oz. (6 Tbs.) unsalted butter, cut into small pieces and softened

     Pinch of table salt

1½   cups heavy cream, chilled

FOR THE MERINGUE

2   tsp. powdered unflavored gelatin

1   cup plus 3 Tbs. granulated sugar

¾   cup egg whites (from 5 to 6 large eggs)

¾   tsp. cream of tartar

TO FINISH THE DESSERT

1   10-inch Angel Food Cake (recipe on p. 107)

     Vegetable oil, for the pan

Early icebox cakes were festive chilled desserts made in molds with layers of cake (be it angel food, sponge cake, or ladyfingers) and custard or cream. Here, slices of angel food cake are layered with a luscious lemon mousse right in the cake pan.

MAKE THE LEMON FILLING

1. Put the lemon zest in a 4-quart or larger bowl and set a medium-mesh sieve on top.

2. In a heavy-duty 4-quart saucepan, whisk the egg yolks and sugar. Add the lemon juice, butter, and salt. Cook over medium-low heat, stirring constantly, until thickened enough to coat the back of a wooden spoon but still pourable, 4 to 5 minutes. (Don't boil or it will curdle.) Pass the thickened curd through the sieve and mix in the zest. Cool, stirring occasionally, about 1 hour.

3. When the lemon curd is cool, beat the cream with an electric mixer on medium speed just until soft peaks form, about 2 minutes. With a large balloon whisk or silicone spatula, gently fold in the lemon curd. Cover the bowl tightly with plastic wrap and refrigerate.

MAKE THE MERINGUE

1. In a small, microwavable bowl, sprinkle the gelatin over 3 Tbs. water; let soften for at least 5 minutes. Microwave on high to melt the gelatin, 15 to 30 seconds.

2. In a heavy-duty nonstick 2-quart saucepan over medium-high heat, combine 1 cup of the sugar and 6 Tbs. water and stir constantly until the syrup is bubbling, 2 to 3 minutes. Remove the pan from the heat.

3. In a stand mixer fitted with the whisk attachment, beat the egg whites on medium-high speed until foamy, 45 seconds. Add the cream of tartar and beat until soft peaks form, 30 seconds. Gradually beat in the remaining 3 Tbs. sugar until stiff peaks form, 1 to 2 minutes.

4. Have ready a 2-cup or larger heatproof liquid measure. Return the pan of syrup to medium-high heat and boil until a candy thermometer registers 248°F (firm-ball stage). Pour the syrup into the measure to stop the cooking and then immediately pour a small amount of syrup over the whites with the mixer off. Immediately beat at high speed for 5 seconds. Stop the mixer and add a larger amount of syrup. Beat at high speed for 5 seconds. Continue with the remaining syrup. Lower

continued on p. 106

the speed to medium, add the gelatin mixture, and beat on medium speed for 2 minutes. Decrease the speed to low and continue beating until the bottom of the bowl is no longer warm to the touch, about 10 minutes.

5. Use a large balloon whisk or silicone spatula to gently fold one-third of the meringue into the lemon cream. Repeat twice more until all of the meringue is folded into the lemon cream.

SPLIT THE CAKE

Unmold the cake according to the recipe on the facing page. Spread two 3-foot-long pieces of parchment or waxed paper on the counter. Position the cake so the top is facing up. Using a long serrated knife, remove and discard the brown top crust. Turn the cake bottom up and split it into 4 even layers. After cutting each layer, use two spatulas to lift a layer off the cake and put it on the parchment or waxed paper. Arrange the layers in the order you cut them so it's easy to assemble the cake.

ASSEMBLE THE CAKE

1. Lightly oil the inside of a clean 10-inch (16-cup) 2-piece metal tube pan.

2. Spread one-quarter of the filling on the bottom of the pan. Place the smallest cake ring on top of the filling. Spread about one-third of the remaining lemon filling on top. Top with the next cake layer. Spread on half of the remaining filling. Repeat with the third cake layer and remaining filling. Top with the last cake layer and lightly press it down. Cover tightly with plastic wrap and refrigerate for at least 12 hours or overnight.

3. To unmold, wet a kitchen towel under very hot water and wring out the excess. Wipe the sides and bottom of the pan to help release the cake smoothly.

4. Set the pan on top of a canister that's smaller than the pan's removable bottom and higher than the pan's sides, and gently press down on the sides of the pan. If it doesn't slide down easily, apply more heat to the sides.

5. Run a long offset spatula between the bottom of the cake and the pan. Run a wire cake tester or wooden skewer around the inner tube. Invert the cake onto a serving plate and remove the tube portion of the pan. Slice and serve the cake. *–Rose Levy Beranbaum*

PER SERVING: 570 CALORIES | 12G PROTEIN | 75G CARB | 26G TOTAL FAT | 15G SAT FAT | 8G MONO FAT | 2G POLY FAT | 295MG CHOL | 220MG SODIUM | 0G FIBER

angel food cake

MAKES ONE 10-INCH CAKE

1½	**cups superfine sugar**
3¾	**oz. (1 cup) sifted cake flour**
¼	**tsp. table salt**
2	**cups egg whites (from about 16 large eggs), at room temperature**
1	**Tbs. fresh lemon juice**
2	**tsp. cream of tartar**
4	**tsp. pure vanilla extract**

1. Position a rack in the lower third of the oven and heat the oven to 350°F.

2. In a small bowl, whisk ¾ cup of the sugar, the flour, and salt until evenly combined. Sift the remaining ¾ cup sugar onto a piece of waxed paper.

3. In the bowl of a stand mixer fitted with the whisk attachment, beat the egg whites on medium-low speed until frothy, about 1 minute. Turn off the mixer and add the lemon juice and cream of tartar. Increase the speed to medium high and beat until soft peaks form, 2 to 3 minutes. Gradually beat in the sifted sugar and continue beating on medium-high speed until very stiff peaks form, 1 to 2 minutes. Beat in the vanilla.

4. One-quarter at a time, sift the flour mixture over the whites and, with a large balloon whisk, fold it in quickly but gently. It's not necessary to incorporate every speck until the last addition of the flour.

5. Using an offset spatula, spread a thin layer of the cake batter onto the sides of a 10-inch (16 cup) 2-piece metal tube pan to ensure smooth sides. Pour the remaining batter into the pan. Run a knife through the batter to eliminate air bubbles and smooth the surface.

6. Bake until golden brown, a wire cake tester inserted in the center comes out clean, and the cake springs back when lightly pressed, 30 to 40 minutes. (A wooden skewer will still have a few moist crumbs clinging to it.) During baking, the center will rise about 2 inches above the pan but will sink to almost level with the pan when done. The surface will have deep cracks, like a soufflé.

7. Immediately invert the cake; if your pan has feet, simply invert it onto the feet. Otherwise, invert the pan onto a long-necked soda or wine bottle, or a large inverted metal funnel that fits into the tube opening to suspend it well above the counter (if using a soda or wine bottle, fill it with sugar, salt, or marbles to keep it from tipping). Cool the cake completely in the pan, about 1½ hours.

8. Loosen the sides of the cake with a long metal spatula and remove the cake (still on the tube section) from the sides of the pan. Loosen the cake from the bottom and tube with the spatula or a thin, sharp knife. (A wire cake tester works well around the tube. To keep the sides attractive, press the spatula firmly against the sides of the pan, moving the spatula up and down as you go around.) Invert the cake onto a flat plate or work surface covered with plastic wrap.

frozen lemon cream cakes with toasted meringue and caramel sauce

SERVES 8

FOR THE CRUST

- 5 oz. (1 cup plus 2 Tbs.) graham cracker crumbs (from 12 to 13 homemade graham crackers, recipe on p. 111, or 9 whole store-bought crackers)
- 1½ oz. (3 Tbs.) unsalted butter, melted
- 2 Tbs. granulated sugar

FOR THE LEMON LAYER

- 2 cups granulated sugar
- 3 to 4 medium lemons, zest finely grated to yield ¼ cup, then juiced to yield 1 cup
- 2 large eggs
- 8 large egg yolks
- ½ lb. (1 cup) unsalted butter, cut into small pieces and softened
- 1½ cups heavy cream, chilled

FOR THE CARAMEL SAUCE

- 1¼ cups granulated sugar
- ⅛ tsp. table salt
- 1¼ cups heavy cream
- ½ tsp. pure vanilla extract

FOR THE MERINGUE

- 1 cup superfine sugar
- 5 large egg whites, at room temperature (about ¾ cup)
- ⅛ tsp. table salt
- ⅛ tsp. cream of tartar

  Fresh blueberries, for garnish

Here, the classic lemon icebox cake becomes an impressive individual frozen dessert boasting a graham cracker crust, layers of lemon curd, lemon cream, and toasted meringue, with a rich caramel sauce and fresh berries.

MAKE THE CRUST

1. Arrange eight 3-inch-diameter, 2-inch-deep round metal ring molds on a rimmed baking sheet lined with parchment.

2. In a large bowl, stir the cracker crumbs, melted butter, and sugar until the crumbs are evenly moist and slightly clump together. Portion the mixture among the molds and pack it in, pressing to compact. Refrigerate.

MAKE THE LEMON LAYER

1. Fill a large bowl about a third full with ice cubes plus a cup or so of water. Set a second bowl (one that holds at least 2 quarts) in the ice bath and put a medium-mesh strainer in the bowl.

2. Combine the sugar and lemon zest in a medium bowl and rub it between your fingers to release the lemon oil into the sugar.

3. In a large heatproof bowl, whisk the lemon juice, eggs, egg yolks, and the sugar mixture. Whisk in the butter pieces. In a 4-quart saucepan, bring 2 inches of water to a bare simmer. Set the bowl over the pot (the water shouldn't touch the bottom of the bowl). Whisk constantly until the mixture thickens and reaches a temperature of 170°F, 5 to 10 minutes. Immediately strain into the bowl in the ice bath. Gently stir every so often until completely cool.

4. Distribute ½ cup of the lemon curd evenly among the 8 ring molds and spread it with the back of a spoon to cover the crust. Put the baking sheet in the freezer.

5. In a stand mixer fitted with the whisk attachment, whip the cream just until soft peaks form, 1 to 2 minutes. With a spatula, gently fold the remaining lemon curd into the whipped cream until well combined. Spoon about ½ cup of lemon cream into each mold (you may not use all of the cream). Cover loosely with plastic and freeze for at least 8 hours or overnight.

MAKE THE CARAMEL SAUCE

1. In a 4-quart heavy-duty saucepan, mix the sugar, salt, and ½ cup water with a wooden spoon. Cook over medium-low heat until the sugar turns golden amber, about 15 minutes. As the sugar cooks, occasionally rinse down the sides of the pan with a wet pastry brush to prevent sugar crystals from forming.

2. Remove the pan from the heat and carefully add the cream—it may splatter a bit. Stir in the vanilla. If the sugar hardened when adding the cream, stir until it's completely dissolved. Let cool to room temperature, about 4 hours. (The sauce may be made several days ahead. Refrigerate and gently reheat just long enough to take off the chill before serving. Leftovers will keep, refrigerated, for about 2 weeks.)

continued on p. 110

MAKE THE MERINGUE

1. Shortly before serving, boil the sugar and ½ cup water in a heavy-duty 2-quart saucepan over medium heat, stirring to dissolve the sugar, until the mixture reaches the soft-ball stage (235° to 240°F on a candy thermometer), 3 to 5 minutes. As the sugar boils, occasionally wash the sides of the pan with a wet pastry brush to prevent sugar crystals from forming.

2. Meanwhile, whip the egg whites and salt in a stand mixer fitted with the whisk attachment on low speed until foamy. Increase the speed to medium, add the cream of tartar, and beat until soft peaks form, about 3 minutes. With the mixer on medium speed, pour the hot sugar syrup in a very thin stream down the side of the bowl. Continue beating on medium-high speed until the egg whites are firm and glossy and the bowl is cool to the touch, 6 to 8 minutes.

ASSEMBLE THE CAKES

Put the cakes on individual serving plates. To unmold, quickly pass the flame of a small kitchen torch around the sides of the rings to loosen them, and then use tongs to slide the rings off. Dollop spoonfuls of meringue over the lemon cream. Using the kitchen torch, lightly brown the meringue. Pool about 2 Tbs. of the caramel sauce next to each cake and garnish with blueberries. Serve immediately.

–Yasmin Lozada-Hissom

PER SERVING: 1 | 110 CALORIES | 10G PROTEIN | 127G CARB | 66G TOTAL FAT | 40G SAT FAT | 19G MONO FAT | 3G POLY FAT | 455MG CHOL | 220MG SODIUM | 1G FIBER

homemade graham crackers

MAKES FORTY-FIVE 2X2-INCH
CRACKERS

- 5   oz. (1 cup) whole-wheat
       graham flour

- 5   oz. (1 cup plus 2 Tbs.)
       all-purpose flour

- ⅓   cup packed light brown
       sugar

- ¾   tsp. baking powder

- ½   tsp. baking soda

- ½   tsp. kosher salt

- ⅛   tsp. ground cinnamon

- 3   oz. (6 Tbs.) cold unsalted
       butter, cut into small pieces

- 3   Tbs. buttermilk

- 3   Tbs. honey

- 1½   Tbs. unsulfured molasses

- ½   tsp. pure vanilla extract

1. Position a rack in the center of the oven and heat the oven to 350°F.

2. Put both flours, the sugar, baking powder, baking soda, salt, and cinnamon in a food processor and pulse until combined. Add the butter and pulse until the mixture resembles coarse meal. In a small bowl, whisk the buttermilk, honey, molasses, and vanilla. Add the wet ingredients to the dry and pulse until a dough begins to form.

3. Remove the dough from the food processor and transfer to a large piece of parchment. Put another piece of parchment over it. Roll the dough into a ⅛-inch-thick, 16x13-inch rectangle. Remove the top sheet of paper, trim the rough edges, and transfer the dough along with the bottom layer of parchment to a baking sheet.

4. With a pizza cutter, divide the dough into 2-inch squares (press just hard enough to cut the dough and not the paper). With a fork, prick each square 3 or 4 times. Bake until golden brown, 15 to 20 minutes. Let cool on the sheet.   *–Rose Levy Beranbaum*

Make Ahead

> You can bake half a batch of graham cracker dough and refrigerate or freeze the rest for later use. Divide the dough in two before rolling it, wrap one half well, and refrigerate for up to 3 days or freeze for up to 1 week until ready to use again for a second batch of crackers. Take the dough out of the refrigerator or freezer at least a couple hours before you plan to bake so it will soften slightly.

classic boston cream pie

FOR THE RUM SYRUP

⅓ cup warm water

¼ cup granulated sugar

2 Tbs. dark rum (such as Myers's®)

FOR THE CAKE

French Butter Sponge Cake (recipe on p. 115)

Pastry Cream, well chilled (remove from the refrigerator and whisk gently to make it smooth; recipe on p. 117)

1 cup toasted sliced almonds

Chocolate Ganache (if made in advance, warm it gently in a heavy saucepan; recipe on p. 117)

FOR THE WHITE ICING

½ cup confectioners' sugar (scoop a dry measure into the sugar container; level it with a metal spatula)

2¼ tsp. very hot water

This American classic is a stunning version of the original dessert created more than 100 years ago. It consists of butter sponge cake layered with pastry cream and a topping of chocolate ganache zigzagged with white icing. Though it's a complex recipe, many of the components can be made in advance.

MAKE THE RUM SYRUP

Stir together the warm water and sugar in a small bowl until the sugar is dissolved. Stir in the rum. Let cool and then cover until ready to use.

SPLIT AND LAYER THE CAKE

1. Trim a very thin layer off the top of the cake with a sharp serrated knife to expose the cake's interior porous structure (you may need to cut as much as ¼ inch off the top if the cake is slightly domed). Slice the cake in half horizontally with the serrated knife (each layer will be about ¾ inch thick).

2. Dot a bit of pastry cream in the center of a 10-inch cardboard disk (or the removable bottom of a 10-inch tart pan) and set the bottom cake layer, cut side up, on the disk. The pastry cream will hold it in place. (If you have a cake turntable, set the disk on that. Otherwise, put the disk on a large cake plate or cake stand.)

3. Use a pastry brush to dab half of the rum syrup all over the cake.

4. Reserve ½ cup of the pastry cream and spread the remainder on the top of the cake. The layer of pastry cream will be about ½ inch thick. Set the second cake layer over the cream, and dab on the remaining rum syrup. With a narrow metal spatula, spread the reserved pastry cream all around the sides of the cake.

5. Supporting the cake in your hand, hold it over a sheet tray or a piece of parchment and gently press the almonds all around the sides of the cake. The nuts that don't stick will fall into the tray or onto the parchment. You won't use all the nuts; snack on the leftovers.

6. Using two large offset spatulas, carefully transfer the cake from the cardboard disk onto a cake plate or cake stand. Pour the warm ganache (if it has started to firm up, warm it gently in a heavy saucepan) onto the center of the top of the cake without letting any run down the sides. Carefully spread the ganache with a large metal icing spatula right to the edges of the cake.

MAKE THE WHITE ICING AND DECORATE THE CAKE

1. In a small bowl, whisk together the confectioners' sugar and hot water. The icing should have a smooth, creamy consistency that's a bit thinner than honey; add a few more drops of water if needed.

2. Scrape the white icing into a zip-top bag, seal, and cut a tiny hole in one corner of the bag to pipe it. Squeeze the icing over the ganache in a decorative pattern like a crosshatch or zigzag. Refrigerate the cake for at least 1 hour.

SLICE THE CAKE WHILE COOL

Twenty or thirty minutes before serving, remove the assembled cake from the refrigerator. Run a sharp knife under hot water and wipe it dry before slicing. You may have to make several progressively deeper cuts (heating the knife each time) to cut through the chocolate without cracking the top. The rest of the cake cuts easily. Put portions on dessert plates and let stand at room temperature for about 20 minutes before serving. Refrigerate any leftovers for up to 2 days.
—Greg Patent

PER SERVING: 500 CALORIES | 10G PROTEIN | 59G CARB | 25G TOTAL FAT | 12G SAT FAT | 9G MONO FAT | 3G POLY FAT | 225MG CHOL | 170MG SODIUM | 1G FIBER

continued on p. 114

how to assemble the boston cream pie

Follow these steps to ensure success in assembling the dessert.

Add a dot of pastry cream to the center of a cardboard disk or bottom of a tart pan. The bottom cake layer will sit on top.

Brush half of the rum syrup over top of the bottom layer.

Spread pastry cream to the outside edge of the cake, then set the second cake layer on top and brush with rum syrup.

Press sliced almonds all over the sides of the cake.

Pour ganache on the center of the top of the cake—don't let it run down the sides.

Spread the ganache to the edges of the cake.

Squeeze the icing over the ganache, then let harden in the refrigerator.

french butter sponge cake

2 oz. (¼ cup) unsalted butter;
more for the pan

Unbleached all-purpose
flour, for the pan

3¾ oz. cake flour (scant 1 cup,
spooned into a dry measure)

7 large eggs, separated

1 cup granulated sugar

2 tsp. pure vanilla extract

¼ tsp. table salt

1. Position a rack in the lower third of the oven; heat the oven to 325°F. Melt the butter in a small saucepan over medium-low heat and set it aside to cool. It must be no hotter than tepid when used.

2. Butter the bottom of a 10-inch springform pan and line it with a round of parchment or waxed paper; butter the paper. Dust the inside of the pan with all-purpose flour; knock out any excess. Sift the cake flour three times onto a sheet of waxed paper, return the flour to the sifter, and set the sifter on the waxed paper.

3. Using the whip attachment on a stand mixer, whip the yolks on medium-high speed until thickened, about 3 minutes. Continue beating on medium high and gradually add ½ cup of the sugar, about 2 Tbs. at a time; beat for 20 to 30 seconds between additions. You may need to stop to scrape the bowl occasionally. Beat on high speed until very thick and pale, about another 3 minutes. When the whip is raised, the yolks should fall into the bowl and form a slowly dissolving ribbon. Beat in the vanilla. Scrape the mixture into a large, wide bowl. Wash and dry the mixing bowl and the whip.

4. Combine the egg whites with the salt in the bowl of the mixer and begin mixing on medium low until frothy, about 1 minute. Increase the speed to medium and mix until the whip leaves distinct traces in the whites and forms peaks that curl softly at their tips when the beater is raised, about 4 minutes. With the mixer running on medium, gradually add the remaining ½ cup sugar, about 2 Tbs. at a time, beating for 20 to 30 seconds between additions. Continue beating on medium to medium-high speed until the whites hold a firm shape and form peaks that curl only very slightly at their tips, another 1 to 2 minutes. Stop beating before the whites form stiff, unwavering upright peaks.

5. Check the melted butter to be sure it's tepid (about 95°F) and liquid. The butter must not be at room temperature or it won't blend into the batter properly. If necessary, rewarm it briefly.

6. Scoop about a quarter of the whites over the yolk mixture and fold together gently with a few broad strokes of a large rubber spatula to lighten the mixture. Rotate the bowl a bit with each fold, and don't be too thorough at this point: It's all right if streaks of white remain. Sift about a third of the cake flour over the mixture and scoop about a third of the remaining whites over the flour. Fold together gently, turning the

continued on p. 116

bowl as you go; but again, don't be too thorough. Sift half of the remaining flour and scoop half of the remaining whites onto the batter and fold in the same manner. Sift on the last of the flour and add the last of the whites; fold gently but thoroughly, only until the batter is an even yellow color.

7. Drizzle half of the tepid butter on top of the batter and partially incorporate it quickly with three or four broad strokes, turning the bowl a little with each fold. Pour on the remaining butter and fold it in only until no butter shows. Carefully scrape the batter into the prepared pan (the pan will be about half full), spread it evenly, and put the pan in the oven immediately.

BAKE THE CAKE
Bake until the cake is golden brown and springs back when gently pressed, about 40 minutes; don't overbake. Let the cake cool in the pan on a rack for 10 minutes. Run a sharp knife around the edge to release the cake from the sides; unclasp and remove the bottom of the pan invert the cake and remove the paper liner. Replace the paper on the cake bottom, cover with another rack, and invert. Let cool completely, right side up. If storing, wrap the cake tightly in plastic when completely cool.

pastry cream

- 2 **cups whole milk**
- 2 **large eggs**
- 2 **large egg yolks**
- ¼ **tsp. table salt**
- ⅔ **cup granulated sugar**
- 1 **Tbs. dark rum (such as Myers's)**
- 2 **tsp. pure vanilla extract**
- ¼ **cup cornstarch (spooned into a dry measure and leveled)**
- 3 **Tbs. cold unsalted butter, cut into pieces**

Make Ahead

Make the pastry cream up to 1 day ahead and refrigerate, covered. The rum syrup and toasted almonds can also be made 1 day in advance.

1. Heat the milk in a heavy 3-quart saucepan over medium heat until very hot. If a skin forms on the milk's surface, remove it. Meanwhile, beat the eggs, egg yolks, and salt in a medium bowl with an electric hand mixer on medium-high speed until slightly thickened, about 3 minutes. With the mixer on medium-high speed, add the sugar, 2 to 3 Tbs. at a time, beating about 30 seconds between additions. Continue beating until the mixture is very thick and pale, about another 3 minutes. On low speed, beat in the rum, vanilla, and cornstarch until smooth. Still on low speed, slowly add the hot milk, just a few dribbles at first and then in tablespoon-size dollops, beating after each addition only until smooth.

2. Scrape the mixture into the saucepan used to heat the milk and add the cold butter pieces. Set the pan over medium heat and stir constantly and gently with a heatproof rubber spatula, scraping all across the bottom and around the sides of the pan. As the mixture heats, it will thicken first at the bottom of the pan, and the mixture will look very lumpy. Decrease the heat slightly and keep stirring as the entire mixture approaches the boiling point and becomes even thicker and lumpier. Switch to a whisk and stir (don't beat) to smooth the pastry cream. The custard won't actually boil because it's so thick. When very thick and smooth (after 7 to 8 minutes), reduce the heat to very low and continue stirring gently with the rubber spatula all over the bottom and sides of the pan for another 1 minute.

3. Remove the pan from the heat and immediately scrape the custard into a medium bowl. Lay a piece of plastic wrap directly on the custard's surface, let cool to room temperature, and then refrigerate overnight.

chocolate ganache

- ⅓ **cup heavy cream**
- 7 **oz. bittersweet or semi-sweet chocolate, chopped**

In a heavy 1-quart saucepan, bring the cream just to a boil over medium heat. Add the chopped chocolate and stir with a small wire whisk. Take the pan off the heat and stir occasionally as the chocolate melts. The ganache should be perfectly smooth. Let cool slightly before using. If it cools beyond a pourable consistency, warm it gently in a heavy saucepan.

apple upside-down cake
(recipe on p. 158)

fruit cakes

fresh pineapple upside-down cake

FOR THE TOPPING

- ¾ **cup packed dark brown sugar**
- 2 **oz. (4 Tbs.) butter**
- 1 **small, ripe pineapple, trimmed, quartered, cored, and cut into ¼-inch-thick slices**

FOR THE CAKE

- 8 **oz. (2 cups) cake flour**
- 2½ **tsp. baking powder**
- ¼ **tsp. table salt**
- ¼ **lb. (½ cup) unsalted butter, at room temperature; more for the pan**
- ¾ **cup granulated sugar**
- 1½ **tsp. finely grated orange zest**
- 1 **tsp. pure vanilla extract**
- 2 **large eggs**
- ⅔ **cup plain nonfat yogurt**

Tangy pineapple and a buttery-sweet brown sugar topping are a good match for this yogurt cake. If you don't have a square pan, a 9x2-inch round pan works, too.

MAKE THE TOPPING

In a small saucepan, combine the brown sugar and butter. Cook over medium heat, stirring often, until the butter is melted and the mixture is smooth. Bring to a boil and pour into the prepared pan. Spread with a spatula to coat the bottom evenly. Scatter or arrange the pineapple slices evenly in the caramel, overlapping them slightly. Gently press the fruit into the caramel.

MAKE THE CAKE

1. Heat the oven to 350°F and lightly butter the sides of an 8-inch square pan.

2. Sift together the cake flour, baking powder, and salt. In a medium bowl, beat the butter with an electric mixer until smooth. Gradually add the sugar and continue beating until fluffy and lighter in color, about 3 minutes. Beat in the orange zest and vanilla. Add the eggs one at a time, beating briefly after each addition. Sprinkle half of the flour mixture over the butter mixture and, on low speed, mix just until the flour disappears. Add the yogurt and mix until just blended. Gently mix in the remaining flour.

3. Scoop large spoonfuls of batter onto the fruit; gently spread the batter evenly in the pan. Lightly tap the pan on the counter to settle the batter. Bake until the cake is golden brown and a pick inserted in the center comes out clean, about 45 minutes. Immediately run a paring knife around the inside edge of the pan. Set a flat serving plate on top of the pan and invert the cake. Let the inverted pan rest for about 5 minutes to let the topping settle. Gently remove the pan and serve the cake warm or at room temperature. *–Abigail Johnson Dodge*

PER SERVING (BASED ON 10 SERVINGS): 370 CALORIES | 4G PROTEIN | 56G CARB | 15G TOTAL FAT | 9G SAT FAT | 15G MONO FAT | 1G POLY FAT | 80MG CHOL | 200MG SODIUM | 1G FIBER

More about Pineapples

Fresh pineapple's tropical aroma and spunky acidity are wonderful winter pick-me-ups. Two common varieties are Golden Ripe and Hawaiian Jet. Golden Ripes should have an overall golden hue; intensely sweet, they're best for eating plain and in blender drinks. Hawaiian Jets have a greenish cast even when ripe; they're not as sweet, tend to keep longer, and are best for grilling or using in cooked desserts.

Choosing

Here are a few ways to tell if a pineapple is ready to eat.

Sniff it: A ripe one has a sweet fragrance with no hint of fermentation (if you do detect a fermenty odor, move along to the next pineapple).

Squeeze it: If it's rock hard, it's probably unripe. If there's a little bit of give, the pineapple is probably nice and ripe. Always pass on fruit with soft spots.

Another clue: A juicy pineapple will feel heavy for its size, but do check to make sure that juice isn't leaking through the bottom, indicating that the fruit is breaking down. Color isn't necessarily an indicator of ripeness. Also, the brighter and greener the leaves, the fresher the pineapple will be. Don't worry about rind color or tugging on a leaf to test for ripeness; both are unreliable indicators of maturity and are influenced by variety.

Storing

A ripe pineapple will keep for up to 3 days at room temperature. It may soften and its rind color may change a bit, but its sweetness and flavor will remain the same. For best flavor, stash your pineapple in the fridge until you're ready to eat it. For slightly longer storage, wrap a whole pineapple in plastic and refrigerate it for up to 5 days.

Prepping

To trim a pineapple: Slice ½ inch off the top and bottom of the pineapple and rest it on a cut end. Slice the rind off in strips, removing as many of the eyes as possible. With a paring knife, cut around and remove any remaining eyes. Quarter the pineapple lengthwise, trim the core from each quarter, and slice according to recipe instructions.

grilled polenta cake with cherry–cassis sauce

SERVES 8

FOR THE CAKE

- 4¼ oz. (8½ Tbs.) unsalted butter, softened
- 3⅜ oz. (¾ cup) unbleached all-purpose flour
- ½ cup finely ground cornmeal
- 1¼ tsp. baking powder
- ⅛ tsp. table salt
- 1 cup granulated sugar
- 3 whole eggs, at room temperature
- 3 egg yolks, at room temperature
- 1 tsp. pure vanilla extract

FOR THE CHERRY SAUCE

- 6 cups fresh sweet or sour cherries (about 2 lb.), pitted and halved
- 3 to 5 Tbs. granulated sugar; more to taste
- 3 Tbs. cassis
- ¼ tsp. fresh lemon juice
- ¼ tsp. freshly ground coarse black pepper (optional)

Grilling this pound cake may sound odd, but it's definitely worth it—the cake gets a toasty texture that contrasts nicely with the soft whipped cream and bold cherry sauce. (You can also use a grill pan, broiler, or toaster oven.)

MAKE THE CAKE

1. Position a rack in the center of the oven and heat the oven to 325°F. Grease an 8½x4½-inch loaf pan with ½ Tbs. of the butter.

2. Sift the flour, cornmeal, baking powder, and salt through a medium-mesh sieve. In a stand mixer fitted with the paddle attachment, cream the remaining 8 Tbs. butter and the sugar on medium-high speed until light and fluffy, 3 to 5 minutes. Scrape the sides of the bowl. In a separate bowl, lightly beat the eggs, egg yolks, and vanilla. With the mixer running on medium speed, very slowly add the egg mixture to the butter a little at a time, until the eggs are completely incorporated. With a spatula, very gently fold in the dry ingredients until just incorporated (don't overmix).

3. Transfer the batter to the prepared loaf pan, smooth the surface, and bake until a skewer inserted in the center comes out clean, about 40 minutes. Cool on a rack for 15 minutes. Run a table knife around the edges, remove the cake from the pan, and cool completely.

MAKE THE SAUCE

Put 4 cups of the cherries in a medium bowl and set aside. In a blender or food processor, purée the remaining 2 cups cherries, sugar (3 Tbs. for sweet cherries; 5 Tbs. for sour), and cassis until smooth. Strain through a fine-mesh sieve. Add the lemon juice and pepper (if using), and then mix the cherry sauce with the reserved cherries. Add more sugar to taste.

FOR SERVING

1 cup heavy cream

2 tsp. confectioners' sugar; more for dusting

2 Tbs. melted unsalted butter

SERVE THE CAKE

1. In a bowl, whip the cream until it forms soft peaks. Add the confectioners' sugar and mix just to combine. Don't overwhip.

2. Prepare a medium charcoal or gas grill fire. Cut the pound cake into ¾-inch slices. Brush each side with the melted butter. Grill the pound cake until golden, 1 to 2 minutes per side.

3. Put one piece of pound cake on each plate. Top with the cherry sauce and a dollop of the cream and dust with more confectioners' sugar. Serve immediately.   *–Joanne Weir*

PER SERVING : 560 CALORIES | 7G PROTEIN | 68G CARB | 30G TOTAL FAT | 18G SAT FAT | 9G MONO FAT | 1.5G POLY FAT | 240MG CHOL. | 140MG SODIUM | 3G FIBER

pitting cherries without a cherry pitter

There are a number of cherry pitters on the market, but you can improvise with one of these common household items if you don't have a pitter handy.

WOODEN SKEWER Insert the point of the skewer into the stem end and gently work it down and around the pit until it loosens enough to be pried out.

PAPER CLIP Unbend a clip into an "S" shape. Work one end of the clip down into the stem end of a cherry until you can hook under and pull out the pit.

DRINKING STRAW Poke and then twist a plastic drinking straw into the blossom end of the cherry to remove a plug of the cherry flesh—this makes an exit for the pit. Next, twist the straw into the stem end, pushing gently but firmly until the pit pops out the other side.

PASTRY TIP As with the drinking straw, press and twist the blossom end of a cherry onto a small star tip to remove a plug. Turn the cherry over and firmly twist the stem end onto the tip until the pit pops out.

berry buttermilk cake with vanilla-scented crème fraîche

FOR THE CRUMB TOPPING

2¼ oz. (½ cup) unbleached all-purpose flour

⅓ cup firmly packed light brown sugar

¼ tsp. kosher salt

2 oz. (¼ cup) unsalted butter, chilled

FOR THE CAKE

2 cups fresh blueberries, raspberries, or a mix

13½ oz. (3 cups) unbleached all-purpose flour; more for the pan and for the berries

4 tsp. baking powder

1 tsp. baking soda

¾ tsp. kosher salt

6 oz. (¾ cup) unsalted butter, softened at room temperature; more for the pan

1½ cups granulated sugar

3 large eggs

2 tsp. pure vanilla extract

1½ cups buttermilk

FOR THE CRÈME FRAÎCHE

1 lb. (2 cups) crème fraîche

1 tsp. pure vanilla extract

1 Tbs. granulated sugar

For the best flavor, make this moist, berry buttermilk cake and its crème fraîche topping 1 day in advance.

MAKE THE CRUMB TOPPING

Mix the flour, brown sugar, and salt in a medium bowl. Cut the butter into chunks and add to the dry mixture. Rub the flour and butter between your fingers until the mixture just comes together and has a nice crumbly texture.

MAKE THE CAKE

1. Rinse the berries well, then spread on paper towels to air-dry for at least 15 minutes. Position a rack in the center of the oven and heat the oven to 350°F. Generously butter and flour a 12-cup bundt pan. In a medium bowl, mix the flour, baking powder, baking soda, and salt.

2. In a stand mixer fitted with a paddle attachment (or in a large bowl, using a hand-held mixer), whip the butter and sugar together on medium-high speed until light and fluffy, about 3 minutes. Add the eggs one at a time, beating well for 15 seconds after each addition. Scrape the bowl, add the vanilla, and continue whipping until the mixture is light and fluffy, 1 to 2 minutes. On low speed, add the dry ingredients one-third at a time, alternating with the buttermilk ½ cup at a time. After the last addition of buttermilk, scrape the bowl, increase the speed to medium, and beat for about 15 seconds to mix the batter fully.

3. Transfer the berries to a medium bowl and toss gently with 2 tsp. flour. Gently fold the berries into the cake batter with a rubber spatula. Scrape the batter into the prepared pan with the rubber spatula, level the batter, and sprinkle with the crumb topping.

4. Bake until a toothpick comes out clean when inserted in the middle of the cake, 45 to 55 minutes. Let the cake rest for 10 minutes, then turn it out onto a rack. Flip the cake over so that the crumb topping is upright. Let cool completely and wrap tightly. Store at room temperature overnight before slicing.

MAKE THE CRÈME FRAÎCHE SERVE

In the bowl of a stand mixer fitted with a whisk attachment or with a hand-held mixer, whip the ingredients until soft peaks form, about 2 minutes. Cover and refrigerate until needed. Slice the cake and serve each slice with a dollop of the crème fraîche.

–Maria Helm Sinskey

PER SERVING: 355 CALORIES | 5G PROTEIN | 48G CARB | 16G TOTAL FAT | 10G SAT FAT | 3G MONO FAT | 1G POLY FAT | 77MG CHOL | 295MG SODIUM | 1G FIBER

lemon chiffon cake with raspberry cream

SERVES 12 TO 14

FOR THE CAKE

9	oz. (2¼ cups) cake flour
1½	cups granulated sugar
1½	tsp. baking powder
½	tsp. table salt
½	cup canola or corn oil
7	large eggs, separated
½	cup water
⅓	cup fresh lemon juice
1½	tsp. finely grated lemon zest
½	tsp. pure vanilla extract
	Pinch of cream of tartar

FOR THE WHIPPED CREAM

2	cups whipping cream
6	Tbs. unsweetened seedless raspberry purée (from about 1 cup raspberries; frozen is fine)
6	Tbs. confectioners' sugar
1	tsp. pure vanilla extract
	Fresh raspberries, for garnish (optional)

Use the whipped cream to frost the whole cake or to garnish individual slices of cake.

MAKE THE CAKE

1. Heat the oven to 325°F. Have ready a 9½- or 10-inch tube pan with sides at least 3¾ inches high.

2. In a large bowl, sift together the cake flour, 1 cup of the sugar, the baking powder, and the salt. Make a well in the center of the flour mixture and put in the oil, egg yolks, water, lemon juice, lemon zest, and vanilla extract. Beat the mixture on medium speed until smooth and thick, at least 3 minutes. Set aside.

3. In a large, clean bowl with clean beaters or a whisk attachment, whisk the egg whites and the cream of tartar on medium speed until the cream of tartar is dissolved and the whites are foamy. Increase the speed to high and beat the whites until the movement of the beaters forms lines in the mixture. Slowly pour in the remaining ½ cup sugar, about 2 Tbs. at a time, and beat the mixture until soft peaks form.

4. With a large rubber spatula, stir about one-third of the egg whites into the yolk mixture. Gently fold in the remaining egg whites until no white streaks remain. Pour the batter into the tube pan, spreading it evenly. Bake until you can gently press your fingers on top of the cake and it feels firm, about 1 hour and 10 minutes. Any cracks that form on the top should look dry.

5. Invert the pan onto a bottle with a narrow neck and cool thoroughly, about an hour and a half. Use a small, sharp knife to loosen the cake from the sides of the pan and the center of the tube, if necessary. Remove the cake from the pan and slide it onto a serving plate.

MAKE THE WHIPPED CREAM

In a large bowl, beat the whipping cream, raspberry purée, confectioners' sugar, and vanilla extract until soft peaks form. Spread the whipped cream over the cooled cake. Garnish with fresh berries, if you like. *–Elinor Klivans*

PER SERVING (BASED ON 14 SERVINGS): 390 CALORIES | 5G PROTEIN | 41G CARB | 23G TOTAL FAT | 9G SAT FAT | 9G MONO FAT | 3G POLY FAT | 155MG CHOL | 150MG SODIUM | 0G FIBER

pecan pineapple upside-down cake

SERVES 10 TO 12

- **7** oz. (14 Tbs.) unsalted butter at room temperature; more for the pan
- **½** cup plus 2 Tbs. light or dark brown sugar
- **Six** to eight ¼-inch-thick fresh pineapple rings
- **¼** to ⅓ cup pecan halves
- **½** cup lightly toasted pecan pieces
- **5½** oz. (1¼ cups) cake flour
- **1** tsp. baking powder
- **½** tsp. freshly grated nutmeg
- **¼** tsp. baking soda
- **¼** tsp. kosher salt
- **1** cup granulated sugar
- **2** large eggs, at room temperature
- **1** tsp. pure vanilla extract
- **½** cup plus 2 Tbs. buttermilk

The classic upside-down cake is even better when made with fresh pineapple and a buttermilk batter enriched with ground pecans.

1. Position a rack in the center of the oven and heat the oven to 350°F. Butter a 10x2-inch round cake pan or 10-inch cast-iron skillet.

2. Combine 6 Tbs. of the butter with the brown sugar in a small saucepan and cook over medium heat, whisking until the butter is melted, the sugar is dissolved, and the mixture is smooth, 1 to 2 minutes. Remove from the heat and immediately pour the mixture in the bottom of the prepared pan, tilting to evenly cover the surface.

3. Set one pineapple ring in the center of the pan. Surround it with several other rings, overlapping them slightly. Cut the remaining rings into quarters or sixths and fill in the spaces around the perimeter of the pan. Set a pecan half, curved side down, in the center of each pineapple ring. If you like, fill in any additional spaces with pecan halves, curved sides down. (You may not need all the pecans.)

4. Finely grind the toasted pecan pieces in a food processor but don't overprocess or you'll make pecan butter. In a small bowl, sift together the cake flour, baking powder, nutmeg, and baking soda. Add the salt and ground pecans, mix well, and reserve.

5. In a stand mixer fitted with the paddle attachment, beat the remaining 8 Tbs. butter with the granulated sugar on medium speed until fluffy, 2 to 3 minutes. Beat in the eggs one at a time, pausing to scrape the bowl. Mix in the vanilla. On low speed, alternate adding the dry ingredients and the buttermilk in five additions, beginning and ending with the dry ingredients, scraping the bowl once or twice, and mixing until the batter is smooth. Pour the batter over the fruit and spread it evenly with a spatula.

6. Bake until the cake is golden brown and springs back when pressed lightly in the center with a fingertip, 40 to 45 minutes. Transfer the cake to a rack and cool in the pan for 15 minutes. Run the tip of a paring knife around the edge of the cake. Cover with a serving plate, and gripping both the cake and the plate, invert the two. Carefully lift off the cake pan, rearranging the fruit if necessary. Allow the cake to cool completely before serving. *—Karen Barker*

PER SERVING (BASED ON 12 SERVINGS): 360 CALORIES | 3G PROTEIN | 43G CARB | 20G TOTAL FAT | 9G SAT FAT | 7G MONO FAT | 2G POLY FAT | 70MG CHOL | 115MG SODIUM | 1G FIBER

how to position the pineapple and pecans

Placing the fruit and nuts carefully will ensure a pretty cake.

Position a pineapple ring in the center of the pan, then surround it with more rings, packing them tightly—it's fine if they overlap slightly. Cut the remaining rings to fill in the spaces around the perimeter of the pan.

Set a pecan half, flat side up, in the center of each pineapple ring. If you like, add more pecan halves to fill in holes.

lemon–poppyseed shortcakes with summer berries

SERVES 9

FOR THE BISCUITS

13½ oz. (3 cups) unbleached all-purpose flour; more as needed

¼ cup plus 2 Tbs. granulated sugar; plus about 3 Tbs. for sprinkling

1½ Tbs. baking powder

¾ tsp. table salt

¼ cup plus 2 Tbs. finely grated, lightly packed lemon zest; more for garnish

2 Tbs. poppyseeds

6 oz. (¾ cup) cold unsalted butter, cut into small pieces

1¼ cups heavy cream; plus about 3 Tbs. for brushing

¼ cup fresh lemon juice

FOR THE BERRIES

2 cups ⅛-inch-thick fresh strawberry slices (from about 1½ pints)

1 cup fresh blueberries

1 cup fresh raspberries

1 cup fresh blackberries

1 to 3 Tbs. granulated sugar, depending on the sweetness of the berries

FOR THE WHIPPED CREAM

1½ cups heavy cream

2 Tbs. granulated sugar

2 Tbs. fresh lemon juice

Whether you get your berries from the grocery store, the farmers' market, or the local pick-your-own place, you'll need to toss them in sugar before you fill your shortcakes. The sugar sweetens them, of course, but—more important—it gets the berries' juices flowing and softens their texture so that they'll settle nicely into the biscuit and make the whole dish feel well integrated.

MAKE THE BISCUITS

1. Line a heavy baking sheet with parchment. Sift the flour, sugar, baking powder, and salt into a large bowl. Add the lemon zest and poppyseeds and toss with a fork to combine. Cut the butter into the flour mixture with a pastry cutter or a fork until the largest pieces of butter are the size of peas. Combine the cream and lemon juice in a liquid measure. Make a well in the center of the flour mixture and pour the cream mixture into the well. Mix with a fork until the dough is evenly moistened and just combined; it should look shaggy and still feel a little dry. Gently knead by hand five or six times to pick up any dry ingredients remaining in the bottom of the bowl and to create a loose ball.

2. Turn the dough out onto a lightly floured work surface and pat it into an 8-inch square, ¾ to 1 inch thick. Transfer the dough to the parchment-lined baking sheet, cover with plastic wrap, and chill for 20 minutes.

3. Meanwhile, heat the oven to 425°F. Remove the dough from the refrigerator and trim about ¼ inch from each side to create a neat, sharp edge (a bench knife or a pastry scraper works well, or use a large chef's knife, being sure to cut straight down). Cut the dough into 9 even squares (about 2½ inches square) and spread them about 2 inches apart on the baking sheet. With a pastry brush or the back of a spoon, brush each biscuit with a thin layer of cream and sprinkle generously with sugar. Bake until the biscuits are medium golden brown on top and the bottoms are golden brown, 18 to 20 minutes.

PREPARE THE BERRIES

Toss the berries with 1 Tbs. sugar and taste. If they're still tart, sprinkle with another 1 to 2 Tbs. sugar. Let sit at room temperature until the sugar dissolves and the berries begin to release their juices, at least 30 minutes but no more than 2 hours.

WHIP THE CREAM

Pour the cream into a cold mixing bowl and beat with a hand-held mixer until it begins to thicken. Add the sugar and lemon juice and, using a whisk, continue to beat by hand until the cream is softly whipped or until the whisk leaves distinct marks in the cream; it should be soft and billowy but still hold its shape.

continued on p. 130

ASSEMBLE THE SHORTCAKES

While the biscuits are still warm, split them in half horizontally with a serrated knife. For each serving, set the bottom half of a biscuit on a plate. Scoop about ½ cup of the berries and their juices over the biscuit. Add a generous dollop of whipped cream and cover with the top half of the biscuit. Top with a small dollop of cream and garnish with lemon zest. —*Katherine Seeley*

PER SERVING: 660 CALORIES | 7G PROTEIN | 62G CARB | 44G TOTAL FAT | 27G SAT FAT | 13G MONO FAT | 3G POLY FAT | 145MG CHOL | 470MG SODIUM | 5G FIBER

4 steps to tender biscuits

1. Cut the butter into the flour mixture with a pastry cutter or a fork until the largest pieces of butter are the size of peas. The butter will melt and create steam when baked, making a flaky biscuit.

2. Make a well and pour in the cream. Mix just until the ingredients start to come together. If your dough is too dry to combine, add more cream, 1 Tbs. at a time.

3. Work the dough until just combined. Knead gently to bring the dough together into a loose ball.

4. Gently pat the dough into a square about 1 inch thick and refrigerate for 20 minutes. This gives the flour a chance to relax and also helps the biscuits hold their shape when baked.

roasted pineapple and coconut shortcakes

SERVES 9

FOR THE PINEAPPLE

- **1 large, ripe pineapple, peeled, quartered lengthwise, and cored**
- **¼ cup unsalted butter, melted**
- **⅔ to ¾ cup packed light brown sugar**

FOR THE SHORTCAKES

- **9 oz. (2 cups) unsifted unbleached all-purpose flour; more as needed**
- **¼ cup granulated sugar**
- **1 Tbs. baking powder**
- **½ tsp. table salt**
- **¼ lb. (½ cup) unsalted butter, chilled and sliced**
- **¾ cup loosely packed sweetened shredded coconut**
- **⅓ cup canned coconut milk**
- **6 Tbs. whole milk**
- **1 tsp. pure vanilla extract**

- **1 cup heavy cream, lightly whipped with 2 Tbs. granulated sugar and 1 Tbs. dark rum**

Canned coconut milk is available in the Asian food section of most grocery stores (don't use "cream of coconut"—it isn't the same thing). Be sure to shake the can of coconut milk well before you open it.

ROAST THE PINEAPPLE

Heat the oven to 400°F. Slice each pineapple quarter lengthwise into 4 strips. Put the strips on a rimmed baking sheet lined with parchment. Brush the strips with some of the melted butter and sprinkle with half the brown sugar. Roast the strips for 10 minutes and then turn them over with tongs. Brush with more butter and top with the remaining brown sugar. Bake until the juices are bubbling in the pan and the pineapple is light gold, another 5 to 10 minutes. Set the baking sheet on a wire rack to cool. Cut each strip crosswise into 5 or 6 chunks.

MAKE THE SHORTCAKES

1. Position a rack in the lower third of the oven and heat to 375°F. Line a large baking sheet with parchment. Sift the flour, sugar, baking powder, and salt into a large bowl. With a pastry blender or two table knives, cut the butter into the dry ingredients until the mixture looks like coarse meal. With a fork, stir in the coconut. Whisk together the coconut milk, whole milk, and vanilla and slowly add to the flour mixture, stirring in with a fork until it forms a dough that leaves the sides of the bowl.

2. Gently knead the dough on a floured work surface four or five times until the dough holds together (it will be soft). With lightly floured hands, pat it into about a 7-inch square that's a generous 1 inch thick (if you like, trim the edges with a sharp knife to even them). Cut the dough into 9 equal squares. Transfer to the prepared baking sheet and bake until pale gold on top and golden on the bottom, 22 to 25 minutes. Transfer the cakes to a wire rack to cool.

ASSEMBLE THE SHORTCAKES

Carefully slice the shortcakes in half with a serrated knife. Spoon between ⅓ and ½ cup roasted pineapple chunks over each biscuit bottom and then spoon a dollop of the lightly whipped cream over the pineapple. Set the shortcake tops on or beside the whipped cream and serve straightaway. *–Flo Braker*

PER SERVING: 520 CALORIES | 5G PROTEIN | 58G CARB | 30G TOTAL FAT | 20G SAT FAT | 8G MONO FAT | 1G POLY FAT | 80MG CHOL | 340MG SODIUM | 2G FIBER

four-layer cake with raspberry whipped cream and mixed berries

SERVES 12

FOR THE CAKE

Nonstick cooking spray
for the pan

10½ oz. (2¾ cups) cake flour

1½ cups granulated sugar

3¾ tsp. baking powder

¾ tsp. table salt

6 oz. (¾ cup unsalted butter,
cut into tablespoon-size
pieces, at room temperature

¾ cup whole or low-fat milk,
at room temperature

1½ tsp. pure vanilla extract

4 large eggs, at room
temperature

FOR THE WHIPPED CREAM

3 cups heavy or whipping
cream

7 Tbs. granulated sugar

2¼ cups raspberry purée
(purée the fruit in a blender
and strain)

6¼ cups fresh berries
(strawberries, blueberries,
raspberries, blackberries,
or a combination, large
berries sliced)

This gorgeous layer cake starts with a vanilla butter cake that is tender, not overly sweet, and impossibly easy. Pair it with whatever berries are in season for a wonderfully fresh dessert.

MAKE THE CAKE

1. Position a rack in the center of the oven and heat the oven to 350°F. Lightly coat two 9x2-inch round cake pans with nonstick cooking spray and line the bottoms with parchment.

2. Sift the cake flour, sugar, baking powder, and salt into the bowl of a stand mixer fitted with the paddle attachment. Mix on low speed (#2 on a KitchenAid® mixer) until the ingredients are well combined.

3. Add the softened butter pieces and mix on low speed for 20 to 30 seconds to mix the butter into the dry ingredients—the mixture should look a little lumpy, with the largest lumps being about the size of a hazelnut. Add the milk and vanilla extract. Mix on medium speed (#5 on a KitchenAid) for 1 min. to thoroughly blend the ingredients and aerate the batter. Scrape the sides of the bowl with a spatula.

4. Add the eggs one at a time, mixing on medium speed for about 15 seconds after each addition. Scrape the bowl after the second egg.

5. Divide the batter equally between the two prepared pans. Use a small offset spatula or spoon to spread the batter evenly in each pan. Bake until the cakes are golden brown and the tops feel firm but spring back a little when tapped lightly with a finger, and a pick inserted in the center of the cake comes out clean, 30 to 35 minutes. Set the pans on a rack, run a table knife around the edge of each cake and let cool in the pans for 30 minutes. Invert the cakes onto the rack, lift the pans, peel off the parchment, and let the cakes cool completely before filling and frosting.

MAKE THE WHIPPED CREAM

1. Chill the bowl and whisk attachment of a stand mixer for 20 minutes in the refrigerator or 5 minutes in the freezer. Pour the cream into the bowl and whisk on medium-high speed until it just starts to thicken. Slow the speed down to medium and gradually pour in the sugar and raspberry purée. Continue to whisk until soft peaks form.

2. Continue to whisk by hand, tasting and adjusting the flavoring, until the cream is smooth, and stiff peaks form (the cream will stand up straight when the whisk is raised). (The purée increases the amount of whipped cream, so you may not need it all; save the extra for topping other desserts.)

ASSEMBLE THE CAKE

1. Level the cakes, if necessary, and slice each cake into two layers, making a total of four layers of cake.

2. Place the bottom layer on a flat serving platter or a cake stand lined with strips of waxed paper to keep it clean while assembling the cake. Top the layer with a scant 1½ cups whipped cream, spreading the cream to the edges of the cake with a metal cake spatula so that it's almost dripping over the sides. Top with 1½ cups berries, making sure some of the berries are around the edges of the cake so you can see them between the layers.

3. Repeat with the next two layers. For the final layer, spread about 1½ cups whipped cream on top of the cake with the spatula. Arrange the berries artfully on top of the cream. *–Katherine Seeley*

PER SERVING (BASED ON 12 SERVINGS): 580 CALORIES | 7G PROTEIN | 59G CARB | 36G TOTAL FAT | 22G SAT FAT | 10G MONO FAT | 1.5G POLY FAT | 185MG CHOL | 330MG SODIUM | 2G FIBER

angel food cake with strawberries and whipped cream

MAKES ONE 10-INCH CAKE;
SERVES 8 TO 10

FOR THE STRAWBERRIES

- ¾ lb. fresh strawberries, hulled and sliced (about 3 cups)
- 2 Tbs. granulated sugar
- 1 Tbs. Grand Marnier® (optional)

FOR THE CAKE

- 1½ cups egg whites (from 11 large eggs)
- 4 oz. (¾ cup plus 2 Tbs.) unbleached all-purpose flour
- 1½ cups granulated sugar
- Pinch of kosher salt
- 2 Tbs. fresh lemon juice
- 1½ tsp. pure vanilla extract

  Lightly sweetened whipped cream, for serving

This dessert—a light cake topped with fresh berries—is a simple and bright way to welcome spring back to the table.

PREPARE THE STRAWBERRIES

Toss the berries with the sugar and Grand Marnier (if using) and refrigerate for at least 1 hour before serving (you can prepare the berries up to 6 hours ahead).

MAKE THE CAKE

1. Put the egg whites in the bowl of a stand mixer fitted with the whisk attachment and let them warm until they're a little cooler than room temperature (about 60°F), about 1½ hours. (To speed up this step, set the mixer bowl in a bowl of lukewarm water and stir the whites occasionally; check the temperature frequently.)

2. Position a rack in the bottom third of the oven and heat the oven to 325°F. Have ready a 10-inch tube pan with removable bottom. Sift together the flour, ½ cup of the sugar, and the salt; set aside.

3. Add the lemon juice to the egg whites and beat on medium-low speed until the mixture is quite frothy and has increased a little in volume, 1 to 2 minutes. Increase the speed to medium and slowly, about a tablespoon at a time, add the remaining 1 cup of sugar. Continue beating until the whites thicken and form soft droopy peaks when the beater is lifted, 6 to 7 minutes from when you began adding sugar. Do not beat the whites until stiff. In the final minute or so of beating, add the vanilla extract. The mixture should be voluminous and light but still fluid enough to pour.

4. Sprinkle about one-fifth of the flour and sugar mixture over the egg whites and with a large spatula, gently fold it in. Continue gently folding in the remaining flour-sugar mixture in four more additions until it's fully incorporated. Gently pour the batter into the ungreased tube pan. Run a spatula once through the batter to eliminate any big air bubbles and then lightly smooth the batter if necessary.

5. Bake until the top is light golden and the cake feels spongy and springs back when touched very lightly, 45 to 55 minutes. Insert the neck of a bottle or a funnel into the tube part of the pan and invert the pan. Let the cake cool completely before removing it from the pan. (Cooling the cake upside down keeps it from collapsing before it cools, and elevating it on a bottle or funnel helps air circulate for faster cooling.)

6. To remove the cake, run a thin knife or spatula around it to loosen it. Lift the cake (still on the tube section) from the pan. Run the knife or spatula between the cake and the bottom of the pan. Invert the cake onto a cake plate and remove the tube section.

7. Slice the cake with a serrated knife using a gentle sawing motion. Serve topped with the strawberries and a dollop of whipped cream.

—Barbara Lynch

PER SERVING (BASED ON 10 SERVINGS): 290 CALORIES | 6G PROTEIN | 46G CARB | 9G TOTAL FAT | 5G SAT FAT | 2.5G MONO FAT | 0G POLY FAT | 35MG CHOL | 100MG SODIUM | 1G FIBER

toasted-almond raspberry roll

FOR THE FILLING

¾ **cup seedless raspberry jam**

1 **cup fresh raspberries**

FOR THE CAKE

8 **oz. sliced almonds (2¼ cups)**

1½ **tsp. baking powder**

Unsalted butter, softened, for the pan

2 **Tbs. unbleached all-purpose flour, for the pan**

8 **large eggs, separated, whites at room temperature**

1 **cup granulated sugar**

¼ **tsp. pure almond extract**

¼ **tsp. kosher salt**

¼ **cup confectioners' sugar, for dusting**

TO FINISH

¾ **cup heavy cream**

1 **Tbs. granulated sugar**

¼ **cup fresh raspberries**

A topping of billowy whipped cream, toasted nuts, and raspberries not only looks pretty but also adds textural notes that make each bite exciting.

MAKE THE FILLING

Put the jam in a bowl and stir to loosen. Add the raspberries and lightly crush with the back of a fork.

MAKE THE CAKE

1. Position a rack in the bottom third of the oven and heat the oven to 350°F.

2. Spread the almonds on a rimmed baking sheet and toast, stirring once or twice, until golden, about 7 minutes. (Leave the oven on.) Cool the almonds to room temperature. Reserve 1½ Tbs. of the almonds for the garnish and pulse the remaining nuts in a food processor until finely ground.

3. In a large bowl, combine the ground nuts with the baking powder and reserve.

4. Butter an 18x13-inch rimmed baking sheet. Line the pan with parchment. Butter the parchment and sprinkle the flour over it, shaking the pan for even coverage and knocking out the excess.

5. In a stand mixer fitted with the whisk attachment, beat the egg yolks, granulated sugar, and almond extract on medium-low speed until combined. Increase the speed to medium high and beat until light and fluffy, about 3 minutes. Fold into the ground nuts until incorporated.

6. In a clean bowl with a clean whisk, beat the egg whites and salt on medium-high speed until medium peaks form. Fold one-third of the beaten whites into the almond mixture to lighten it. Gently fold in the remaining whites until the batter is evenly colored, with no streaks of white. Transfer the batter to the prepared pan, gently spreading it with an offset spatula.

7. Bake, rotating the pan halfway through, until golden brown, set to the touch, and beginning to pull away from the sides of the pan, 18 to 20 minutes. Immediately loosen the cake from the sides of the pan with a paring knife. Sift the confectioners' sugar evenly over the cake.

8. While the cake is still hot, lay a clean, lint-free kitchen towel over it. If the towel is long, extend one end about 1½ inches beyond a short side of the cake; don't worry about the other end. Invert a large rack or cutting board over the towel. Holding both the baking sheet and the rack with protected hands, invert the cake. Remove the baking sheet and parchment.

9. Using both hands and starting from the short end with the shortest towel overhang, roll the cake and the towel up together. Let cool for 30 minutes.

10. Carefully unroll the cake; it should look wavy and both ends should curl. (It's OK if there are some small cracks.) Let cool completely, 10 to 15 minutes.

11. Using an offset spatula, spread the filling over the cake to within 1½ inches of the far short edge and to within ½ inch of the other edges. Be sure to coax the filling into the interior of the closer curled end so that when the cake is sliced there will be filling in the center of the spiral.

12. Reroll the cake without the towel this time. The filling may squish out of the ends a bit, which is fine.

FINISH THE CAKE

1. With a serrated knife and a sawing motion, trim the ends of the cake. Using two large spatulas, transfer the cake to a serving platter.

2. Chill a metal bowl and the beaters of an electric mixer or a whisk. Beat the cream and granulated sugar to medium peaks. Spoon dollops of whipped cream on top of the cake. Scatter the reserved almonds over the cream and garnish with the raspberries. Slice with the serrated knife and serve. *–Karen Barker*

PER SERVING (BASED ON 12 SERVINGS). 350 CALORIES | 9G PROTEIN | 41G CARB | 19G TOTAL FAT | 6G SAT FAT | 9G MONO FAT | 3G POLY FAT | 145MG CHOL | 125MG SODIUM | 3G FIBER

classic strawberry shortcake

SERVES 6

FOR THE STRAWBERRIES

1	lb. ripe fresh strawberries, hulled (about 4 cups)
2	Tbs. granulated sugar; more to taste

FOR THE BISCUITS

9	oz. (2 cups) unbleached all-purpose flour; more for rolling
⅓	cup plus 1 Tbs. granulated sugar
2½	tsp. baking powder
¼	tsp. baking soda
½	tsp. kosher salt
¼	lb. (½ cup) cold unsalted butter, cut into ½-inch pieces
1	large egg
¼	cup heavy cream; more for brushing
¼	cup buttermilk

FOR THE WHIPPED CREAM

1½	cups heavy cream
2	Tbs. granulated sugar

These biscuits get their light, tender texture from buttermilk and baking powder, and their rich flavor from an egg, cream, and lots of butter. This simple dessert is best made at the height of strawberry season, using the juiciest, sweetest strawberries you can find.

PREPARE THE STRAWBERRIES

Put one-third of the berries in a medium bowl and, using a potato masher, crush them into a chunky purée. Slice the remaining berries ¼ inch thick and stir them into the mashed berries along with the sugar. Taste the berries, adding more sugar if necessary. Let the berries sit at room temperature for at least 30 minutes and up to 2 hours.

MAKE THE BISCUITS

1. Position a rack in the center of the oven and heat the oven to 425°F. Line a large heavy-duty baking sheet with parchment.

2. Sift the flour, ⅓ cup of the sugar, the baking powder, and baking soda into a large bowl. Stir in the salt. Using a pastry blender, a fork, or your fingertips, work the butter into the dry ingredients until the mixture resembles coarse cornmeal.

3. In a small bowl, beat the egg and heavy cream with a fork. Mix in the buttermilk. Make a well in the center of the flour mixture and pour in the cream mixture. Mix with the fork until the dough is evenly moistened and just comes together; it will still look a little shaggy. Gather the dough and gently knead it three or four times. If the dough seems dry and doesn't form a cohesive mass, work in more cream, 1 tsp. at a time.

4. Transfer the dough to a lightly floured surface and roll it into a ¾-inch-thick disk. With a sharp 2½-inch biscuit cutter, press straight down to cut the dough into rounds and lift straight up to remove (don't twist the cutter or it will seal the sides of the biscuits and interfere with rising). Transfer the rounds to the prepared baking sheet. Gather the dough scraps, gently knead them together, reroll, and cut out more biscuits until you have a total of 6.

5. Lightly brush the biscuit tops with cream (about 1 Tbs.) and sprinkle with the remaining 1 Tbs. sugar. Bake, rotating the baking sheet once, until the biscuit tops are lightly browned, 10 to 15 minutes. Serve the biscuits warm. (They can be baked 10 to 12 hours ahead and reheated in a 350°F oven before serving.)

WHIP THE CREAM

In a large, chilled metal bowl, whip the heavy cream and sugar to soft peaks with an electric hand mixer. (Use immediately or refrigerate, covered, for up to 2 hours. If necessary, lightly rewhip before using.)

TO ASSEMBLE

Using a serrated knife, split the warm biscuits in half horizontally and transfer the bottoms to six dessert plates. Spoon about three-quarters of the macerated berries and their juice evenly over the biscuit bottoms. It's OK if some of the berries spill out onto the plate. Top with a generous dollop of whipped cream and cover each with a biscuit top. Spoon more berries and cream over each shortcake and serve immediately. *–Karen Barker*

PER SERVING: 630 CALORIES | 7G PROTEIN | 59G CARB | 42G TOTAL FAT | 26G SAT FAT |
12G MONO FAT | 2G POLY FAT | 165MG CHOL | 330MG SODIUM | 3G FIBER

Make Ahead

> The biscuits can be baked 10 to 12 hours ahead and reheated in a 350°F oven before serving. The strawberries can be macerated up to 2 hours ahead. The cream can be whipped up to 2 hours ahead and refrigerated, covered. If necessary, lightly rewhip before using.

blueberry–lime pound cake

FOR THE CAKE

½   **lb. (1 cup) unsalted butter, softened; more for the pan**

10½   **oz. (2⅓ cups) all-purpose flour; more for the pan**

1½   **tsp. baking power**

¼   **tsp. plus ⅛ tsp. table salt**

1¾   **cups granulated sugar**

2   **tsp. finely grated lime zest**

6   **oz. cream cheese, softened**

4   **large eggs plus 1 large egg yolk, at room temperature**

2½   **cups room-temperature fresh blueberries (about 13 oz.), washed and drained on paper towels**

FOR THE GLAZE

4   **oz. (1 cup) confectioners' sugar**

2   **Tbs. fresh lime juice; more as needed**

Lime zest and a tangy lime juice glaze add zip to the sweet summer flavor of fresh blueberries in this moist, tender pound cake. The cream cheese is an unusual ingredient for pound cake, but it lends the typically springy crumb an exceptional richness and tenderness and helps the cake stay moist and fresh for several days.

Position a rack in the center of the oven and heat the oven to 350°F. Butter and flour a 12-cup Bundt pan.

MAKE THE CAKE

1. Sift the flour, baking powder, and salt into a medium bowl. Put the sugar and lime zest in a food processor and pulse 20 times, or until the zest is in small pieces. (If you don't have a food processor, omit this step and blend the zest into the flour.)

2. In a stand mixer fitted with the paddle attachment or in a large bowl, using a hand-held mixer, beat the butter and cream cheese in a large bowl on medium speed until smooth, about 1 minute. Add the sugar mixture and beat on medium until light and fluffy, 1 to 2 minutes. With the mixer still running, add the whole eggs one at a time, mixing well after each addition and stopping the mixer to scrape the bowl twice. Beat in the egg yolk. Reduce the mixer speed to low and slowly add the flour mixture. Stop the mixer one last time to scrape the bowl and then beat at medium speed until the batter is smooth and light, about 20 seconds. With a rubber spatula, gently fold the blueberries into the batter.

3. Transfer the batter to the prepared pan, spreading it evenly with the spatula. Run a knife through the batter or tap the pan lightly against the counter to eliminate any air pockets. Bake until a wooden skewer inserted in the center comes out clean, 50 to 55 minutes. Set the pan on a wire rack to cool for 10 minutes and then invert onto the rack, remove the pan, and let cool completely.

GLAZE THE CAKE

In a spouted measuring cup or bowl, whisk the confectioners' sugar and lime juice together until smooth. The glaze should be thin enough to pour. If not, add more lime juice, 1 tsp. at a time. Put a baking sheet under the rack to catch drips and drizzle the glaze over the top and sides of the cake. Let the glaze set fully before transferring to a cake plate and serving. *–Nicole Rees*

PER SERVING: 360 CALORIES | 5G PROTEIN | 48G CARB | 17G TOTAL FAT | 10G SAT FAT | 4.5G MONO FAT | 1G POLY FAT | 110MG CHOL | 140MG SODIUM | 1G FIBER

> Be sure to use room-temperature berries. Cold fruit straight from the refrigerator will prevent your dessert from baking evenly.

Buying and Storing Blueberries

You can judge some fruit with your nose, but not blueberries. Use your eyes first: Blueberries should have a lovely silvery-white bloom over the dark blue. Look for pints free of small, purplish or greenish immature berries, a sign that they were picked before their peak. Then use the "heft" test: Berries should be plump and heavy. The sure-fire way of judging blueberries is to taste a few, because sweetness is variable even within the same pint.

At home, pick through them, discarding any squishy berries that may turn moldy and infect their healthy neighbors. Store the berries in the coldest part of the refrigerator, but not in a drawer, where it's too humid. To keep them dry, don't wash them until you're ready to use them. (Blueberries can lose moisture during storage and shrink slightly. For baking, this can work in your favor, because the flavor becomes concentrated.)

You can also freeze blueberries. Rinse them in a colander, dry thoroughly on paper towels, and then spread them on rimmed baking sheets in a single layer until frozen solid. Once frozen, place in plastic storage bags.

polenta pound cake
with blueberries and thyme

Fresh thyme in both the cake and the blueberries adds savory herbal notes to this not-too-sweet dessert. Serve with sweetened whipped cream, if you like.

FOR THE BLUEBERRIES

- ¼ cup granulated sugar
- 1 tsp. chopped fresh thyme
- 1 pint fresh blueberries, picked over
- 1½ tsp. finely grated lemon zest
- Pinch of kosher salt

FOR THE CAKE

- ½ lb. (1 cup) unsalted butter, softened; more for the pan
- 6⅔ oz. (1⅔ cups) cake flour; more for the pan
- ⅓ cup polenta (cornmeal)
- 2 Tbs. finely chopped fresh thyme
- ¼ tsp. kosher salt
- 1⅓ cups granulated sugar
- 5 large eggs, at room temperature
- 1 Tbs. fresh lemon juice
- 2 tsp. pure vanilla extract

MAKE THE BLUEBERRIES

In a small saucepan, combine the sugar, thyme, and 2 Tbs. water. Cook over low heat, stirring, until the sugar dissolves. Add the blueberries, lemon zest, and salt. Raise the heat to medium high and bring the mixture to a boil. Cook, stirring occasionally, until the syrup thickens slightly and the berries are warm but most are still whole, 1 to 2 minutes. Remove from the heat. (The blueberries will keep, covered and refrigerated, for 1 day; the thyme flavor will become more intense. Reheat gently just before serving.)

MAKE THE CAKE

1. Position a rack in the center of the oven and heat the oven to 325°F. Butter and flour a 9x5-inch loaf pan.

2. In a small bowl, whisk together the flour, polenta, thyme, and salt.

3. In a stand mixer fitted with the paddle attachment or in a large bowl, using a hand-held mixer, beat the softened butter and sugar on medium-high speed until fluffy, about 2 minutes. Add the eggs one at a time, mixing well after each addition. Add the lemon juice and vanilla and mix briefly to combine. Reduce the speed to low and add the flour mixture gradually until just combined.

4. Scrape the batter into the prepared pan and smooth the top, then tap the pan on the counter to pop any large air bubbles. Bake until a tester inserted in the center comes out with just a few small, moist crumbs attached, 1¼ to 1½ hours. (If the top starts to get too dark, lay a piece of foil loosely over the cake.) Cool in the pan on a rack for 30 minutes, then invert onto a serving plate or cutting board. Slice and serve warm or at room temperature, topped with the blueberries.
–Aimee Olexy

PER SERVING: 440 CALORIES | 6G PROTEIN | 56G CARB | 22G TOTAL FAT | 13G SAT FAT | 6G MONO FAT | 1.5G POLY FAT | 145MG CHOL | 75MG SODIUM | 1G FIBER

sweet corn cake with blueberry-lavender compote

SERVES 10 TO 12

FOR THE CAKE

6	oz. (¾ cup) unsalted butter, softened; more for the pan
4½	oz. (1 cup) unbleached all-purpose flour
2	tsp. baking powder
¼	tsp. table salt
2¼	oz. (½ cup) sifted stone-ground yellow cornmeal
1	cup cooked fresh corn kernels (from about 1 large ear)
½	cup sour cream, at room temperature
¾	cup granulated sugar
3	large eggs, at room temperature and lightly beaten

FOR THE COMPOTE

1	cup granulated sugar
2	tsp. dried lavender
1¼	cups cooked fresh corn kernels (from about 2 medium ears)
1	cup fresh blueberries

A lavender-scented topping lends an elegant touch to this rustic cake. To cook the corn, boil it in lightly salted water until tender—3 to 5 minutes, depending on how fresh the corn is. You can skip sifting the cornmeal if you'd like a coarser texture in the cake.

MAKE THE CAKE

1. Position a rack in the center of the oven and heat the oven to 350°F. Butter the sides and bottom of a 9x2-inch round cake pan. Fit a round of parchment in the bottom of the pan and butter that as well.

2. Sift the flour, baking powder, and salt into a medium bowl. Whisk in the cornmeal; set aside.

3. Purée the corn kernels in a food processor until smooth. Strain the purée through a fine-mesh sieve, pressing with a rubber spatula to extract the liquid; scrape any purée off the bottom of the sieve into the liquid and then discard the remaining solids. Measure ¼ cup of the strained corn liquid and transfer to a small bowl (discard any excess liquid). Stir in the sour cream.

4. In a stand mixer fitted with the paddle attachment, beat the butter and sugar on medium-high speed until fluffy, about 2 minutes. Stop and scrape the sides of the bowl. On low speed, slowly pour in the beaten eggs, mixing until incorporated and stopping midway to scrape the sides. (The mixture will be loose and curdled-looking.)

5. On low speed, add one-third of the flour mixture and mix until just blended. Add one-third of the sour cream–corn mixture and mix until just blended. Alternate adding the remaining flour and sour cream mixtures in two additions each. Do not overmix.

6. Scrape the batter into the cake pan and spread it evenly with a spatula. Bake until the cake is golden brown and springs back when lightly pressed in the center, 30 to 35 minutes. Transfer to a rack to cool for 10 to 15 minutes. Run a knife around the edge of the pan and then gently invert the cake onto the rack, removing the pan. Remove the parchment, turn the cake right side up onto the rack, and let cool completely.

MAKE THE COMPOTE

1. Combine the sugar and ⅔ cup water in a small saucepan. Bring to a simmer over medium-high heat, stirring frequently until the sugar has dissolved completely. Remove from the heat. Add the lavender and stir to combine. Let infuse for 10 minutes, then strain the syrup into a small bowl and let cool.

2. When ready to serve the cake, stir the corn and blueberries into the syrup. Cut the cake into wedges, and top each serving with about 3 Tbs. of the mixture, letting most of the syrup drain off the spoon before sprinkling the blueberries and corn over the cake.

–Maryellen Driscoll

PER SERVING (BASED ON 12 SERVINGS): 320 CALORIES | 4G PROTEIN | 46G CARB | 15G TOTAL FAT | 9G SAT FAT | 4G MONO FAT | 1G POLY FAT | 85MG CHOL | 140MG SODIUM | 2G FIBER

chocolate strawberry shortcakes

SERVES 9

FOR THE CHOCOLATE BISCUITS

10 oz. (2¼ cups) unbleached all-purpose flour

1½ oz. (about ¼ cup plus 3 Tbs.) unsweetened Dutch-processed cocoa powder, such as Droste®

¼ cup granulated sugar; plus about 3 Tbs. for sprinkling

1½ Tbs. baking powder

¾ tsp. table salt

4½ oz. (9 Tbs.) cold unsalted butter, cut into small pieces

6½ oz. semisweet chocolate, grated or finely chopped (the food processor works well); more for garnish

1¼ cups heavy cream; plus about 3 Tbs. for brushing

1½ tsp. pure vanilla extract

FOR THE STRAWBERRIES

5 cups ⅛-inch-thick straw-berry slices (from about 3 pints fresh berries)

1 to 3 Tbs. granulated sugar, depending on the sweetness of the berries

FOR THE WHIPPED CREAM

1½ cups heavy cream

2 Tbs. granulated sugar

¾ tsp. pure vanilla extract

Whole fresh strawberries for garnish (optional)

Cocoa and semisweet chocolate give the biscuits an intense flavor close to that of a brownie, but with a light, flaky texture.

MAKE THE BISCUITS

1. Line a heavy baking sheet with parchment. Sift the flour, cocoa powder, sugar, baking powder, and salt into a large bowl. Toss with a fork to combine. Cut the butter into the dry ingredients with a pastry cutter or a fork until the largest pieces of butter are the size of peas. Add the grated chocolate and toss to combine. Combine the cream and vanilla in a liquid measure. Make a well in the center of the flour mixture and pour the cream into the well. Mix with a fork until the dough is evenly moistened and just combined; it should look shaggy and still feel a little dry. Gently knead by hand five or six times to pick up any dry ingredients remaining in the bottom of the bowl and to create a loose ball.

2. Turn the dough out onto a lightly floured work surface and pat it into an 8-inch square, ¾ to 1 inch thick. Transfer the dough to the parchment-lined baking sheet, cover with plastic wrap, and chill for 20 minutes. Meanwhile, heat the oven to 425°F. Remove the dough from the refrigerator and trim about ¼ inch from each side to create a neat, sharp edge (a bench knife or a pastry scraper works well, or use a large chef's knife, being sure to cut straight down). Cut the dough into 9 even squares (about 2½ inches square) and spread them about 2 inches apart on the baking sheet. With a pastry brush or the back of a spoon, brush each biscuit with a thin layer of cream and sprinkle generously with sugar. Bake until the biscuits look a little dry and are mostly firm to the touch (they should spring back slightly when gently pressed), 18 to 20 minutes.

PREPARE THE BERRIES

Toss the berries with 1 Tbs. sugar and taste. If they're still tart, sprinkle with another 1 to 2 Tbs. sugar. Let sit at room temperature until the sugar dissolves and the berries begin to release their juices, at least 30 minutes but no more than 2 hours.

WHIP THE CREAM

Pour the cream into a cold mixing bowl and beat with a hand-held mixer until it begins to thicken. Add the sugar and vanilla extract and, using a whisk, continue to beat by hand until the cream is softly whipped or until the whisk leaves distinct marks in the cream; it should be soft and billowy but still hold its shape.

ASSEMBLE THE SHORTCAKES

While the biscuits are still warm, split them in half horizontally with a serrated knife. For each serving, set the bottom half of a biscuit on a plate. Scoop about ½ cup of the berries and their juices over the biscuit. Add a generous dollop of whipped cream and cover with the top half of the biscuit. Top with a small dollop of cream and garnish with some grated chocolate and a berry or two and serve.

—Katherine Eastman Seeley

PER SERVING: 660 CALORIES | 8G PROTEIN | 61G CARB | 46G TOTAL FAT | 28G SAT FAT | 14G MONO FAT | 2G POLY FAT | 130MG CHOL | 470MG SODIUM | 7G FIBER

Make Ahead

- You can make the biscuits several hours in advance. You can even bake them a day ahead, or freeze them for up to 3 months, although their texture will suffer slightly. Just before serving, reheat the prepared biscuits in a 200°F oven until warmed through.

- Slice the berries hours ahead of time and refrigerate them. Half an hour before assembling the shortcakes, toss the berries with the sugar and let them sit at room temperature.

- Under-whip the whipped cream and refrigerate it, covered, until ready to serve. Then use a whisk to finish whipping.

peach cake with apricot and vanilla glaze

SERVES 8

- ¼ lb. (½ cup) unsalted butter, at room temperature; more for the pan
- 6¾ oz. (1½ cups) unbleached all-purpose flour; more for the pan
- 1½ tsp. baking powder
- ½ tsp. table salt
- 1 cup plus 2 tsp. granulated sugar
- ½ vanilla bean, or 1¼ tsp. pure vanilla extract
- 2 large eggs, at room temperature
- ⅔ cup whole milk
- 2 firm but ripe peaches (about 5 oz. each), pitted and sliced about ¹⁄₁₆ inch thick
- ¼ cup apricot jelly
- 2 tsp. brandy

This peach dessert feels traditional but has a hint of the unexpected with the warmth of a vanilla bean. This cake is best served the day it's baked.

1. Position a rack in the center of the oven and heat the oven to 350°F. Generously butter and flour a 10x2-inch fluted quiche pan or a 9x2-inch round cake pan.

2. In a medium bowl, whisk together the flour, baking powder, and salt; set aside. In a large bowl, beat the butter with an electric mixer until smooth. Add 1 cup of the sugar. Split the vanilla bean (if using) with a paring knife and scrape out the seeds. Add them to the bowl; reserve the pod. Beat on medium speed, scraping the sides, until the mixture is well combined and has some body, about 3 minutes. If using vanilla extract, beat in 1 tsp. now. Add the eggs, one at a time, beating well after each addition. Add half of the flour mixture and mix on low speed until just blended. Add the milk and mix until just blended. Add the remaining flour mixture and mix until just blended.

3. Pour the batter into the prepared pan and spread evenly. Arrange the peach slices, overlapping slightly, on top of the batter in a circular pattern (you might not need all the slices) and sprinkle with the remaining 2 tsp. sugar. Bake until a toothpick inserted into the center of the cake comes out clean, 50 to 55 minutes.

4. While the cake bakes, make the glaze. Put the apricot jelly, brandy, and the empty vanilla bean pod (if using) in a small saucepan and heat on medium low until syrupy. Remove from the heat, cover, and let the vanilla bean infuse for 20 minutes. Remove the bean. If using vanilla extract, stir in ¼ tsp. now.

5. When the cake is done, let it cool on a wire rack for 20 minutes. Run a small knife around the inside edge of the pan to loosen the cake. Remove the cake from the pan and transfer to a serving plate. Just before serving, reheat the glaze to liquefy it and brush it over the peaches. *–Abigail Johnson Dodge*

PER SERVING: 360 CALORIES | 5G PROTEIN | 55G CARB | 14G TOTAL FAT | 8G SAT FAT | 4G MONO FAT | 1G POLY FAT | 85MG CHOL | 270MG SODIUM | 1G FIBER

individual dried apricot and cranberry upside-down cakes

SERVES 6

FOR THE CARAMEL

1   cup granulated sugar

3   Tbs. water

FOR THE FRUIT

12   dried apricots

1   cup fresh orange juice

     Pinch of ground cinnamon

⅓   cup dried cranberries

FOR THE POLENTA CAKES

3¾   oz. (¾ cup) yellow cornmeal

5¾   oz. (1¼ cups plus 1 Tbs.) unbleached all-purpose flour

⅓   cup granulated sugar

2½   tsp. baking powder

¼   tsp. salt

¼   tsp. ground cinnamon

¾   cup buttermilk

     Reserved fruit poaching liquid (from above)

3   oz. (6 Tbs.) unsalted butter, melted and cooled

1   large egg

The cornmeal flavor of these polenta cakes is a delicious complement to the dried fruit. You can line the ramekins with the caramel and fruit a day ahead. These little gems are best served warm, but they're good at room temperature, too.

MAKE THE CARAMEL

1. Lightly butter six 8-oz. ramekins.

2. In a heavy saucepan, stir the sugar and water together. Cook over medium heat, stirring frequently, until the sugar is completely dissolved. Turn the heat to high and boil until the sugar is light amber. Keep a close watch; the sugar will go from medium to deep amber quite quickly. Immediately pour the caramel into the ramekins and swirl each one right away to coat the bottom evenly. Set aside to cool.

PREPARE THE FRUIT

In a small saucepan, combine the apricots, orange juice, and cinnamon. Cover and simmer until the apricots are plump and tender, about 12 minutes. Add the cranberries and simmer for 2 minutes. Strain, reserving the poaching liquid. Set aside ¼ cup of the liquid to flavor the cake batter and save the rest to moisten the caramel. Put the fruit on a plate to cool completely. Cut each apricot into thirds. Arrange the fruit decoratively in each of the caramel-lined ramekins.

MAKE THE CAKE

1. Set a baking sheet on the center rack of the oven and heat the oven to 350°F. In a medium bowl, whisk the cornmeal, flour, sugar, baking powder, salt, and cinnamon until blended. In a small bowl, whisk the buttermilk, the reserved ¼ cup poaching liquid, the melted butter, and the egg. Pour the wet ingredients over the dry ingredients and fold until the batter is just blended. Add 1 tsp. of the remaining poaching liquid to each ramekin; swirl to distribute. Spoon the batter into the ramekins. Tap the ramekins on the counter to settle the batter.

2. Set the ramekins on the heated baking sheet and bake until the edges are browned and a pick inserted in the center comes out clean, 25 to 30 minutes. Immediately run a paring knife around the inside edge of each ramekin and invert onto serving plates. Let the inverted ramekins rest for 5 minutes to let the topping settle. Gently remove the ramekins and serve. *–Abigail Johnson Dodge*

PER SERVING: 520 CALORIES | 7G PROTEIN | 94G CARB | 14G TOTAL FAT | 8G SAT FAT | 4G MONO FAT | 1G POLY FAT | 70MG CHOL | 250MG SODIUM | 3G FIBER

peaches and cream shortcakes

FOR THE SHORTCAKE BISCUITS

- **9 oz. (2 cups) unbleached all-purpose flour; more for rolling and cutting the biscuits**

- **2 Tbs. light brown sugar**

- **2½ tsp. baking powder**

- **¼ tsp. table salt**

- **¼ tsp. ground nutmeg, preferably freshly grated**

- **3 oz. (6 Tbs.) unsalted butter, chilled in the freezer for 15 minutes**

- **1 cup plus 1 tsp. heavy whipping cream**

- **1 Tbs. demerara sugar**

- **Marinated Peaches (recipe on p. 152)**

- **Honey Whipped Cream (recipe on p. 152)**

The deep flavor of brown sugar in this syrup is the perfect complement to fresh peaches. You can make the syrup a couple of weeks ahead and refrigerate it, tightly covered. Don't add the peaches too far ahead, though, as they will turn brown after a couple of hours in the marinade. Use a delicately flavored honey, such as orange blossom or clover, so the whipped cream doesn't outshine the peaches.

MAKE THE BISCUITS

1. Position a rack in the center of the oven and heat the oven to 400°F. Line a baking sheet with parchment or a nonstick liner.

2. Put the flour, brown sugar, baking powder, salt, and nutmeg in a food processor fitted with a steel blade. Pulse briefly to blend. Cut the butter into small pieces and add to the food processor. Pulse until the butter is cut into pieces the size of large breadcrumbs, 6 to 8 pulses. With the food processor running, immediately pour 1 cup of the cream through the feed tube and process just until the ingredients are moistened.

3. Turn the mixture out onto a lightly floured work surface and knead a few times just until smooth. Pat the dough into a ¾-inch-thick round or rectangle. Dip a 2¾-inch round plain-edge biscuit cutter in flour and then cut straight down through the dough to form the biscuits. (Dip the cutter in flour before cutting each biscuit and don't twist the cutter, because it will seal the edges and keep the shortcakes from rising as they bake.)

4. Transfer the shortcakes to the lined baking sheet, leaving at least an inch between them. Gather the scraps together, knead briefly to smooth the dough, and shape into a ¾-inch-thick round or rectangle. Cut out more shortcakes. Repeat as often as necessary to use most of the dough (there will be a little left over).

5. With a pastry brush, lightly coat the tops of the biscuits with the remaining 1 tsp. cream and then lightly sprinkle them with demerara sugar.

6. Bake until the bottoms are slightly golden, 14 to 16 minutes. Remove the baking sheet from the oven and let the biscuits cool completely on a rack before serving.

continued on p. 152

Variations

- Instead of the amaretto, stir peach schnapps, Grand Marnier, Cointreau, or a dessert wine, such as Muscat (Moscato), Muscat Canelli, or Sauternes into the brown-sugar syrup.
- For deeper flavor, replace the light brown sugar with dark brown.
- For lighter flavor, replace the light brown sugar with granulated.

ASSEMBLE THE SHORTCAKES

Using a serrated knife, slice each biscuit in half horizontally. Set the bottom half on an individual serving plate and spoon about one-eighth of the marinated peaches, a scant ¼ cup, over the biscuit. Cover the peaches with a generous spoonful of whipped cream. Put the top of the biscuit on the cream. Drop a small dollop of whipped cream on the biscuit top, if you wish. Repeat with the remaining biscuits. If you have any peach slices left, arrange them around the plates. Serve immediately. —*Carole Bloom*

PER SERVING: 600 CALORIES | 6G PROTEIN | 63G CARB | 37G TOTAL FAT | 23G SAT FAT | 10G MONO FAT | 1.5G POLY FAT | 125MG CHOL | 230MG SODIUM | 2G FIBER

marinated peaches

MAKES ABOUT 2 CUPS

½ cup firmly packed light brown sugar

1 Tbs. Amaretto

4 large ripe peaches (about 1½ lb.)

1. Combine the sugar and ¼ cup water in a small heavy-based saucepan and bring to a boil over medium-high heat. Remove from the heat and let the sugar syrup cool. Stir in the amaretto.

2. Bring a large saucepan of water to a boil. Fill a large bowl with ice water. Using a small, sharp knife, cut a small X in the pointed end of each peach. Plunge the peaches into the boiling water for 1 minute. With a slotted spoon, remove the peaches from the water and put them into the bowl of ice water to stop the cooking. When the peaches are cool enough to handle, use a small, sharp knife to gently peel the skin off the peaches, starting at the X. If the skins don't peel off easily, return the peaches to the boiling water for another 30 to 60 seconds.

3. Halve the peaches lengthwise and remove the pits. Slice each half lengthwise into ½-inch-thick slices and put them in a medium bowl. Pour the amaretto sugar syrup over the peaches and stir gently to coat completely. Cover the bowl tightly with plastic wrap and let the peaches marinate in the refrigerator for at least 30 minutes and up to 2 hours before using.

honey whipped cream

MAKES ABOUT 3 CUPS

1½ cups cold heavy cream

5 Tbs. honey

1. Pour the heavy cream into the chilled bowl of an electric stand mixer or into a large chilled mixing bowl. Use the whisk attachment on the stand mixer or a hand-held mixer to whip the cream on medium speed until it begins to thicken slightly.

2. Turn the mixer off and add the honey. If necessary, scrape the sides of the bowl to push the honey into the cream. Whip the cream on medium-high speed until it holds soft peaks. Use right away.

More about Peaches

All peaches are classified as either freestone or cling. The flesh of a cling peach clutches at the stone of the fruit, while freestone varieties relinquish their seed more readily. You'll rarely find cling peaches at the market: Their firm flesh holds up well when cooked and is prized by commercial canners. The peaches you find at the grocery or farmers' market are almost always freestones.

Choosing peaches

A perfectly ripe peach should be firm. The only soft places will be the bruises left by other people pinching the peach before you got there. A ripe peach feels heavy in the palm of your hand; it will give a little and feel more voluptuous. Look for the golden or creamy background color of the skin at the stem end of the peach. Don't be duped by a provocative blush color (varieties are being developed that are nearly 90% blush). The background color of the skin is important.

Size is crucial, too. Bigger is better when it comes to peaches. Bigger peaches seem to be sweeter, more fully developed in flavor. Sniff the peach you're considering: You can smell the nectar in a riper peach.

Storing peaches

Supermarket peaches are often smaller, picked greener, and stored longer. But if imperfect peaches are all that's available, you can ripen peaches in a brown paper bag or a ripening bowl.

If you've picked firm, ripe fruit with good background color at the stem end, the peaches will soften in 3 or 4 days, and a lovely fragrance will beckon you. They'll keep in the refrigerator for a couple of days longer.

Don't wash peaches until you're ready to use them or they're likely to develop mold.

Prepping peaches

When preparing peaches for cooking, the trick is to remove the skin while keeping as much flesh as you can on the peach. The best way to do this is to quickly blanch the peaches before you peel them.

To blanch: Bring a large pot of water to a boil. While the water heats, cut an X into the bottom of each peach. Drop the peaches into the boiling water and cook just until the skin begins to loosen, 30 to 60 seconds. Drain the peaches and then plunge them into cold water to stop them from cooking further. The peel should slip right off.

To slice a peach: Run a small knife from stem to tip, cutting right through to the pit. Turn the peach in your hand, making one cut after another and let the slices fall into a bowl. Once exposed to the air, peach flesh tends to turn brown quickly. To keep the color bright, sprinkle the slices with a bit of lemon juice.

cinnamon–walnut shortcakes
with caramelized plums

FOR THE BISCUITS

¼ **lb. (½ cup) cold butter, cut into small pieces**

12 **oz. (2⅔ cups) unbleached all-purpose flour; more for dusting**

⅓ **cup granulated sugar**

1½ **Tbs. baking powder**

1½ **tsp. ground cinnamon**

½ **tsp. table salt**

⅛ **tsp. ground nutmeg**

¾ **cup (about 3 oz.) walnuts, toasted and very roughly chopped**

1 **cup plus 2 Tbs. cold heavy cream; more for brushing**

1 **tsp. pure vanilla extract**

1 **Tbs. demerara or turbinado sugar**

FOR THE CARAMELIZED PLUMS

1 **Tbs. unsalted butter**

⅓ **cup granulated sugar**

Large pinch of kosher salt

5 **firm medium plums, each cut into 10 wedges**

FOR THE WHIPPED CREAM

1 **cup cold heavy cream**

¼ **cup cold sour cream**

3 **Tbs. confectioners' sugar**

The warm flavor of these biscuits makes these shortcakes extra special. If you're making the biscuits in a hot kitchen, try to keep the ingredients as cold as possible for the flakiest texture. It's OK to use underripe plums if that's all you can find—the caramelization softens and sweetens the fruit.

MAKE THE BISCUITS

1. Line a large rimmed baking sheet with parchment.

2. Chill the butter pieces in the freezer for about 15 minutes. Meanwhile, in a large bowl, whisk the flour, sugar, baking powder, cinnamon, salt, and nutmeg. With a pastry blender, cut in the cold butter until the mixture resembles a very coarse meal strewn with pieces of butter the size of peas and pistachios. Add the walnuts and toss with a fork to distribute them.

3. Combine the cream with the vanilla in a liquid measuring cup. Make a well in the center of the flour mixture and pour the cream into the well. With a fork, work your way around the bowl, pulling the dry ingredients into the wet and mixing until the ingredients are mostly moistened and a rough dough forms. Gently knead the dough a few times in the bowl to pick up any dry ingredients in the bottom of the bowl and bring it together into a loose ball. Transfer the dough to the parchment-lined baking sheet and pat into a ¾-inch-thick round. Refrigerate for about 20 minutes.

4. Position a rack in the center of the oven and heat the oven to 450°F.

5. Dip a 3-inch round plain-edge biscuit cutter in flour and cut straight down through the dough without twisting to form the biscuits. (Dip the cutter in flour before cutting each biscuit.) Carefully move the biscuits to one end of the baking sheet. Gather the dough scraps together, knead briefly to smooth the dough, and pat into a ¾-inch-thick round on the other end of the baking sheet. Cut out more biscuits. Repeat one more time. You can use the remaining scraps to make an additional biscuit or two, but those won't have as nice a texture as the others.

6. Spread the biscuits out over the baking sheet. Lightly brush their tops with cream and then sprinkle with the demerara sugar.

7. Put the baking sheet in the oven and lower the temperature to 425°F. Bake until the biscuits are deeply browned on top and bottom, 20 to 25 minutes. Let them cool on a rack while you make the caramelized plums.

continued on p. 156

ROAST THE PLUMS

1. In a 12-inch heavy-duty skillet, melt the butter over medium heat. Add the sugar, salt, and 1 Tbs. water. Swirl the pan to moisten and dissolve the sugar. Cook until the mixture becomes a bubbling golden caramel, 3 to 5 minutes. Immediately remove the pan from the heat.

2. Carefully add the plum wedges to the pan, spreading them out evenly. Set the pan over medium heat and cook, shaking the pan every 30 seconds or so, until the plums start to release their juices, 2 to 3 minutes. Turn the plums with tongs and cook until soft (but not mushy) and golden brown along some of the cut edges, 1 to 5 minutes more. Pour the contents of the pan into a medium bowl and cover to keep warm.

MAKE THE WHIPPED CREAM

Using a chilled bowl and beaters, whip the heavy cream with a hand-held or stand mixer on medium speed until it thickens slightly. Add the sour cream and confectioners' sugar and whip on medium-high speed until it holds medium peaks. Use right away.

ASSEMBLE THE SHORTCAKES

Using a fork, split each biscuit in half horizontally. Set the bottom halves on serving plates and spoon 5 or 6 plum wedges onto each biscuit. Dollop the cream on the plums and drizzle with some of the caramelized plum juice. Perch the tops of the biscuits on the cream. If you have plums left, arrange them on the plates alongside the shortcakes. *–Kim Masibay*

PER SERVING: 690 CALORIES | 8G PROTEIN | 63G CARB | 46G TOTAL FAT | 25G SAT FAT | 12G MONO FAT | 7G POLY FAT | 125MG CHOL | 420MG SODIUM | 3G FIBER

gingery plum cake

SERVES 8 TO 10

FOR THE CAKE

- 3 oz. (6 Tbs.) unsalted butter, at room temperature; more for the pan
- 6 oz. (1⅓ cups) unbleached all-purpose flour; more for the pan
- 1 tsp. ground ginger
- ¾ tsp. baking powder
- ¼ tsp. baking soda
- ¼ tsp. table salt
- 1 cup packed light brown sugar
- 2 large eggs
- 1 tsp. pure vanilla extract
- ⅔ cup (5½ oz.) sour cream

FOR THE TOPPING

- 1 plum (or pluot or ripe apricot), halved, pitted, and cut into ⅛- to ¼-inch slices
- 2 tsp. finely grated fresh ginger
- 3 Tbs. firmly packed light brown sugar
- 1 Tbs. unbleached all-purpose flour

  Whipped cream, for garnish (optional)

Add the fruit after the cake batter has been baking for 15 minutes to keep it from sinking to the bottom. Feel free to substitute apricots or pluots for the plums.

MAKE THE CAKE

1. Position a rack in the center of the oven and heat the oven to 350°F. Lightly butter a 9x2-inch round cake pan. Line the bottom with a parchment round cut to fit the pan and lightly flour the sides, tapping out the excess.

2. In a medium bowl, whisk the flour, ground ginger, baking powder, baking soda, and salt. In a stand mixer fitted with the paddle attachment (or with a hand-held mixer), beat the butter and sugar on medium high until well blended and fluffy, about 3 minutes. Add the eggs, one at a time, beating on medium speed until just blended and adding the vanilla with the second egg. Using a wide rubber spatula, fold in half the dry ingredients, then the sour cream, and then the remaining dry ingredients. Scrape the batter into the prepared pan and spread evenly. Bake for 15 minutes.

MAKE THE TOPPING

1. Meanwhile, make the topping. Combine the sliced fruit and the grated ginger in a small bowl and toss until the ginger is well distributed. Add the sugar and flour. Using a table fork, mix the ingredients to coat the fruit evenly. After the cake has baked for 15 minutes, scatter the topping evenly over the cake, working quickly. Don't worry about the fruit looking perfect—this is a rustic cake. Continue baking until a toothpick inserted in the center of the cake comes out clean, another 35 to 40 minutes.

2. Let the cake cool on a rack for 15 minutes. Run a knife around the inside edge of the pan. Using a dry dishtowel to protect your hands, lay a rack on top of the cake pan and, holding onto both pan and rack, invert the cake. Lift the pan from the cake. Peel away the parchment. Lay a flat serving plate on the bottom of the cake and flip the cake one more time so that the fruit is on top. Serve warm or at room temperature, with whipped cream if you like. *–Abigail Johnson Dodge*

apple upside-down cake

FOR THE APPLES

2   lb. (about 4 large) sweet apples that hold their shape when cooked, peeled, quartered, and cored, each quarter sliced into 3 wedges

1   large lemon, finely grated to yield 1 Tbs. zest (reserve for the cake) and squeezed to yield 1 Tbs. juice

3   oz. (6 Tbs.) unsalted butter, cut into 6 pieces

    Pinch of table salt

FOR THE TOPPING

    Unsalted butter, softened, for the pan

1   cup granulated sugar

1   tsp. ground cinnamon

FOR THE CAKE

4½ oz. (1 cup) unbleached all-purpose flour

1   tsp. baking powder

¼   tsp. ground cardamom

¼   tsp. table salt

3   oz. (6 Tbs.) unsalted butter, cut into ½-inch cubes and slightly softened

¾   cup granulated sugar

1   tsp. pure vanilla extract

1   large egg

2   large egg yolks

½   cup whole milk

The flower pattern that's revealed once this cake is inverted will be defined best by an apple that holds its shape. A sweet variety will complement the nutty brown butter in which the apples are cooked. Serve the cake on its own or with vanilla ice cream. The cake can be baked up to 1 day ahead and kept covered at room temperature.

PREPARE THE APPLES

1. In a large bowl, toss the apples with the lemon juice.

2. In a heavy-duty 12-inch skillet, cook the butter over medium heat until it has a nutty fragrance and there are brown bits on the bottom of the skillet, about 4 minutes. Immediately add the apples and salt and toss gently with a heatproof spatula until well coated. Cook, uncovered, for 5 minutes, tossing once. Toss again, cover, and cook, tossing every 2 to 3 minutes, until the apples are tender, 6 to 8 minutes.

3. Uncover and cook, stirring gently, until some of the apples begin to brown and any liquid has evaporated, about 2 minutes more. Set aside until cool enough to handle.

MAKE THE TOPPING

1. Butter a 9x2-inch round cake pan, line the bottom with parchment, and butter the parchment. Have ready a pastry brush and a small bowl of water.

2. Put the sugar, cinnamon, and ⅓ cup water in a 2- to 3-quart saucepan and cook over medium heat, stirring, until the sugar dissolves. Stop stirring and, using the pastry brush dipped in the water, wash any sugar crystals from the side of the pan. Continue to cook, without stirring, until the caramel begins to color; then swirl the pan until the caramel turns an even, deep amber, about 3 minutes. Immediately pour the caramel into the prepared cake pan, swirling to evenly coat the bottom. Let cool.

3. Starting in the center of the pan, arrange the cooled apple slices on the caramel in slightly overlapping, tightly packed concentric circles; set aside.

MAKE THE CAKE

1. Position a rack in the lower third of the oven and heat the oven to 350°F.

2. In a medium bowl, whisk the flour, baking powder, cardamom, and salt.

3. In a stand mixer fitted with the paddle attachment, beat the butter on medium speed until smooth and creamy, about 1 minute. Scrape the bowl and beater with a rubber spatula. Add ¼ cup of the sugar, the reserved lemon zest, and vanilla and beat on medium-high speed until well combined, about 1 minute. Scrape the bowl and beater.

4. With the mixer on medium speed, slowly sprinkle in the remaining ½ cup sugar, taking 20 to 30 seconds to add it. Increase the speed to medium high and beat until pale and creamy, 3 to 4 minutes, stopping once to scrape the bowl and beater. Add the egg and beat on medium speed until combined, about 1 minute. Add the yolks and beat until incorporated, 1 minute. (It's OK if the batter looks curdled.) With the mixer on low speed, alternately add the dry ingredients in three additions and the milk in two additions; scrape the bowl and beater as necessary and mix each addition just until smooth.

5. Using the rubber spatula, spread the batter evenly over the apples. Tap the pan down on the counter once or twice to settle the batter. Bake until the cake springs back when gently pressed and a toothpick inserted in the center comes out clean, 40 to 45 minutes.

6. Transfer the cake to a rack and run a small, sharp knife around the edge to release it from the pan. Cool the cake in the pan for 20 minutes.

7. Holding the pan between your palms, rotate it briskly back and forth on the countertop to release the apples from the bottom. Invert the cake onto a cake plate and slowly remove the pan and the parchment. If any apples have shifted, reposition them. Let the cake cool for at least 1 hour before serving. —*Greg Patent*

PER SERVING: 370 CALORIES | 3G PROTEIN | 56G CARB | 16G TOTAL FAT | 9G SAT FAT | 4.5G MONO FAT | 1G POLY FAT | 95MG CHOL | 130MG SODIUM | 2G FIBER

Apples that Hold Their Shape

Choose one of these varieties when making the upside-down cake.

Rome: Softens but holds it shape nicely. Quite juicy, with a complex sweet-tart flavor.

Golden Delicious: Holds its shape fairly well but gets a bit mushy. Very juicy but flavor lacks complexity.

Granny Smith: Holds its shape fairly well. Flavor is not as appley as others, but is fine when teamed with a softer, perfumy apple.

Braeburn: Great texture—soft but still holds its shape. Flavor is on the sweet side.

how to create a flower pattern

To arrange the apples in a flower pattern, begin in the center and put the prettier side of each apple slice face down, because that's the side you'll see.

The side of the pan guides the placement of the final circle. Make sure one end of each apple slice touches the pan as you overlap the slices.

caramelized pear upside-down cake

SERVES 8

FOR THE TOPPING

2 medium firm-ripe Bosc pears (about 1 lb.)

FOR THE CARAMEL

1 cup granulated sugar

¼ tsp. fresh lemon juice

2 oz. (4 Tbs.) unsalted butter, cut into 4 pieces

FOR THE CAKE

6¾ oz. (1½ cups) unbleached all-purpose flour

1¾ tsp. baking powder

½ tsp. ground ginger

½ tsp. ground cinnamon

¼ tsp. table salt

½ cup whole milk

1½ tsp. pure vanilla extract

¼ lb. (½ cup) unsalted butter, softened

1 cup packed light brown sugar

2 large eggs

This stunning cake is delicious warm or at room temperature.

Position a rack in the center of the oven and heat the oven to 350°F. Butter the bottom and sides of a 9x2-inch round cake pan (don't use a springform pan, as the caramel might leak out during baking). Line the bottom of the pan with a round of parchment and butter the top of the paper.

MAKE THE TOPPING

Peel, core, and cut the pears lengthwise into ¼-inch-thick slices. Arrange the pear slices on the bottom of the pan in a circle around the edge, overlapping them slightly, with the pointed ends toward the center. If necessary, cut a little off the pointed ends to make the slices fit better. Or if the pear slices don't reach all the way to the middle, arrange a few of the shorter slices in the center to cover the bottom of the pan.

MAKE THE CARAMEL

1. Fill a cup measure halfway with water and put a pastry brush in it; this will be used for washing down the sides of the pan to prevent crystallization.

2. In a heavy-duty 2-quart saucepan, stir the sugar, lemon juice, and ¼ cup cold water. Brush the sides of the pan with water to wash away any sugar crystals. Bring to a boil over medium-high heat and cook, occasionally brushing down the sides of the pan, until the mixture starts to color around the edges, 5 to 8 minutes. Gently swirl the pan once to even out the color and prevent the sugar from burning in isolated spots. Continue to cook until the sugar turns medium amber, about 30 seconds more. (Once the mixture begins to color, it will darken very quickly, so keep an eye on it.)

3. Immediately remove the pan from the heat and whisk in the 4 Tbs. of butter one piece at a time, until they are completely melted. Carefully pour the hot caramel evenly over the pears (it should spread over the pears and onto the bottom of the pan).

continued on p. 162

MAKE THE CAKE

1. Sift the flour, baking powder, ginger, cinnamon, and salt into a medium bowl. Stir to combine. In a small bowl, stir together the milk and vanilla.

2. In the bowl of a stand mixer fitted with the paddle attachment, beat the butter on medium-high speed until light and fluffy, about 1 minute.

3. Turn the mixer to medium and slowly add the brown sugar. Increase the speed to high and continue to mix until lightened in texture and color, 2 to 3 minutes total. Reduce the speed to medium and add the eggs one at a time, beating well after each addition and scraping the sides of the bowl as needed.

4. Reduce the speed to low and alternate adding the flour mixture and milk mixture in five additions, beginning and ending with the flour. Mix each addition just enough to incorporate, as overmixing will lead to a tougher cake. Scrape the sides of the bowl one last time and mix briefly to blend well.

5. Spoon the batter in large dollops over the pears and smooth it into an even layer with an offset spatula. Bake the cake until the top is golden brown and a toothpick inserted in the center comes out clean, 35 to 45 minutes. Transfer the pan to a wire rack to cool for 10 minutes.

6. Run a knife around the edge of the pan. Turn a cake plate upside down on top of the cake pan and, using pot holders, carefully invert the cake pan onto the plate. *–Tish Boyle*

PER SERVING: 510 CALORIES | 5G PROTEIN | 80G CARB | 20G TOTAL FAT | 12G SAT FAT | 5G MONO FAT | 1G POLY FAT | 100MG CHOL | 200MG SODIUM | 2G FIBER

gingerbread cake with root-beer–poached pears

FOR THE GINGERBREAD

- ½ oz. (1 Tbs.) unsalted butter, softened
- 2 Tbs. granulated sugar
- 1 cup vegetable oil
- ¼ cup unsulfured molasses
- 3 large eggs
- 9 oz. (2 cups) unbleached all-purpose flour
- 2 tsp. baking soda
- 1 tsp. ground ginger
- 1 tsp. ground cinnamon
- ¾ tsp. table salt
- 1¾ cups packed dark brown sugar
- 1 cup root beer, preferably an artisanal brand

FOR THE PEARS

- 4 firm-ripe Bosc pears, peeled, halved, and cored
- 4 12-fl.-oz. bottles root beer, preferably an artisanal brand

  Freshly grated zest of 2 medium lemons

FOR SERVING

- 1 cup heavy cream
- 1 Tbs. confectioners' sugar

Root beer's aromatic, spicy sweetness makes it a great poaching liquid for pears. Serve both the gingerbread cake and the pears warm or at room temperature.

MAKE THE GINGERBREAD

1. Position a rack in the center of the oven and heat the oven to 350°F. Coat an 8-inch square cake pan with the butter and lightly dust with the granulated sugar. In a small bowl, stir the oil, molasses, and eggs until combined. In a large bowl, whisk the flour, baking soda, ginger, cinnamon, and salt.

2. In a small pot, bring the brown sugar and root beer to a boil. Meanwhile, add the molasses mixture to the flour and stir to combine. Add the hot root beer mixture and quickly beat until combined. Pour the batter into the prepared pan and bake until a toothpick inserted in the center of the cake comes out clean, 35 to 45 minutes. Let cool in the pan on a wire rack until warm, about 40 minutes. Invert the pan to remove the cake and turn the cake right side up. (The cake may be prepared up to 4 hours ahead.)

POACH THE PEARS

In a medium saucepan, combine the pears, root beer, and lemon zest. Bring the mixture to a slow simmer over medium-low heat and cook until the pears are tender, 20 to 30 minutes. With a slotted spoon, carefully transfer the pears to a plate. Bring the poaching liquid to a boil and boil until reduced to a syrup, about 15 minutes (watch carefully towards the end because it can burn quickly); you should have about ¾ cup. (The pears and syrup may be prepared up to 4 hours ahead. If the syrup thickens, reheat before serving.)

TO SERVE

In a chilled medium bowl, beat the cream and sugar with a hand mixer until soft peaks form, about 3 minutes. Cut the gingerbread into 8 pieces of whatever size you choose and place one on each of 8 plates. Arrange a pear half against each piece of gingerbread and drizzle each with the syrup. Top with a dollop of whipped cream and serve. *–Bruce Aidells*

PER SERVING: 800 CALORIES | 11G PROTEIN | 112G CARB | 39G TOTAL FAT | 11G SAT FAT | 15G MONO FAT | 12G POLY FAT | 115MG CHOL | 550MG SODIUM | 4G FIBER

brown-butter almond cake with roasted pears

SERVES 12 TO 14

- 5 oz. (10 Tbs.) unsalted butter; more for the pan
- 5 oz. (1 cup) whole almonds
- 1½ cups granulated sugar
- 3¾ oz. (1 cup) cake flour
- 2 tsp. baking powder
- Pinch of table salt
- 2 Tbs. dark rum
- 1 tsp. pure vanilla extract
- ¼ cup sour cream
- 9 large egg whites, ideally at room temperature
- ¼ cup sliced almonds
- Roasted Pears with Caramel Sauce (optional; recipe on the facing page)
- Confectioners' sugar, for dusting (optional)

You can make this cake ahead and store it in the freezer in a double layer of plastic wrap for up to 4 weeks. To defrost the cake, unwrap it, set it on a rack, cover it loosely with a towel, and let it sit at room temperature for about 2 hours.

1. Heat the oven to 350°F. Butter a 10-inch springform pan and line the bottom with a round of parchment or waxed paper.

2. Spread the whole almonds on a baking sheet and heat them in the oven, shaking the pan every couple of minutes, until lightly toasted and aromatic, 5 to 9 minutes.

3. In a small saucepan over medium heat, melt the butter and then continue to cook it for 5 to 7 minutes. Watch it carefully and when you see brown flecks in the bottom of the pan, immediately pour the butter into a medium bowl, scraping the pan with a spatula to get all the flecks. Set aside to let cool slightly.

4. In a food processor, pulse the whole almonds and ¾ cup of the sugar until finely ground. Pour the mixture into a medium bowl and stir in the cake flour, baking powder, and salt. Set aside.

tips for boosting the cake's flavor

Toast the almonds before processing to deepen their flavor. Let them cool and then pulse them with the sugar until they have a gritty, almost sandy texture. The sugar helps absorb the oils and prevents the ground nuts from turning into a paste.

Brown the butter well for an even nuttier taste. Swirl the milk solids around in the melted butter until the flecks turn a deep hazelnut brown. Transfer to a heatproof bowl to stop the cooking.

5. Stir the rum, vanilla extract, and sour cream into the browned butter.

6. In a stand mixer or in a large, clean, dry bowl, using a hand-held mixer, beat the egg whites, beginning on low speed until they start to foam. Increase the speed to medium high and beat until the whites barely hold peaks. Beat in the remaining ¾ cup sugar in a very slow, steady stream; continue beating the whites until they hold soft peaks.

7. Scoop a large dollop of the egg whites into the butter mixture and stir it in. Gently fold half of the almond mixture into the remaining egg whites and then half of the butter mixture into the egg whites. Repeat, ending with the butter mixture.

8. Pour the batter into the prepared pan. Smooth the top with a spatula and give the pan a quick spin to even out the batter. Sprinkle with the sliced almonds. Bake on the center rack of the oven until well risen and golden, 45 to 50 minutes. The center of the cake should spring back when pressed lightly.

9. Let the cake cool in the pan on a rack until warm to the touch, about 30 minutes. Run a knife around the inside edge of the pan and carefully flip the cake onto the rack to release it from the pan. Peel off the parchment. Gently flip the cake again onto a serving plate. Serve warm or at room temperature, dusted lightly with confectioners' sugar or with the roasted pears and caramel sauce below.
–Katherine Eastman Seeley

PER SERVING (BASED ON 14 SERVINGS): 280 CALORIES | 5G PROTEIN | 30G CARB | 15G TOTAL FAT | 6G SAT FAT | 6G MONO FAT | 2G POLY FAT | 25MG CHOL | 120MG SODIUM | 2G FIBER

roasted pears with caramel sauce

SERVES 12 TO 14

3 **medium-size ripe Anjou or Bartlett pears**

3 **Tbs. granulated sugar**

2 **Tbs. unsalted butter, cut into 6 pieces**

¾ **cup heavy cream**

1. Heat the oven to 375°F. Peel and halve the pears lengthwise. Using a melon baller or a paring knife, cut out the stems and seeds.

2. Set the pears in a 10-inch ovenproof skillet. Sprinkle with the sugar and dot with the butter. Roast the pears, turning them every 10 minutes, until they're soft and the sugar and fruit juices have caramelized in the pan, 35 to 55 minutes. Transfer the pears to a cutting board and let cool slightly before slicing thinly.

3. Meanwhile, set the skillet on the stove over medium-high heat. Add the cream and bring it to a simmer. Stir with a wooden spoon until the caramel in the pan dissolves into the cream to make a smooth sauce. Simmer to thicken slightly, 3 to 5 minutes. To serve, pool some of the caramel sauce on a plate. Spread a few pear slices in a fan shape over the sauce.

cranberry and almond bundt cake

MAKES 1 LARGE BUNDT CAKE
OR 12 MINIATURE BUNDT
CAKES

- ½ **lb. (1 cup) unsalted butter, softened at room temperature; more for the pan**
- 6¾ **oz. (1½ cups) unbleached all-purpose flour; more for the pan**
- 1½ **tsp. baking powder**
- ¼ **tsp. table salt**
- 7 **oz. (about ⅔ cup) almond paste (not marzipan)**
- 1 **cup granulated sugar**
- 4 **large eggs, at room temperature**
- 1 **tsp. pure vanilla extract**
- ¼ **cup milk, at room temperature**
- 1½ **cups fresh or thawed frozen cranberries, picked through, rinsed, and coarsely chopped**
- **Confectioners' sugar, for dusting (optional)**

This cake is made to last; it will hold up for as long as a week, and you can bake it up to a month ahead of time and freeze it. It's a good option to bring to a party instead of a plate of cookies.

1. Position a rack in the center of the oven and heat the oven to 350°F. Butter and flour a 10- or 12-cup Bundt or kugelhopf pan (or twelve 1-cup mini bundt pans). Tap out any excess flour.

2. Sift together the flour, baking powder, and salt. In a stand mixer fitted with the paddle attachment (or in a large bowl, using a hand-held mixer), beat the butter and almond paste in a large bowl on medium speed until smooth, 1 to 2 minutes. Add the sugar and beat until light and fluffy, about 2 minutes. Beat in the eggs one at a time, stopping the mixer to scrape the bowl after each addition. Beat in the vanilla. With the mixer on low speed, alternate adding the flour mixture and the milk, beginning and ending with the flour. Stop the mixer at least one last time to scrape the bowl and then beat at medium speed until the batter is smooth, about 20 seconds. Fold in the cranberries with a rubber spatula.

3. Spoon the batter into the prepared pan (or pans), spreading it evenly with a rubber spatula. Run a knife through the batter to eliminate any air pockets. Bake until a wooden skewer inserted in the center comes out clean, 40 to 45 minutes (about 20 minutes for mini cakes). Set the pan on a rack to cool for 20 minutes. Invert the cake onto the rack, remove the pan, and let the cake cool completely. If you're making the cake ahead, wrap it while still barely warm. Serve at room temperature, dusting the top with confectioners' sugar, if you like. *–Nicole Rees*

cranberry upside-down cake

MAKES ONE 9-INCH ROUND
CAKE; SERVES 12

- ½ lb. (1 cup) very soft unsalted butter; more for the pan
- 1 cup very firmly packed light brown sugar
- ¼ tsp. ground cinnamon
- 2 cups cranberries, fresh or frozen (thawed, rinsed, and dried), at room temperature
- 1 cup granulated sugar
- 1 large egg yolk, at room temperature
- 2 large eggs, at room temperature
- ⅔ cup sour cream, at room temperature
- 1 tsp. pure vanilla extract
- ½ tsp. table salt
- 7 oz. (1¾ cups) cake flour
- 1 tsp. baking powder
- ¼ tsp. baking soda

This humble, comforting cake is a natural for Thanksgiving or Christmas, but you don't have to wait for a special occasion to make it.

1. Position a rack in the lower third of the oven and heat the oven to 350°F. Lightly butter the bottom and sides of a 9-inch round cake pan with sides at least 2½ inches high. (A springform pan will work; just be sure to set it on a foil-lined baking sheet to catch any leaks.)

2. Put ¼ cup of the butter in the buttered pan. Put the pan in the oven until the butter melts, about 5 minutes. Remove the pan from the oven and stir in the brown sugar and cinnamon until well combined. Spread the brown sugar mixture evenly over the bottom of the pan and spread the cranberries evenly over the sugar.

3. Put the remaining ¾ cup butter in a medium bowl. Using a wooden spoon, cream the butter with the granulated sugar and egg yolk until blended, about 20 seconds. Switch to a whisk and stir in the eggs one at a time. Whisk until the batter is smooth and the sugar begins to dissolve, about 30 seconds. Whisk in the sour cream, vanilla, and salt. Sift the cake flour, baking powder, and baking soda directly onto the batter. Using the whisk, combine the ingredients until the mixture is smooth and free of lumps.

4. Spread the batter evenly over the cranberry mixture in the cake pan. Bake until the center of the cake springs back when gently touched and a skewer inserted in the center comes out with only moist crumbs clinging to it, 50 to 65 minutes. Set the pan on a rack to cool for 5 to 10 minutes (the cranberry syrup in the bottom of the pan will be too thick if you wait longer). Run a knife between the cake and sides of the pan. Invert the cake onto a serving plate and remove the pan. Let cool for at least 15 minutes more before serving. This cake is best served warm and fresh. *–Nicole Rees*

spiced rum fruitcake

SERVES 10

FOR THE FRUIT

¾ **cup dark rum**

4 **oz. dried apricots, chopped into ¼- to ½-inch pieces (¾ cup lightly packed)**

3 **oz. dried apples, chopped into ¼- to ½-inch pieces (1 cup lightly packed)**

3 **oz. currants or dark raisins (¾ cup lightly packed)**

½ **tsp. freshly grated orange zest**

FOR THE BATTER

5 **oz. (10 Tbs.) unsalted butter, softened; more for the pan**

5 **oz. (1 cup plus 1 Tbs.) unbleached all-purpose flour**

½ **tsp. ground cinnamon**

½ **tsp. ground allspice**

¼ **tsp. ground cardamom**

⅛ **tsp. freshly grated nutmeg**

Pinch of ground cloves

⅔ **cup packed dark brown sugar (preferably muscovado)**

⅓ **cup granulated sugar**

3 **large eggs, at room temperature**

½ **tsp. pure vanilla extract**

¼ **tsp. table salt**

3½ **oz. crystallized ginger, finely chopped (½ cup)**

Dark rum, as needed for brushing

If you can find it, use musco-vado sugar. Made from sugar cane juice, it has a smoky, spicy complexity, with notes of butterscotch.

SOAK THE FRUIT

1. Put the rum, dried fruit, and orange zest in 2-quart sauce-pan, cover, and warm over medium heat until hot, 2 to 3 minutes. Remove from the heat and let cool. Refrigerate for a minimum of 24 hours and up to 3 days.

2. Before making the cake, bring the fruit to room temperature and drain, reserving any liquid for basting. (If the fruit was very dry, it may have absorbed all the liquid.)

MAKE THE CAKE

1. Position a rack in the center of the oven and heat the oven to 325°F. Butter an 8½x4½-inch metal loaf pan. Line the pan with two strips of parchment in opposite directions, leaving an overhang for easy removal of the cake.

2. In a medium bowl, whisk the flour with the cinnamon, allspice, cardamom, nutmeg, and cloves. In a stand mixer fitted with the paddle attachment (or in a large bowl, using a hand-held mixer), beat the butter and both sugars on medium-high speed until fluffy and no lumps of brown sugar remain, 1 to 2 minutes, stopping to scrape the bowl as needed. Beat in the eggs one at a time, scraping the bowl and mixing for 30 to 60 seconds after each addition. Beat in the vanilla and salt. Add 2 Tbs. of the flour mixture to the bowl and beat briefly. Reserve 2 Tbs. of the flour mixture and add the rest to the batter; beat on low speed for 10 seconds to incorporate the flour and then on medium high for 1 minute.

3. Combine the crystallized ginger with the drained fruit. Scrape the batter into the center of the bowl. Put the marinated fruit on top of the batter and then sprinkle the reserved flour evenly over the fruit. Using a rubber spatula, fold the fruit into the batter until it's evenly distributed. Scrape the batter into the prepared pan, pressing it in to eliminate air pockets and smoothing the top to make it level. Bake for 15 minutes and then reduce the temperature to 300°F and bake until the center of the cake has risen slightly and a cake tester inserted in the middle comes out clean or with a few moist crumbs, about 1½ hours.

4. Remove the cake and let it cool in its pan on a wire rack for 20 to 30 minutes. Use the parchment overhang to lift the cake from the pan. Place it on the rack, peel down the parchment sides, and cool completely. When cool, brush the cake with 2 to 3 Tbs. of the reserved fruit-soaking liquid or fresh rum. Wrap tightly in plastic and then in foil; store the cake at room temperature for a minimum of 48 hours before serving.

5. If serving within a week of baking, you do not need to baste the cake again. For longer storage, baste once a week with 1 to 2 Tbs. of rum and wrap in fresh plastic and foil. The cake will keep at room temperature for at least 3 weeks. *–Nicole Rees*

PER SERVING: 400 CALORIES | 4G PROTEIN | 59G CARB | 13G TOTAL FAT | 8G SAT FAT | 3.5G MONO FAT | 0.5G POLY FAT | 95MG CHOL | 95MG SODIUM | 3G FIBER

tips for making tasty fruitcake

USE GOOD-QUALITY DRIED FRUIT. Fruitcake is only as good as its fruit. Instead of using super-sweet, artificial-tasting candied fruit, experiment with your favorite dried varieties: apricots, figs, cherries, and cranberries all work. But be sure to presoak the fruit you use—it will up the flavor and add moisture to your cake.

MIX YOUR BATTER THOROUGHLY. Since traditional fruitcake recipes don't include baking powder or baking soda, volume depends on thorough mixing. Adding a couple of tablespoons of flour to the batter before beating in the rest helps emulsify and aerate the batter.

KEEP THE TEMPERATURE LOW. Due to its dense nature, fruitcake is best baked at a low temperature for a longer time—about an hour and a half for an 8½x4½-inch loaf pan.

BASTE YOUR CAKE. Use the rum that remains after soaking the fruit to baste your cooled cake. It makes it extra moist and flavorful and helps preserve the cake. If you plan to keep your fruitcake for longer than a week, baste it each week thereafter with a tablespoon or two of fresh rum.

chocolate roulade with
raspberry filling
(recipe on p. 176)

showstoppers & special-occasion cakes

hot chocolate layer cake with homemade marshmallows

FOR THE CAKE

6	oz. (¾ cup) unsalted butter; more for the pans
13½	oz. (3 cups) unbleached all-purpose flour; more for the pans
¾	cup canola oil
4½	oz. bittersweet chocolate, finely chopped
3	cups granulated sugar
2¼	oz. (¾ cup) unsweetened natural cocoa powder
3	large eggs, at room temperature
¾	cup buttermilk, at room temperature
2	Tbs. pure vanilla extract
2½	tsp. baking soda
½	tsp. kosher salt

FOR THE FROSTING

2½	cups heavy cream
3	oz. (6 Tbs.) unsalted butter
1	vanilla bean, split lengthwise and seeds scraped out
6	oz. bittersweet chocolate, finely chopped
2	cups granulated sugar
6	oz. (2 cups) unsweetened natural cocoa powder; more for decorating
½	cup Lyle's Golden Syrup®
¼	tsp. kosher salt

All the rich flavor of hot choco-late—in cake form. Homemade marshmallows—easier to make than you think—piled on top seal the deal.

MAKE THE CAKE

1. Position racks in the bottom and top thirds of the oven and heat the oven to 350°F.

2. Butter three 9x2-inch round cake pans and line each with a parchment round. Butter the parchment, then dust with flour and knock out the excess.

3. In a 3-quart saucepan, combine the butter, oil, chopped chocolate, and 1 cup water. Heat over medium heat until melted.

4. In a large bowl, whisk the flour, sugar, and cocoa powder. Pour the hot chocolate mixture into the sugar mixture and whisk until combined. Whisk in the eggs, one at a time, then whisk in the butter-milk, vanilla, baking soda, and salt. Portion the batter evenly among the prepared pans.

5. Set two pans on the top rack and the third on the lower rack. Stagger the pans on the oven racks so that no pan is directly over another. Bake, swapping and rotating the pans' positions after 20 minutes, until a toothpick inserted in the center of each cake comes out clean, 35 to 40 minutes. Cool on racks for 10 minutes. Invert the cakes onto the racks, remove the parchment, and cool completely.

MAKE THE FROSTING

In a 4-quart saucepan over low heat, combine the cream, butter, and vanilla bean and seeds and stir until the butter is melted. Remove the vanilla bean and whisk in the chopped chocolate until melted. Whisk in the sugar, cocoa powder, syrup, and salt until smooth—be sure the cocoa powder dissolves completely. Pour into a 9x13-inch pan and freeze until firm, about 2 hours, or refrigerate overnight.

MAKE THE MARSHMALLOWS

1. Pour ¾ cup cold water into the bowl of a stand mixer. Sprinkle the gelatin over the water. Attach the bowl to the mixer and fit it with the whisk attachment.

2. Clip a candy thermometer to a 3-quart saucepan; don't let the tip of the thermometer touch the bottom of the pan. In the saucepan, boil the granulated sugar, corn syrup, salt, and ¾ cup water over

FOR THE MARSHMALLOWS

3 ¼-oz. envelopes unflavored powdered gelatin

2 cups granulated sugar

1 cup light corn syrup

¼ tsp. kosher salt

1 tsp. pure vanilla extract

1 cup plus 2 Tbs. confectioners' sugar; more as needed

Make Ahead

You can bake, cool, wrap, and store the cake layers at room temperature for up to 1 day or freeze for up to 1 month. You can refrigerate the frosting for up to 3 days. The assembled cake can be refrigerated for up to 4 hours (return to room temperature before serving). Wrapped well, leftover marshmallows keep at room temperature for up to 1 month.

medium heat without stirring until the mixture reaches 234° to 235°F, about 10 minutes. With the mixer on low speed, pour the hot sugar mixture into the gelatin in a slow, thin stream.

3. Add the vanilla, carefully increase the speed to high, and beat until the mixture has thickened and cooled, about 5 minutes (the bottom of the bowl should be just warm to the touch). Line a 9x13-inch pan with foil, leaving an overhang on two sides. Sift 1 Tbs. of the confectioners' sugar into the bottom of the pan, then pour the marshmallow mixture into the pan and sift another 1 Tbs. confectioners' sugar on top. Let sit at room temperature until set, at least 2 hours.

ASSEMBLE THE CAKE

1. Remove the frosting from the freezer or refrigerator. Transfer to the bowl of a stand mixer fitted with the paddle attachment and beat on medium speed for 2 minutes to soften. Change to a whisk attachment and beat at medium-high speed until light and fluffy, about 3 minutes.

2. Put a cake layer on a flat serving platter or a cake stand lined with strips of waxed paper to keep it clean while icing. Top the layer with 1½ cups of the frosting, spreading it evenly with an offset spatula to the cake's edge. Repeat with another cake layer and 1½ cups frosting. Top with the last cake layer.

3. Put 1½ cups of the frosting in a small bowl. With an offset spatula, spread this frosting in a thin layer over the top and sides of the cake. Refrigerate the cake until the frosting firms enough to seal in the crumbs, 20 to 30 minutes.

4. Spread the remaining frosting in a smooth layer over the top and sides of the cake. If necessary, you can rewhip the remaining frosting to loosen and lighten it. Remove the waxed paper strips.

5. Use the foil overhang to lift the marshmallow from the pan. Using a knife that has been dipped in cold water, cut along the edge of the marshmallow to release it from the foil. Transfer to a cutting board and remove the foil. Put the remaining 1 cup confectioners' sugar in a medium bowl. Cut the marshmallow into cubes of different sizes, from ¼ to ¾ inch (you will need to continue to dip the knife in cold water as you cut the marshmallows). The marshmallows will be very sticky—dip the cut edges in the confectioners' sugar to make them easier to handle. As you work, toss a few cubes at a time in the sugar to coat, then shake in a strainer to remove the excess. Mound the marshmallows on top of the cake (you'll need only a third to half of them). Sift some cocoa powder over the marshmallows. *–Rebecca Rather*

PER SERVING: 1,080 CALORIES | 14G PROTEIN | 161G CARB | 47G TOTAL FAT | 23G SAT FAT | 17G MONO FAT | 4.5G POLY FAT | 130MG CHOL | 350MG SODIUM | 8G FIBER

chocolate confetti chiffon cake with almond crunch

SERVES 12 TO 14

FOR THE TOPPING

- **1** large egg white
- **1¼** cups sliced almonds
- **2** Tbs. granulated sugar

FOR THE CAKE

- **10** oz. (1½ cups) miniature semisweet chocolate chips
- **9** oz. (2¼ cups) cake flour
- **1½** cups granulated sugar
- **1** tsp. baking powder
- **½** tsp. table salt
- **½** cup canola or corn oil
- **7** large eggs, separated
- **⅔** cup water
- **1** tsp. pure vanilla extract
- **½** to 1 tsp. pure almond extract
- **2** Tbs. almond-flavored liqueur, such as Amaretto (optional)
- **¼** tsp. cream of tartar

FOR THE GLAZE

- **1½** cups confectioners' sugar
- **3** to 4 Tbs. milk
- **½** tsp. pure almond extract (optional)

The sweet coating on the baked almonds keeps its crunch for several days.

PREPARE THE TOPPING

1. Heat the oven to 325°F. Have ready an ungreased nonstick baking sheet.

2. In a medium bowl, whisk the egg white with a fork until foamy, about 30 seconds. Stir in the nuts until they're evenly coated. Sprinkle the sugar over the nuts and stir the mixture. Spread the nuts in a single layer onto the baking sheet. Bake for 5 minutes. Stir the nuts with a wooden spoon to loosen them from the baking sheet. Bake until golden, another 5 to 8 minutes. Remove the nuts from the oven and immediately stir them to loosen them from the baking sheet. The nuts will become crisp as they cool. Set aside.

MAKE THE CAKE

1. Heat the oven to 325°F. Have ready a 9½- or 10-inch tube pan with sides at least 3¾ inches high.

2. In a food processor, pulse the chocolate chips until some of them are finely grated and the rest have formed small crumbs.

3. In a large bowl, sift together the cake flour, 1 cup of the sugar, the baking powder, and salt. Make a well in the center and put in the oil, egg yolks, water, vanilla, almond extract, and Amaretto. Beat the mixture on medium speed until smooth and thick, at least 3 minutes. Fold in the reserved chocolate chips. Set aside.

4. In a large, clean bowl with clean beaters or in a stand mixer with the whisk attachment, whisk the egg whites and the cream of tartar on medium speed until the cream of tartar is dissolved and the whites are foamy. Increase the speed to high and beat the whites until the movement of the beaters forms lines in the mixture. Slowly pour in the remaining ½ cup sugar, about 2 Tbs. at a time, and beat the mixture until soft peaks form.

5. With a large rubber spatula, stir about one-third of the egg whites into the yolk mixture. Gently fold in the remaining egg whites until no white streaks remain. Pour the batter into the tube pan, spreading it evenly. Bake until you can gently press your fingers on top of the cake and it feels firm, about 1 hour and 15 minutes. Any cracks that form on the top should look dry.

6. Invert the pan onto a bottle with a narrow neck and cool thoroughly, about 1 hour and 30 minutes. Use a small, sharp knife to loosen the cake from the sides of the pan and the center of the tube, if necessary. Remove the cake from the pan and slide it onto a serving plate.

MAKE THE GLAZE

In a small bowl, stir together the confectioners' sugar, milk, and almond extract, adding enough milk to make a smooth glaze with a thick, syrupy consistency. Set aside 2 Tbs. of the glaze. Spread the remaining glaze over the top of the cake, letting it drip down the sides of the cake and into the center hole; you may not need to use all of it. Cover the top of the cake with the prepared almonds. Drizzle the reserved glaze over the almonds. *–Elinor Klivans*

PER SERVING (BASED ON 14 SERVINGS): 460 CALORIES | 8G PROTEIN | 64G CARB | 21G TOTAL FAT | 5G SAT FAT | 10G MONO FAT | 4G POLY FAT | 105MG CHOL | 140MG SODIUM | 2G FIBER

chocolate roulade with raspberry filling

SERVES 12

FOR THE CHOCOLATE SPONGE CAKE

- 3 oz. bittersweet chocolate, chopped
- 2 Tbs. warm water
- Softened butter, for the pan
- Unbleached all-purpose flour, for the pan
- 9 large eggs, separated
- 1 cup granulated sugar
- 1⅛ oz. (6 Tbs.) unsweetened Dutch-processed cocoa powder, sifted; more for dusting
- ⅛ tsp. table salt

FOR THE FILLING AND SAUCE

- 1 12-oz. package frozen raspberries, thawed
- 2 large egg whites
- ½ cup plus 2 Tbs. granulated sugar; more to taste
- Table salt
- 5 oz. (10 Tbs.) unsalted butter, softened at room temperature
- 2 tsp. raspberry liqueur, such as Chambord®
- ½ tsp. fresh lemon juice; more to taste
- Pinch of table salt

When you need a showstopper holiday dessert, look no further than this elegant rolled cake (shown on p. 170), which is inspired by the French bûche de Noël, or yule log.

MAKE THE CAKE

1. Position a rack in the center of the oven and heat the oven to 350°F. In a double boiler, melt the chocolate with the warm water. Let cool to room temperature.

2. Grease the bottom of an 18x13-inch rimmed baking sheet (a standard half sheet pan) with the softened butter. Line the pan with parchment; butter and then flour the parchment.

3. With an electric mixer, whip the egg yolks in a large bowl on medium-high speed until light in color and beginning to thicken, 2 to 3 minutes in a stand mixer, or 3 to 5 minutes with a hand-held mixer. Add ½ cup of the sugar and whip until very thick and pale yellow, about 2 minutes. Reduce the speed to low and mix in the melted chocolate. With a rubber spatula, stir in the cocoa and salt until blended.

4. In a clean, dry bowl with clean, dry beaters (any grease will keep the whites from whipping), whip the egg whites with an electric mixer at medium speed until they're frothy and begin to increase in volume, about 30 seconds. In a steady stream, add the remaining ½ cup sugar. Increase the speed to medium high and whip until soft peaks form, 2 to 3 minutes in a stand mixer, or 4 to 6 minutes with a hand-held mixer.

5. With a rubber spatula, fold the whites into the chocolate mixture in two equal additions. You can fold in the first half vigorously to lighten the yolks, but fold in the second half gently, mixing just until the batter is evenly colored with no streaks of white. Don't overmix. Scrape the batter into the baking pan, gently spreading and smoothing it to make sure it's level. Bake until the top springs back lightly when touched, 22 to 25 minutes.

6. Meanwhile, spread a clean dishtowel (at least as big as the cake pan) on the counter. Using a sieve, dust the towel with cocoa powder, completely covering it (this will keep the cake from sticking to the towel as it cools).

FOR THE GLAZE

3 Tbs. heavy cream

¾ cup granulated sugar

½ cup plus 1½ Tbs. water

1½ oz. (½ cup) unsweetened Dutch-processed cocoa powder

1½ tsp. unflavored powdered gelatin

FOR SERVING

¾ cup heavy cream

2 tsp. granulated sugar

½ tsp. pure vanilla extract

Make Ahead

You can make the cake and filling and assemble the roulade (without the glaze) a day ahead. Wrap the unglazed roulade with plastic, refrigerate it, and glaze it the next day. You can prepare the garnishes ahead, too, but whip the cream close to serving time.

7. Immediately after taking the cake from the oven, run a small knife around the inside edge to loosen it from the pan. Invert the cake pan onto the towel in one quick motion. Remove the pan. Carefully peel off the parchment. Using both hands and starting from one of the short ends, roll up the cake and the towel together. Let cool to room temperature.

MAKE THE FILLING AND SAUCE

1. Put the thawed raspberries in a food processor and process until completely puréed. Pass the purée through a fine-mesh sieve to strain out the seeds. You should have about 1 cup of purée.

2. Fill a wide pot or straight-sided skillet with 1 to 2 inches of very hot water. In the bowl of an electric mixer, whisk the egg whites, ½ cup of the sugar, and a generous pinch of salt until blended. Set the bowl in the pot of hot water; make sure the water comes up to at least the level of the mixture in the bowl. Whisk until the mixture is almost hot (about 120°F), about 90 seconds. Take the bowl out of the water. With an electric mixer on medium-high speed, whip the whites until cool and thick, 2 to 3 minutes. Reduce the speed to medium, add the butter, 1 Tbs. at a time, and mix until the butter is completely incorporated. The filling should be soft and loose; it will firm up as it chills. (If it seems very runny, refrigerate it for up to 20 minutes.) With the mixer on low speed, blend in 2 Tbs. of the raspberry purée and the liqueur. Set the filling aside.

3. Make the sauce by stirring together the remaining raspberry purée, the remaining 2 Tbs. sugar, the lemon juice, and salt. Add more sugar or lemon juice to taste.

FILL AND ROLL THE ROULADE

Carefully unroll the cooled, towel-wrapped cake. Spread the filling over the cake, covering it evenly to within 2 inches of the edges. Reroll the cake, without the towel this time. The filling may squish out of the ends a bit; this is fine. Line a rimmed baking sheet with foil and set a wire rack on the foil. Slide two large metal spatulas (or a spatula and your hand) under the roulade and transfer it to the rack. (Or, if working ahead, transfer it to a large sheet of plastic, wrap it snugly, and refrigerate for up to a day; transfer to the rack before glazing.)

continued on p. 178

GLAZE THE ROULADE

1. In a large saucepan, combine the cream, sugar, ½ cup of the water, and the cocoa. Bring the mixture to a boil and then reduce the heat to a simmer, whisking often, until very thick, like hot fudge sauce, 8 to 10 minutes from when the mixture began simmering. Pay close attention: This mixture boils over easily. Remove the pan from the heat.

2. While the mixture is cooling, bloom the gelatin in the remaining 1½ Tbs. water. Melt the bloomed gelatin over very hot water or in the microwave (see the sidebar on the facing page). Whisk the gelatin into the chocolate mixture and strain the glaze through a medium-mesh sieve into a metal bowl. Let the glaze cool at room temperature until thick but still pourable, 5 to 10 minutes; the glaze should be about 110° to 120°F. (If you've made the cake ahead, unwrap it and put it on a rack set over a foil-lined baking sheet.)

3. Pour the glaze over the roulade, using an offset spatula to help the glaze cover the top and sides evenly. Don't worry about covering the ends; they'll be trimmed later. Refrigerate, uncovered, for at least 30 minutes or up to 4 hours.

Variations

Mocha: Substitute 1 Tbs. instant espresso powder and 2 oz. bittersweet chocolate, melted and cooled to room temperature, for the raspberry purée and liqueur in the filling recipe. Omit the sugar and lemon juice used for the raspberry sauce. Garnish with the sweetened whipped cream and 36 chocolate-covered espresso beans.

Orange–Vanilla: Substitute the scraped seeds of 1 vanilla bean, ½ tsp. pure vanilla extract, and the finely grated zest of 1 orange for the raspberry purée and liqueur in the filling recipe. Omit the sugar and lemon juice used for the raspberry sauce. Garnish with ½ cup candied orange zest.

Chocolate–Peppermint: Substitute ½ tsp. pure peppermint extract for the raspberry purée and liqueur in the filling recipe. Add two to three drops of red food coloring to the filling if you like. Omit the sugar and lemon juice used for the raspberry sauce. Garnish each slice with fresh mint sprigs or with crushed candy canes or peppermint candies.

GARNISH AND SERVE

1. With a whisk or hand-held mixer, whip together the cream, sugar, and vanilla until soft peaks form.

2. The glaze will have "glued" the roulade to the rack, so slide a metal spatula between it and the rack to release it. Transfer the roulade to a serving platter, using two large offset spatulas to get underneath and pressing the spatulas against the rack as you go. Trim the ends of the roulade. Fill a tall container with hot water and have a dishtowel handy so that you can clean and dry the knife after cutting each slice. Using a long, sharp knife, cut ¾-inch straight slices, or cut pieces on an angle, rinsing and drying the knife after each slice. Garnish with a small pool of raspberry sauce and a dollop of whipped cream next to each slice. *–Emily Luchetti*

how to "bloom" gelatin

Gelatin is what gives the cake's glaze a gorgeous sheen. Working with gelatin (a stabilizer derived from animal collagen) isn't difficult, but before adding it to a recipe, it must be softened and then melted. For powdered gelatin, the softening process is also known as "blooming."

GELATIN TIPS

- For every 2 tsp. powdered gelatin, use about ¼ cup liquid for blooming.

- One ¼-oz. packet of Knox® brand powdered gelatin contains about 2¼ tsp.

- Always add softened gelatin to warm or hot mixtures; adding the gelatin to a cold mixture will make it firm up immediately, creating an unpleasant stringy or lumpy texture.

- Although powdered gelatin is the form most widely used by home cooks, sheet gelatin is preferred by some pros. The sheets are standardized regardless of thickness or dimension, so two sheets equal 1 tsp. Knox brand powder (other powder brands may differ in their gelling power). Soften sheet gelatin by soaking it in cold water for about 10 minutes. Squeeze it to drain excess liquid before you melt it into the liquid ingredients in the recipe.

- Sprinkle or "rain" the powdered gelatin evenly over its softening liquid to keep lumps from forming.

- Set the gelatin aside for a few minutes until it swells or "blooms" as it absorbs the liquid.

- Melt the gelatin either in a hot water bath or in a microwave (for about 10 seconds on high) until it becomes translucent. Use your fingers to check that all the granules have totally dissolved.

bourbon chocolate cake

SERVES 8 TO 10

FOR THE CAKE

6   oz. (¾ cup) unsalted butter; more for the pan

11 oz. semisweet chocolate, chopped

6   large eggs, separated, at room temperature

¾   cup packed light brown sugar

1   oz. (¼ cup) unbleached all-purpose flour

¼   cup bourbon

1   tsp. pure vanilla extract

½   tsp. kosher salt

FOR SERVING

1   cup heavy cream

1   to 2 Tbs. granulated sugar

Confectioners' sugar, for dusting

This mousse-like cake really does melt in your mouth. It can be baked up to a day before serving and stored lightly wrapped at room temperature. If you don't have a 9x3-inch cake pan, use a 9x2-inch pan (a standard size sold in supermarkets) and construct a parchment collar so the cake has room to rise; for more information, see the sidebar on the facing page. For this cake, it's worth splurging on the best chocolate you can buy, such as Callebaut®.

MAKE THE CAKE

1. Position a rack in the center of the oven and heat the oven to 350°F.

2. Butter a 9x3-inch cake pan (or line a shallower one with a collar as directed on the facing page). Line the bottom of the pan with a round of parchment and butter the parchment. Set the cake pan in a roasting pan large enough to accommodate it.

3. Melt the chocolate and butter over a double boiler. Remove from the heat and let cool slightly.

4. With an electric mixer, beat the egg yolks with the brown sugar on medium speed until very pale, thick, and fluffy, about 3 minutes. Reduce the speed, add the chocolate mixture, and mix just to combine. Add the flour, mixing just to combine and scraping the bowl as needed. Blend in the bourbon and vanilla. Transfer to a large mixing bowl and set aside.

make your shallow cake pan deeper

If your 9-inch cake pan is less than 3 inches deep, make a paper collar to support the cake as it rises. Cut two 6x16-inch strips of parchment. Fold the two strips lengthwise to get two 3x16-inch strips. Butter one side of each strip. Line the inside edge of the pan with the strips, nestling them into each other, with the folded edge on the top and the buttered side facing in.

5. In a clean mixing bowl with clean beaters, beat the egg whites with the salt on high speed until they hold soft peaks, 1 to 2 minutes. With a rubber spatula, fold one-third of the egg whites into the chocolate mixture to lighten it, and then gently fold in the remaining whites. Scrape the batter into the prepared cake pan.

6. Set the roasting pan on the oven rack and add enough warm tap water to come halfway up the sides of the cake pan. Bake until the top feels set, 40 to 45 minutes. Remove the cake pan from the water bath and run a paring knife around the inside of the pan (or the inside of the parchment collar) to loosen the cake and then let the cake cool completely in the cake pan on a rack. When the cake is completely cool, loosen the sides once more with a paring knife. Cover the cake with a serving plate and invert the cake onto the plate. The bottom of the cake is now the top. Peel off the parchment. (Don't worry if the surface looks a little ragged; you'll be dusting with confectioners' sugar.)

TO SERVE
In a chilled bowl with chilled beaters, beat the cream and sugar to medium-soft peaks. Dust the top of the cake generously with confectioners' sugar, slice, and serve each slice with the whipped cream.
–Karen and Ben Barker

PER SERVING (BASED ON 10 SERVINGS): 510 CALORIES | 6G PROTEIN | 41G CARB | 35G TOTAL FAT | 21G SAT FAT | 11G MONO FAT | 2G POLY FAT | 200MG CHOL | 320MG SODIUM | 2G FIBER

white chocolate soufflé cakes with raspberry–chocolate sauce

SERVES 6

FOR THE RASPBERRY–CHOCOLATE SAUCE

- ½ cup fresh raspberries, rinsed, or ¾ cup thawed frozen raspberries
- 3 oz. bittersweet or semi-sweet chocolate, chopped
- 1 oz. (2 Tbs.) unsalted butter
- 1 Tbs. granulated sugar

FOR THE SOUFFLÉ CAKES

- Softened butter and granulated sugar, for the ramekins
- 3 large eggs, separated, at room temperature
- 3 Tbs. unbleached all-purpose flour
- ⅛ tsp. table salt
- ¾ cup whole milk
- 6 oz. white chocolate preferably El Rey® or Callebaut), finely chopped
- ¼ tsp. pure vanilla extract
- Scant ¼ tsp. cream of tartar
- 2 Tbs. granulated sugar

This recipe provides a flavor twist on the molten chocolate cake. Put a ball of raspberry-flavored ganache in each ramekin and top with cake batter; as the cakes bake, the ganache melts into a warm, sumptuous sauce.

MAKE THE SAUCE

1. Put a metal or Pyrex pie plate or cake pan in the freezer to chill.

2. Purée the raspberries in a food processor. Transfer the purée to a fine-mesh sieve set over a small bowl. Strain the purée by pressing and scraping with a rubber spatula. Discard the seeds.

3. In a medium heatproof bowl set in or over a skillet of barely simmering water, combine the chocolate, butter, sugar, and 2 Tbs. of the raspberry purée (save any extra for another use). Stir frequently with a rubber spatula until melted and smooth. Scrape into a puddle on the chilled plate and return to the freezer until firm, 20 to 30 minutes. When the raspberry–chocolate mixture is firm, use a teaspoon to scrape it into 6 rough balls. Keep the balls on the plate and refrigerate until ready to use.

MAKE THE SOUFFLÉ CAKES

1. Lightly butter six 6-oz. ramekins or custard cups. Coat with sugar and tap out the excess.

2. Put the 3 egg yolks in a medium bowl near the stove and have another large, clean bowl at hand. Combine the flour and salt in a small, heavy saucepan. Whisk in just enough of the milk to make a smooth paste. Whisk in the remaining milk. Set the pan over medium heat and cook, whisking constantly, until the mixture has the consistency of a thick cream sauce, 2 to 3 minutes. Whisk about 2 Tbs. of the hot sauce into the yolks to warm them up gently. Scrape the yolks back into the saucepan and cook for a minute or two, whisking constantly, until the mixture becomes a thick pastry cream; it should be about as thick as store-bought mayonnaise. Use a rubber spatula to scrape the pastry cream into the clean bowl. Add the white chocolate and whisk until it's fully melted and incorporated into the warm pastry cream. Stir in the vanilla. Set aside for a few minutes until tepid.

3. In a clean, dry bowl, beat the egg whites and cream of tartar on medium speed in a stand mixer (or on high with a hand-held mixer) until the whites mound gently. Gradually beat in the sugar and beat until the whites form medium-stiff peaks when you lift the beaters; the tips should curl over but still look moist, glossy, and flexible. With a rubber spatula, fold about one-quarter of the whites into the white chocolate pastry cream to lighten it. Scrape the remaining whites into the cream and gently fold in until blended, taking care not to deflate the whites.

4. Take the raspberry–chocolate balls out of the refrigerator and put one in the center of each ramekin. Divide the batter evenly among the ramekins and level the tops gently with the back of a spoon. You can now heat the oven and bake right away or cover the ramekins with plastic and refrigerate for up to 2 days.

5. When you're ready to bake, position a rack in the lower third of the oven and heat the oven to 375°F. Remove the plastic and put the ramekins on a baking sheet. Bake until the cakes are puffed and golden brown on top—they'll quiver when tapped and seem soft in the center, 16 to 18 minutes. Let cool for a few minutes before serving.
–Alice Medrich

making a hidden sauce

Start by pouring a mixture of melted chocolate and butter into a puddle on a pie plate. Freeze until firm and then scoop into 6 rough balls.

Put one chocolate ball in the center of each ramekin and spoon the batter on top. As the cakes bake, the chocolate melts into a warm, sumptuous sauce.

chocolate–pomegranate torte

FOR THE CAKE

- 2 oz. (4 Tbs.) softened unsalted butter, cut into 4 pieces; more for the pan
- 6 oz. bittersweet chocolate (70% or 72% cacao)
- 3 large eggs, separated
- ¾ cup granulated sugar
- ¼ tsp. table salt
- ⅛ tsp. cream of tartar
- 2¼ oz. (½ cup) unbleached all-purpose flour

FOR THE POMEGRANATE JELLY

- 1 medium Pink Lady or Braeburn apple
- 1½ cups pure unsweetened pomegranate juice
- ¼ cup plus 2 Tbs. granulated sugar
- 12 fresh or frozen cranberries

FOR THE GLAZE

- 6 oz. bittersweet chocolate (70% or 72% cacao), chopped medium fine
- 3 oz. (6 Tbs.) unsalted butter, cut into 6 pieces
- 1 Tbs. honey or light corn syrup
- Pinch of table salt
- Fresh pomegranate seeds, for garnish (optional)

For the best flavor and texture, make this elegant cake and spread it with the jelly a day or two before serving. Glaze it on the day you serve it.

MAKE THE CAKE

1. Position a rack in the center of the oven and heat the oven to 350°F. Lightly grease the sides of a 9x2-inch round cake pan and line the bottom with parchment.

2. Finely grate 2 oz. of the chocolate and set aside. Coarsely chop the remaining chocolate and combine with the butter and 3 Tbs. water in a heatproof bowl. Set the bowl in a skillet of barely simmering water and stir frequently until the mixture is melted and smooth. Set aside.

3. In a large bowl, whisk the egg yolks with ½ cup of the sugar and the salt until thick and lightened in color.

4. In a stand mixer fitted with the whisk attachment, beat the egg whites and cream of tartar at medium-high speed until soft peaks have formed, about 2 minutes. With the motor running, gradually add the remaining ¼ cup sugar, beating to stiff peaks, 1 to 2 minutes more.

5. Whisk the warm chocolate and the flour into the yolk mixture. With a rubber spatula, fold one-quarter of the whites into the chocolate batter. Scrape the remaining whites into the chocolate mixture and sprinkle the grated chocolate on top. Fold together. Pour the batter into the prepared pan and spread it evenly.

6. Bake until a toothpick inserted in the center of the cake comes out smudged with a few moist crumbs, about 25 minutes. Cool in the pan on a rack for 10 minutes. Run a knife around the edge of the cake and invert it onto another rack. Remove the pan and parchment and invert the cake onto the first rack (it's normal for the cake to have a crusty exterior that may crack with handling). Let cool completely.

MAKE THE POMEGRANATE JELLY

1. Grate enough of the apple (including the peel) to yield ¾ cup. In a medium saucepan, bring the grated apple, pomegranate juice, sugar, and cranberries to a simmer over medium heat. Simmer, covered, until the apple is softened and the mixture has thickened a little, about 10 minutes. Uncover and continue to simmer, stirring occasionally at first and then constantly towards the end, until the liquid has evaporated and the mixture is reduced to ¾ cup, about 5 minutes.

2. With a rubber spatula, press the pulp through a medium-mesh strainer into a bowl until you can't get any more juice out of the pulp. Scrape all of the juice clinging to the bottom of the strainer into the bowl and discard the pulp in the strainer.

3. Brush away any loose crumbs and easily detachable crusty pieces from the sides and top of the cake. Transfer the cake to a cardboard round or tart pan bottom.

4. Stir the jelly to blend it, scrape it onto the cake, and spread it evenly over the top. Let the jelly cool until it's set, about 1 hour. At this point, the cake may be covered with an inverted cake pan, wrapped in plastic (the pan keeps the plastic from touching the cake), and stored at room temperature for up to 2 days.

MAKE THE GLAZE AND FINISH THE CAKE
1. Put the chocolate, butter, honey, and salt in a heatproof bowl set in a skillet of barely simmering water. Stir gently until the chocolate melts and the mixture is perfectly smooth. Remove from the heat and stir in 2 Tbs. cool water. Let cool to room temperature without stirring. If not using right away, cover and store at room temperature.

2. Set the cake on a rack set over a baking sheet. With an offset spatula, spread ⅓ cup of the glaze around the sides of the cake and on top of the jelly (be careful not to disturb the jelly) to smooth the surfaces and glue on any crumbs. Rewarm the remaining glaze gently to 90°F in a skillet of barely simmering water—the glaze should have the consistency of thick, pourable cream.

3. Scrape all of the glaze onto the top of the cake. Spread the glaze over the top and all around the sides. For the shiniest glaze, work quickly and use as few strokes as possible. Scoop up any excess glaze from the baking sheet and use it to cover bare spots.

4. Garnish with pomegranate seeds (if using) and let the cake rest on the rack for 10 minutes. Transfer to a cake plate and let sit at room temperature until set, 15 to 30 minutes, or up to several hours before serving. *–Alice Medrich*

PER SERVING: 350 CALORIES | 5G PROTEIN | 41G CARB | 20G TOTAL FAT | 11G SAT FAT | 6G MONO FAT | 2.5G POLY FAT | 70MG CHOL | 105MG SODIUM | 3G FIBER

coconut-cream meringue cake

SERVES 16

FOR THE CAKE

- ½ lb. (1 cup) unsalted butter, softened; more for the pans
- 13½ oz. (3 cups) unbleached all-purpose flour
- 4 tsp. baking powder
- ½ tsp. kosher salt
- 1 cup unsweetened coconut milk, well shaken, at room temperature
- 1 Tbs. pure vanilla extract
- 2 cups granulated sugar
- 2 large eggs, at room temperature
- ⅔ cup sour cream, at room temperature
- 6 large egg whites, at room temperature

FOR THE FILLING

- 2 cups heavy cream
- 3 large egg yolks
- ¾ cup granulated sugar
- 2 Tbs. unbleached all-purpose flour
- 1 cup sweetened coconut flakes, toasted
- 1 oz. (2 Tbs.) unsalted butter, softened
- 1 Tbs. pure vanilla extract
- Pinch of kosher salt

FOR THE MERINGUE

- 3 cups granulated sugar
- 1½ cups egg whites (about 10 large), preferably pasteurized, at room temperature

This cake owes its stunning looks to a billowy meringue frosting that's spiked and browned all over with a kitchen torch.

MAKE THE CAKE

1. Position racks in the bottom and top thirds of the oven and heat the oven to 350°F.

2. Butter three 9x2-inch round cake pans and line each with a parchment round. Butter the parchment.

3. In a medium bowl, mix the flour, baking powder, and salt. In a 1-cup liquid measure, mix the coconut milk with the vanilla.

4. In a stand mixer fitted with the paddle attachment, beat the butter and sugar on medium-high speed until light and fluffy, 3 to 5 minutes. Scrape down the bowl. Add the eggs one at a time, beating well after each addition.

5. Add about one-third of the flour mixture and mix on low speed until incorporated. Add half of the coconut milk and mix until incorporated. Continue adding the flour mixture and coconut milk, alternating the two and ending with the flour. Add the sour cream and mix until incorporated. Pour the batter into a large bowl.

6. In a clean mixer bowl and using the whisk attachment, beat the egg whites on high speed until soft peaks form, 2 to 3 minutes. Using a spatula, gently stir a large spoonful of the whites into the batter to loosen it, and then fold the remaining egg whites gently into the batter.

7. Portion the cake batter evenly among the prepared cake pans. Level the batter with a spatula. Set two pans on the top rack and the third on the lower rack. Stagger the pans on the oven racks so that no pan is directly over another. Bake, swapping and rotating the pans' positions after 15 minutes, until a toothpick inserted in the center of each cake comes out clean, 25 to 30 minutes total. Cool on racks for 10 minutes. Invert the cakes onto the racks, remove the parchment, and cool completely.

MAKE THE FILLING

1. In a medium bowl, whisk 1½ cups of the cream and the egg yolks.

2. Combine the sugar and flour in a medium saucepan. Add the cream mixture and cook, whisking, over medium heat until smooth, 2 minutes. Bring to a simmer and cook, whisking, until thickened to a pudding consistency, 8 to 10 minutes. Remove from the heat. Stir in the coconut, butter, vanilla, and salt and let cool to room temperature.

3. With an electric hand mixer, whip the remaining ½ cup cream to soft peaks. With a spatula, gently fold the whipped cream into the filling.

ASSEMBLE THE CAKE

Put a cake layer on a flat serving platter or a cake stand lined with strips of waxed paper to keep it clean while icing. Top the layer with half of the filling, spreading it evenly with an offset spatula almost to the cake's edge. Repeat with a second cake layer and the remaining filling. Top with the last cake layer.

MAKE THE MERINGUE

1. Put the sugar and egg whites in the metal bowl of a stand mixer (make sure it's clean) and set over a pot of simmering water. Whisk constantly until the sugar melts completely, 3 to 4 minutes. Rub a small amount between your fingers to make sure all of the sugar grains have melted.

2. Transfer the bowl to the mixer, fitted with the whisk attachment, and whisk at low speed until the mixture becomes completely opaque and begins to thicken, about 4 minutes. Raise the speed to medium and beat until thickened to soft peaks that barely hold their shape and flop over when the beater is lifted, 5 to 7 minutes. Finally, raise the speed to high and beat until glossy and thickened to medium-firm peaks that stand up stiffly but curl slightly at the tip when the beater is lifted, about 4 minutes more.

3. Using an offset spatula, apply the meringue thickly over the entire cake—don't worry about spreading it smooth or you'll overwork the meringue (you may not need all of it). Then, repeatedly poke your fingertips into the meringue, pulling it into spikes all over the cake. Remove the waxed paper strips.

4. Using a kitchen torch, brown the meringue by holding the torch 2 to 3 inches from the meringue and waving the flame over the cake until it's browned all over. *–Rebecca Rather*

PER SERVING: 700 CALORIES | 9G PROTEIN | 96G CARB | 32G TOTAL FAT | 21G SAT FAT | 8G MONO FAT | 1.5G POLY FAT | 145MG CHOL | 250MG SODIUM | 1G FIBER

Make Ahead

You can bake, cool, wrap, and store the cake layers at room temperature for up to 1 day or freeze for up to 1 month. You can refrigerate the assembled cake (without the meringue topping) for up to 4 hours before decorating it. Wait to make the meringue until you're ready to finish the cake.

spiking meringue

Once the cake is frosted, use your fingers to fluff and pull the meringue into spikes all over the cake. Work your way around the cake and keep at it until you're happy with the results.

white chocolate macadamia cake with raspberries and white chocolate buttercream

SERVES 16

FOR THE CAKE

- 12 oz. (1½ cups) unsalted butter, softened; more for the pans
- 14 oz. (3½ cups) cake flour
- 1½ tsp. baking powder
- ¾ tsp. baking soda
- ¾ tsp. kosher salt
- 2⅓ cups granulated sugar
- 2 tsp. pure vanilla extract
- 3 large eggs, at room temperature
- 1½ cups buttermilk, at room temperature
- 6½ oz. white chocolate, chopped (1⅓ cups)
- 4 oz. (1 cup) chopped toasted macadamia nuts

FOR THE WHITE CHOCOLATE LEAVES

- 9 to 12 organic lemon leaves, preferably different sizes
- 6 oz. white chocolate, coarsely chopped (1¼ cups)

FOR THE BUTTERCREAM

- 4 large eggs
- 4 large egg yolks
- 2 cups granulated sugar
- 1½ lb. (3 cups) unsalted butter, softened
- ½ tsp. kosher salt
- 8 oz. white chocolate, melted and cooled to room temperature

White chocolate leaves and a sleek coat of buttercream give this three-layer stunner a dressed-up look.

MAKE THE CAKE

1. Position racks in the bottom and top thirds of the oven and heat the oven to 350°F. Butter three 9x2-inch round cake pans and line each with a parchment round. Butter the parchment.

2. Combine the flour, baking powder, baking soda, and salt in a medium bowl.

3. In a stand mixer fitted with the paddle attachment, beat the butter and sugar on medium speed until light and fluffy, 3 to 5 minutes. Scrape the bowl. Add the vanilla and then the eggs one at a time, beating well after each addition.

4. Add about one-third of the flour mixture and mix on low speed until incorporated. Add half of the buttermilk and mix until incorporated. Continue adding the flour mixture and the buttermilk, alternating between the two and ending with the flour. The batter will be thick and glossy. Fold in the white chocolate and macadamia nuts.

5. Portion the cake batter evenly among the prepared cake pans. Level the batter with a spatula. Set two pans on the top rack and the third on the lower rack. Stagger the pans on the oven racks so that no pan is directly over another. Bake, swapping and rotating the pans' positions after 15 minutes, until a toothpick inserted in the center of each cake comes out clean, 28 to 35 minutes total. Cool on racks for 10 minutes. Invert the cakes onto the racks, remove the parchment, and cool completely.

MAKE THE WHITE CHOCOLATE LEAVES

1. Wash the leaves and dry them with paper towels. Line two rimmed baking sheets with parchment.

2. Put the white chocolate in a metal bowl over a saucepan of barely simmering water and whisk until melted and smooth.

3. Using a small pastry brush, paint a thick coat of chocolate on the underside of each leaf. Don't let chocolate drip over the sides of the leaves, or they will be difficult to peel off later.

4. Place the leaves, chocolate side up, on the prepared baking sheet and leave in a cool, dry place or refrigerate until the chocolate has set.

5. Hold the leaf stem and peel the leaf carefully away from the chocolate. Transfer the chocolate leaves to the other prepared baking sheet and refrigerate until ready to use.

FOR THE FILLING

2 **cups raspberry jam**

2 **cups (8 oz.) fresh raspberries**

FOR THE DECORATION (OPTIONAL)

¼ **to ⅓ cup fresh raspberries**

3 **to 6 small sprigs fresh mint**

MAKE THE BUTTERCREAM

1. In a stand mixer fitted with the whisk attachment, whip the eggs and egg yolks on high speed until thick and lightened, about 5 minutes.

2. Meanwhile, clip a candy thermometer to a 3-quart saucepan; don't let the tip touch the bottom of the pan. Combine the sugar with ½ cup water in the pan and simmer over medium heat until it reaches 234° to 235°F. Transfer the sugar mixture to a heatproof measuring cup. With the mixer running on low speed, pour the sugar mixture down the side of the bowl into the egg mixture in a slow, thin stream. Increase the speed to medium and beat until the mixture has cooled (the bowl should be barely warm to the touch), 6 to 8 minutes. Add the butter 4 Tbs. at a time, beating on medium speed until incorporated, about 20 seconds for each addition. (Don't worry if the mixture looks thin at first; it'll thicken as you add more butter.) After all the

continued on p. 190

making white chocolate leaves

Paint the undersides of organic lemon leaves (look for them at a flower shop) with melted white chocolate, and then peel the leaves away once the chocolate has set. Make sure no chocolate drips over the sides of the leaves, or they'll be difficult to peel off.

Make Ahead

You can bake, cool, wrap, and store the cake layers at room temperature for up to 1 day or freeze for up to 1 month. The white chocolate leaves will keep in the refrigerator for up to 2 days. You can refrigerate the frosted cake (without the decorations) for up to 4 hours. Return to room temperature before decorating.

butter has been added, add the salt, raise the speed to medium high, and beat until thick and glossy, about 1 minute. Fold the white chocolate into the buttercream.

ASSEMBLE THE CAKE

1. Put a cake layer on a flat serving platter or a cake stand lined with strips of waxed paper to keep it clean while icing. Top the layer with 1 cup of the jam, spreading it evenly with an offset spatula to the cake's edge. Scatter 1 cup of the raspberries evenly over the jam. Repeat with a second cake layer, the remaining 1 cup jam, and the remaining 1 cup raspberries. Top with the last cake layer.

2. Put 2 cups of the buttercream in a small bowl. With an offset spatula, spread this buttercream in a thin layer over the top and sides of the cake. Refrigerate the cake until the buttercream is firm enough to seal in the crumbs, 20 to 30 minutes.

3. Spread the remaining buttercream in a thick, smooth layer over the entire cake. Remove the waxed paper strips.

4. Decorate the cake with the white chocolate leaves, fresh raspberries, and mint leaves, if using. Before serving, let sit at room temperature until the chocolate leaves soften slightly, about 30 minutes.
–Rebecca Rather

PER SERVING: 1,180 CALORIES | 10G PROTEIN | 130G CARB | 72G TOTAL FAT | 41G SAT FAT | 22G MONO FAT | 3G POLY FAT | 290MG CHOL | 290MG SODIUM | 2G FIBER

spiced carrot cakes with candied carrots and pistachios

SERVES 8

FOR THE CAKES

- **2** cups carrot juice
- **1** 1-inch piece fresh ginger, peeled and finely grated
- **3** oz. (6 Tbs.) unsalted butter, softened; more for the molds
- **6¾** oz. (1½ cups) unbleached all-purpose flour; more for the molds
- **1½** tsp. ground allspice
- **1** tsp. ground cinnamon
- **½** tsp. ground star anise
- **½** tsp. baking soda
- **¼** tsp. table salt
- **¼** cup packed light brown sugar
- **2** large eggs
- **¼** cup chopped unsalted pistachios, for garnish

FOR THE CANDIED CARROTS

- **2** cups granulated sugar
- **2** large carrots, peeled and cut into long julienne strands to yield 1 cup
- **1** cinnamon stick
- **1** whole star anise

Make Ahead

You can make the cakes up to 1 day ahead and the candied carrots up to 2 hours ahead.

Candied carrots and a finer crumb set this variation apart from traditional carrot cake.

MAKE THE CAKES

1. Combine the carrot juice and ginger in a medium saucepan and bring to a boil over medium heat. Boil until reduced to ¾ cup, about 25 minutes. Let cool to room temperature.

2. Position a rack in the center of the oven and heat the oven to 325°F. Butter and flour 8 baba au rhum molds (2¼ to 2½ inches tall). Set aside on a large rimmed baking sheet.

3. In a medium bowl, whisk the flour, allspice, cinnamon, star anise, baking soda, and salt. In a large bowl using a hand-held mixer or in a stand mixer fitted with the paddle attachment, cream the butter and brown sugar on medium speed until light and fluffy, 1 to 2 minutes. On medium-low speed, add one of the eggs, mix until mostly blended, and then add the second egg. On low speed, alternate adding the flour mixture and the carrot juice reduction in two additions each. Mix each addition until just combined.

4. Spoon the batter into the prepared molds, filling each a little more than half full. Swirl the batter with a skewer to smooth the tops. Bake the cakes until a cake tester inserted in the centers comes out clean, 20 to 22 minutes. Cool the cakes on a rack for 10 minutes and then carefully invert to remove from the molds. Cool the cakes upright on the rack. The cakes may be served warm or at room temperature.

MAKE THE CANDIED CARROTS

1. Bring the sugar and 2 cups of water to a boil in a medium saucepan over high heat. Add the carrots, cinnamon stick, and star anise. Reduce the heat to maintain a simmer; simmer gently, stirring occasionally, until the carrots are translucent, soft, and slightly sticky to the touch, about 30 minutes. Discard the cinnamon and star anise. Remove the carrots with a slotted spoon and set aside. Reserve the syrup.

2. To serve, dip each cake in the syrup for about 3 seconds, put it on a dessert plate, and drizzle with about 1 tsp. syrup. Garnish with the candied carrots and pistachios. *—Jehangir Mehta*

PER SERVING: 460 CALORIES | 6G PROTEIN | 85G CARB | 12G TOTAL FAT | 6G SAT FAT | 3.5G MONO FAT | 1G POLY FAT | 75MG CHOL | 200MG SODIUM | 2G FIBER

chocolate — espresso mousse torte

SERVES 12

1 Tbs. softened unsalted butter for the pan

12 oz. semisweet chocolate (55% to 60% Cacao), coarsely chopped or broken into pieces (2 slightly heaping cups)

1 cup heavy cream

1 Tbs. instant espresso granules

6 large eggs, at room temperature

½ cup granulated sugar

1⅛ oz. (¼ cup) unbleached all-purpose flour

1 Tbs. confectioners' sugar

¼ tsp. ground cinnamon

Be sure to wrap your springform pan with heavy-duty aluminum foil (or two layers of regular foil); even the best pans can let water in. This torte is delicious alone or with lightly sweetened whipped cream.

1. Position a rack in the center of the oven and heat the oven to 400°F. Generously butter a 10-inch springform pan and wrap the bottom and sides in heavy-duty aluminum foil. Have ready a roasting pan just big enough to accommodate the springform, and put a kettle of water on to boil.

2. Grind the chocolate in a food processor until it reaches the consistency of coarse meal, about 30 seconds. Bring the cream to a boil in a small saucepan over medium heat. Add the cream to the food processor and process until smooth, about 10 seconds. Dissolve the espresso powder in 1 Tbs. hot water and add it to the food processor. Process until fully incorporated, about 10 seconds. Transfer the espresso-flavored ganache to a large bowl.

3. In the bowl of a stand mixer fitted with the whisk attachment, whip the eggs, sugar, and flour at just under high speed until pale, light, and fluffy and at least doubled in volume (if not tripled), about 6 minutes. Add about one-third of the egg mixture to the ganache and mix with a rubber spatula until combined. Add the remaining egg mixture and gently fold together until just combined and no obvious streaks of egg remain.

4. Pour the batter into the prepared springform pan. Set the pan inside the roasting pan and fill the roasting pan with 1 to 1½ inches of boiling water. Bake until a dry crust forms on the top of the torte and the edges seem set but the center is still a bit wobbly when you jiggle it, 15 to 20 minutes. Remove the torte from the water bath and its foil wrap. Cool the torte on a wire rack to room temperature and then refrigerate until cold and completely set, at least 3 hours or overnight.

5. To unmold, carefully remove the springform ring. Put a piece of plastic wrap over the top of the torte. Invert the torte onto a baking sheet and remove the pan bottom; use a thin-bladed knife to help separate the torte and pan bottom if necessary. Invert the torte again onto a serving plate and remove the plastic wrap. Just before serving, put the confectioners' sugar and cinnamon in a small fine-mesh strainer and sift over the top of the torte.

6. To cut the torte as cleanly as possible, dip your knife in hot water to heat the blade and wipe dry before each cut. Or for a cleaner cut, use unwaxed dental floss. *–Greg Case and Keri Fisher*

PER SERVING (BASED ON 20 SERVINGS): 290 CALORIES | 5G PROTEIN | 30G CARB | 19G TOTAL FAT | 11G SAT FAT | 6G MONO FAT | 0.9G POLY FAT | 135MG CHOL | 45MG SODIUM | 2G FIBER

chocolate soufflé layer cake with mascarpone cream and raspberries

MAKES ONE 11X16-INCH
THIN SHEET CAKE, ENOUGH
FOR FOUR LAYERS;
THE ASSEMBLED CAKE
SERVES 8 TO 10

Nonstick cooking spray

1 oz. (2 Tbs.) unsalted butter

8 oz. good-quality bittersweet or semisweet chocolate, chopped

¼ cup strong coffee or whiskey, or a mix

7 large eggs

1 cup granulated sugar

¼ tsp. table salt

Confectioners' sugar, for dusting

Mascarpone Cream (recipe on p. 197)

Rich Chocolate Glaze, at room temperature (recipe on p. 197)

1½ cups fresh raspberries, rinsed and dried

There's no flour in the cake, so it's amazingly tender and luscious. The filling is tender enough to make slicing the cake easy yet it's firm enough to hold up the layers, thanks to the mascarpone added to the cream.

1. Position the rack in the center of the oven and heat the oven (not a convection oven) to 375°F. Grease a jellyroll pan or half sheet pan (about 11x16 inches) and line the bottom and long sides with parchment. Grease the parchment or spray it with nonstick cooking spray.

2. In a small heavy-based saucepan (or a double boiler), melt the butter, chocolate, and coffee or whiskey over very low heat, stirring occasionally with a whisk. Take care not to let the chocolate scorch and heat only until the chocolate has melted. Remove from the heat, whisk until the mixture is smooth and glossy, and set aside to cool slightly while you beat the eggs.

3. Separate the egg yolks and whites into two large clean mixing bowls. Using an electric mixer (either a hand-held or stand mixer) on medium high, beat the egg whites until soft peaks form. Add about 2 Tbs. of the sugar and beat on high speed for about 30 seconds. Set aside.

4. Without cleaning the beaters or whip, beat the egg yolks on medium high, with the salt and the remaining sugar, until the mixture becomes light and thick and forms a ribbon trail when the beaters are lifted, about 3 minutes with a hand-held mixer, slightly less in a stand mixer. Turn the mixer to low speed, add the chocolate, and mix until completely blended, scraping the sides of the bowl with a rubber spatula as needed.

5. With a clean whisk, vigorously beat the whites until a definite peak forms, about another 30 seconds.

6. Transfer about one-third of the whites into the bowl with the chocolate and fold them in with a rubber spatula. The whites should be smooth and blend into the chocolate thoroughly. Now scrape all of the chocolate mixture at once into the bowl with the remaining whites. Fold together lightly to blend, but don't overwork—try to preserve as much volume as possible. Scrape the batter into the prepared pan and smooth the top with the spatula. Give the pan a gentle rap on the table to release any large air bubbles.

continued on p. 196

7. Put the pan in the oven and bake for 15 minutes. Turn the oven down to 325°F and let the cake bake for another 5 minutes. The cake should look puffed, and a toothpick inserted in the center should come out clean.

8. Transfer the pan to a cooling rack. Moisten a clean, light (not terry-cloth) dishtowel and wring it out completely so it's just barely damp. Cover the cake with the towel; the cake will sink slightly as it cools. Once the cake has cooled, slide the pan into the fridge until chilled, 1 to 2 hours. This will help the trimming and assembly process.

TRIM AND ASSEMBLE THE CAKE

1. Lift the towel off the cake. Carefully loosen the parchment from the pan and run a knife along the edges to free the cake from the parchment. Dust the top of the cake generously with confectioners' sugar. Lay a large piece of parchment, a large cutting board, or a dry dishcloth perfectly flat over the cake, pulling taut on both ends, and with a deep breath, invert the cake onto a work surface, long side facing you. Gently peel away the parchment.

2. With a large, sharp knife, carefully trim about ¼ inch off the edges to get an even rectangle. Use a slow sawing motion to avoid tearing the cake; a light coating of confectioners' sugar on the knife will prevent sticking. Cut the rectangle crosswise into four even panels, each about 4x10 inches. Slide a long spatula or a long, wide knife, like a bread knife, under the first panel and carefully transfer it to a flat serving platter.

3. Tuck strips of parchment, plastic wrap, or foil under the edges of the cake layer and over the plate to keep the plate clean during assembly. Spread one-third of the Mascarpone Cream evenly over the cake layer. Sprinkle one-third of the berries over the cream and press them in gently. Top with a second cake panel and another third of the cream and berries. Top with a third cake panel and the remaining cream and berries. Arrange the final cake layer on top and press gently. Dust the top of the cake generously with more confectioners' sugar. Drizzle the chocolate glaze over the top of the cake. Carefully slide the parchment strips away from the plate. Refrigerate the cake until about 15 minutes before serving.   *–Randall Price*

PER SERVING (BASED ON 10 SERVINGS): 630 CALORIES | 9G PROTEIN | 57G CARB | 42G TOTAL FAT | 26G SAT FAT | 9G MONO FAT | 3G POLY FAT | 235MG CHOL | 130MG SODIUM | 5G FIBER

mascarpone cream

MAKES ENOUGH TO FILL ONE
4-LAYER CAKE

1   **cup mascarpone cheese**

1¼ **cups heavy or whipping
    cream**

3   **Tbs. granulated sugar**

1   **tsp. pure vanilla extract**

In a medium bowl, beat the mascarpone, cream, sugar, and vanilla with an electric mixer on low speed until blended. Increase the speed to medium high and beat until the cream is thick and firm peaks form (don't overbeat or the mixture will curdle). Keep refrigerated until ready to assemble.

rich chocolate glaze

MAKES ABOUT 1 CUP GLAZE,
ENOUGH FOR 1 CAKE
AND EXTRA SAUCE

¼   **cup heavy or whipping
    cream**

¼   **cup light corn syrup**

4   **oz. semisweet chocolate,
    chopped**

1   **Tbs. unsalted butter**

1   **Tbs. whiskey or liqueur
    (optional)**

In a small saucepan, mix the cream with the corn syrup. Stir over medium heat until the syrup dissolves, and then bring the mixture to a full boil. Remove from the heat, and add the chocolate all at once. Let stand for 2 minutes and then whisk until smooth. Whisk in the butter and then the alcohol, if using. Keep at room temperature if using the same day; otherwise, cover and refrigerate for up to 4 days.

chocolate mousse layer cake

MAKES ONE 9-INCH CAKE;
SERVES 12

FOR THE CHOCOLATE CAKE

Vegetable oil or nonstick cooking spray, for the pan

Unbleached all-purpose flour, for the pans

6 oz. (1½ cups) cake flour

1 oz. (6 Tbs.) unsweetened natural cocoa powder

2 tsp. baking powder

¼ tsp. baking soda

¼ tsp. table salt

1 cup granulated sugar

¼ cup vegetable oil

1 large egg

2 tsp. pure vanilla extract

FOR THE MOUSSE

2 cups heavy cream

¾ oz. (¼ cup) unsweetened natural cocoa powder

13 oz. bittersweet chocolate, chopped

¼ lb. (½ cup) unsalted butter, at room temperature and cut into small pieces

2 tsp. pure vanilla extract or 1 to 2 Tbs. brandy or Cointreau

Pinch of table salt

7 large egg whites, at room temperature

½ cup granulated sugar

FOR DECORATING THE CAKE
see pp. 200–201

The simplest way to decorate this cake is to press chopped, toasted walnuts onto the sides. For a more dramatic look, try wrapping the cake in a chocolate band and topping it with white chocolate curls, as shown here.

MAKE THE CAKE

1. Position a rack in the center of the oven and heat the oven to 325°F. Lightly grease a 9x2-inch round cake pan, line the bottom with parchment, and flour the sides (but not the bottom).

2. Sift the cake flour, cocoa powder, baking powder, baking soda, and salt into a large bowl. Add the sugar and whisk until well blended. Measure the oil into a 1-cup liquid measure, add the egg and vanilla, and mix with a fork to blend. Add the egg-oil mixture to the dry ingredients and then add 1 cup water. Whisk until the dry ingredients are just moist, about 1 minute, scraping the bowl. Pour the batter into the prepared pan.

3. Bake until a pick inserted in the center of the cake comes out clean, 32 to 34 minutes. Let cool on a rack for 20 minutes. Lightly grease a wire rack, invert the cake onto it, lift off the pan, peel off the paper, and let the cake cool completely.

MAKE THE MOUSSE

1. Set up an ice bath: Fill a large bowl with cold water and ice.

2. Combine the cream and cocoa in a large saucepan set over medium heat. Bring to a full boil, whisking occasionally to blend in the cocoa. Slide the pan off the heat and immediately add the chopped chocolate and the butter; whisk slowly until melted and smooth.

3. Scrape the chocolate mixture into a large bowl. Add the vanilla and salt. Set over the ice bath and stir constantly with a rubber spatula, scraping the sides very frequently, until the chocolate cools to room temperature (don't stop stirring or lumps will form). Remove the bowl from the ice bath.

4. Put the whites in a large, clean bowl. Whip with an electric mixer on medium-low speed until very foamy. Increase the speed to medium high and beat until the whites form very loose, soft peaks. Slowly add the sugar. Keep beating until the whites are shiny and form floppy peaks.

5. Working quickly, scoop about a third of the whites into the cooled chocolate mixture and fold together with a rubber spatula or a whisk until blended. Scrape the remaining whites into the chocolate and fold together gently but thoroughly. Scoop out about 1 cup of the mousse into a bowl, cover, and refrigerate for finishing touchups. Use the rest of the mousse to assemble the cake.

ASSEMBLE THE CAKE

1. Set the ring of a 9-inch springform pan on a large, flat cake plate. To cut the cake into layers, it helps if the cake is slightly chilled. Set the cake, bottom side up, on a parchment-lined work surface. Cut into three equal layers. Set aside without separating the layers.

2. Gently flip the top cake layer (really the bottom) upside down and center it in the springform ring so the mousse can flow over the edge to frost the sides; handle the cake carefully (if it breaks, just piece it together). Scoop about one-third of the mousse (a heaping 2 cups) onto the cake layer in the ring and gently spread to cover. Flip the next cake layer (the center) on top of the mousse and press gently to level it, if necessary. Scoop half of the remaining mousse over the layer and spread gently. Flip the remaining cake layer upside down and set it on top of the mousse. Press gently to level it. Spread on the remaining mousse and smooth the top; the cake should fill the ring (don't worry if a little mousse leaks out of the bottom).

3. If you're decorating the cake with nuts, add enough mousse to the top layer of the cake so it comes to the rim of the springform ring. Smooth the top with a metal spatula or the flat, straight edge of a long knife. Pull an icing comb or a long serrated knife across the mousse, making a wavy pattern. If the pattern doesn't hold, pop the cake in the fridge for 5- to 10-minute intervals so the mousse starts to set, and then try again. (If you're wrapping the cake with a chocolate band, skip this step.) Put the cake in the fridge for at least 6 hours and up to 24.

DECORATE THE CAKE

1. Take the cake from the fridge. Run a long, thin knife or metal spatula under hot water and dry it well. Slide the warm knife between the cake and the ring, pressing the knife against the ring, to loosen the cake. Carefully release the springform clasp; gently pry it all the way open. Lift off the ring and clean the plate edge. If you're decorating the cake with nuts, mold strips of foil around the cake plate to keep it clean. Chill the cake. Decorate the cake as directed on pp. 200–201.

2. Once decorated, keep the cake refrigerated and serve it within 8 hours. Remove from the fridge 10 to 15 minutes before serving.
–Abigail Johnson Dodge

cutting cake into layers

Choose your longest serrated knife. Place the section of the blade near the handle one-third of the way down the side of the cake (use a ruler, eyeball it, or use two toothpicks to divide the cake into three equal layers and then use the picks as guide when cutting). With a firm, slow sawing motion, cut around the cake at this level. Focus on where the blade enters the cake (not the knife tip). When you've made a full circle and cut through the layer, place the knife two-thirds of the way down the cake and repeat, creating three layers in all.

Decorating Ideas

Choose one of these three decorating ideas—topping with chopping nuts, adding chocolate shavings and curls, or adding a chocolate band and curls.

Simple chopped nuts

You'll need:

- **7 oz. (1½ cups) whole walnuts**

1. Heat the oven to 400°F. Toast the walnuts on a baking sheet in a single layer until golden and aromatic, 12 to 15 minutes, stirring every 5 minutes. Let cool, then chop them into medium-fine pieces.

2. Scoop up a handful of nuts in one hand and pat them onto the side of the cake. Many will fall off but you'll be left with a single layer of nuts. Repeat, rotating the cake to cover all the sides; you'll have extra nuts. Sprinkle more chopped nuts on the top. Brush extra nuts off the plate before removing the foil strips.

Shavings and curls

You'll need:

- **1 10- to 12-oz. thick block of bittersweet, semisweet, milk, or white chocolate**

1. Set out two large (11x17-inch) sheets of parchment or waxed paper.

2. Start with shavings: Rub the chocolate with your palm to warm it slightly. Wrap a sheet of paper towel or plastic wrap around half of the chocolate block so it's easier to grip. Drag a vegetable peeler across the side of the chocolate block, letting the shavings fall on the paper. As your hand warms the chocolate, turn the block around. You'll get larger shavings from the warmer side. Stop when you have 1½ to 2 cups.

3. Then make curls: Curls are made with the same technique as for shavings, only the chocolate must be a bit warmer. Microwave the chocolate block very, very briefly, using 5-second jolts on high, until it feels just slightly warm. One or two 5-second bursts should be sufficient; white chocolate needs even less time. Use the peeler as for shavings, but apply a bit more pressure. If the chocolate still makes shavings or won't give big curls, it isn't warm enough, so heat it again for 5 seconds. If it melts against the peeler, it's too warm, so let it cool. Let the curls fall in an even, single layer on the other sheet of paper until the curls cover the paper.

4. Using a soupspoon, scoop up some shavings. Starting at the bottom of the cake and using light pressure, gently drag the spoon up the side so the shavings stick; continue until the sides of the cake are covered. Arrange the curls on the top. Brush extra shavings off the plate before removing the foil strips.

Chopped nuts

Shavings and curls

Chocolate bands and curls

You'll need:

6 oz. bittersweet chocolate

1 10- to 12-oz. thick block of white, milk, semisweet, or bittersweet chocolate

1. Finely chop the 6 oz. bittersweet chocolate in a food processor or with a chef's knife. Set a 16x8-inch rectangle of waxed paper on a large cutting board. Get the cake from the fridge.

2. Melt the chocolate: Put half the chopped chocolate in the top of a small double boiler and melt it over simmering water (or in a microwave, using short bursts). When the chocolate is melted, smooth, and warm, take the bowl off the heat. Add the remaining chopped chocolate and stir vigorously with a rubber spatula until melted and smooth (1). Scrape the chocolate onto the waxed paper and use an offset metal spatula to spread it as evenly as possible to cover the entire rectangle, just passing the edges.

3. Let the chocolate set until it's pliable but not stiff. It should look more matte than glossy and should bend but not snap if you lift up a corner of the paper; this takes 3 to 20 minutes at room temperature (if it's going slowly, you can pop it in the fridge, but check the chocolate every minute because once it starts to set, it hardens quickly).

4. With a sharp paring knife, trim the short edges to neaten them, cutting through the chocolate and the paper. If the chocolate sticks to the knife, it hasn't set enough, so let it cool for a few minutes more. Cutting through the chocolate and paper, cut the rectangle lengthwise into two 4-inch-wide bands.

5. Position one band so the long cut edge touches the plate. Wrap it around the cake, pressing gently (2). When the band is exactly where you want it, peel away the paper (3). Don't touch the bare chocolate or it will show fingerprints. Position the other band, cut edge down, on the opposite side so it covers the outside of the cake completely; the bands will overlap slightly. Remove the paper. If the top edges of the bands don't flop onto the cake, nudge them gently (using parchment to avoid prints). If they don't bend easily, don't force them; the cake is pretty with straight edges as well.

6. Using the block of chocolate, make the curls as described in "Shavings and Curls." Arrange the curls on top of the cake.

Chocolate bands

flourless chocolate cake with chocolate glaze

MAKES ONE 9-INCH CAKE;
SERVES 12 GENEROUSLY

FOR THE CAKE

- 6 oz. (¾ cup) unsalted butter, cut into 6 pieces; more for the pan
- 12 oz. bittersweet chocolate, coarsely chopped (2 ¼ cups)
- 5 large eggs
- 1 cup granulated sugar
- 1½ tsp. pure vanilla extract
- ¼ tsp. table salt
- ¾ oz. (¼ cup) unsweetened natural cocoa powder, sifted if lumpy; more for the pan

FOR THE GLAZE

- 4 oz. bittersweet chocolate, coarsely chopped (¾ cup)
- 1½ oz. (3 Tbs.) unsalted butter

To slice this cake (or any dense, sticky cake), heat the knife first, either by dipping it in a tall container of very hot water or by holding it under hot running water for a few seconds. Then wipe it dry before cutting the cake. The knife will cool quickly, and the cake will start sticking, so expect to rinse and repeat several times. A crème brûlée torch, if you have one, is also handy for heating up a knife.

MAKE THE CAKE

1. Position a rack in the middle of the oven and heat the oven to 300°F. Lightly butter the bottom of a 9x2-inch round cake pan and line it with a round of parchment. Lightly butter the parchment and the sides of the pan and dust with cocoa powder. Tap out any excess.

2. Melt the chocolate and butter in the microwave or in a medium metal bowl set in a skillet of barely simmering water, stirring with a rubber spatula until smooth. Remove the bowl from the water bath and set aside to cool slightly. In the bowl of a stand mixer fitted with the whisk attachment, combine the eggs, sugar, vanilla, salt, and 2 Tbs. water. Beat on medium-high speed until the mixture is very foamy, pale in color, and doubled in volume, 2 minutes. Reduce the mixer speed to low and gradually pour in the chocolate mixture. Increase the speed to medium high and continue beating until well blended, about 30 seconds. Add the cocoa powder and mix on medium low just until blended, about 30 seconds.

3. Pour the batter into the prepared pan. Bake until a pick inserted in the center comes out looking wet with small gooey clumps, 40 to 45 minutes. Don't overbake. Let cool in the pan on a rack for 30 minutes. If necessary, gently push the edges down with your fingertips until the layer is even. Run a small knife around the edge of the pan to loosen the cake. Cover the cake pan with a wire rack and invert. Remove the pan and parchment and let the cake cool completely. The cake may look cinched in around its sides, which is fine. Transfer to a cake plate. Cover and refrigerate the cake until it's very cold, at least 6 hours or overnight.

GLAZE THE CAKE

Melt the chocolate and butter in the microwave or in a medium metal bowl set in a skillet of barely simmering water, stirring with a rubber spatula until smooth. Pour the warm glaze over the chilled cake and, using an offset spatula, spread the glaze evenly to within ¼ inch of the edge. Refrigerate the cake until the glaze is set, 20 to 40 minutes. Before serving, remove the cake from the refrigerator and let it come to room temperature, 20 to 30 minutes. To serve, cut the cake into small, if not tiny, slices using a hot knife. *–Abigail Johnson Dodge*

PER SERVING (BASED ON 12 SERVINGS): 420 CALORIES | 6G PROTEIN | 37G CARB | 33G TOTAL FAT | 18G SAT FAT | 5G MONO FAT | 1.5G POLY FAT | 125MG CHOL | 80MG SODIUM | 3G FIBER

chocolate irish whiskey cake

FOR THE CAKE LAYERS

Unsalted butter, for the pans

10 oz. (2¼ cups) unbleached all-purpose flour

2 cups granulated sugar

2¼ oz. (¾ cup) unsweetened natural cocoa powder

1½ tsp. baking powder

1½ tsp. baking soda

1 tsp. table salt

2 large eggs

1 cup whole milk

½ cup canola oil

1½ tsp. pure vanilla extract

1 cup hot coffee

FOR THE COFFEE–WHISKEY WHIPPED CREAM

1 Tbs. instant espresso granules

¼ cup Irish whiskey, such as Jameson®

3 cups heavy cream

3 Tbs. packed dark brown sugar

TO FINISH THE CAKE

1 4-oz. block semisweet chocolate (about 1 inch thick), at room temperature

1 4-oz. block white chocolate (about 1 inch thick), at room temperature

This recipe reimagines the classic whiskey-spiked irish coffee as a decadent mocha layer cake filled with coffee–whiskey whipped cream and topped with white and dark chocolate shavings.

MAKE THE CAKE

1. Position racks in the upper and lower thirds of the oven and heat the oven to 350°F. Butter three 9x2-inch round cake pans and line the bottoms with parchment. Butter the parchment.

2. In a stand mixer fitted with the whisk attachment (or in a large bowl, using a hand-held mixer), briefly blend the flour, sugar, cocoa, baking powder, baking soda, and salt on low speed. Add the eggs, milk, oil, and vanilla and mix at low speed, scraping the bowl as necessary, until the mixture is thick and creamy, like chocolate frosting, about 5 minutes. With the mixer running, gradually add the hot coffee, mixing at low speed just until combined. The batter will be quite thin. Portion the batter equally among the pans. Bake, switching positions and rotating the pans halfway through, until a tester inserted in the center of the cake comes out with only a few crumbs clinging to it and the center feels firm to the touch, 20 to 25 minutes. Let the cakes cool completely in the pans on racks.

MAKE THE COFFEE–WHISKEY WHIPPED CREAM

Clean and chill the mixing bowl and whisk attachment. In a measuring cup, stir the instant espresso into the whiskey until completely dissolved. In the chilled bowl, whip the cream, brown sugar, and whiskey mixture on medium-high speed until medium peaks form, 2 to 3 minutes.

FINISH THE CAKE

1. Run a thin knife around the inside edge of the cake pans and turn the cakes out onto a large cutting board; peel off the parchment.

2. Transfer one layer to a cake plate and spread a third of the whipped cream on top, leaving a ½-inch border; repeat with the second layer. Put the top layer in place and spread the remaining whipped cream out to the edge.

3. To make the chocolate shavings, put a piece of waxed paper or foil on a baking sheet. Microwave each block of chocolate on medium power for 20 to 30 seconds to soften slightly, then draw a vegetable peeler along the chocolate bar's edge, letting the curls fall onto the waxed paper. Make enough curls of both colors to top the cake generously, 1½ to 2½ oz. each. Refrigerate the shavings to make them easier to handle. Arrange the shavings on top of the cake and serve.

–Gale Gand

PER SERVING: 610 CALORIES | 7G PROTEIN | 66G CARB | 37G TOTAL FAT | 17G SAT FAT | 14G MONO FAT | 4G POLY FAT | 120MG CHOL | 450MG SODIUM | 3G FIBER

tips for pretty cake layers

The most accurate way to distribute the batter among the three pans is by weight. A full batch of batter weighs about 3 lb. 3 oz., so each pan should get about 1 lb. 1 oz.

For the bottom two layers, spread the whipped cream with an offset spatula to within ½ inch of the edge. The extra space will keep it from spilling over when the cake is assembled.

Apply a little pressure when you place a layer on top of the whipped cream to help the cream spread just to the edge.

strawberries and corn-cream layer cake with white chocolate cap'n crunch crumbs

MAKES ONE 8-INCH CAKE;
SERVES 8

FOR THE CAKE

Nonstick cooking spray

¼ lb. (½ cup) unsalted butter, softened

1 cup plus 2½ Tbs. granulated sugar

¼ cup packed light brown sugar

3 large eggs, at room temperature

½ cup buttermilk, at room temperature

6 Tbs. grapeseed or canola oil

2½ tsp. pure vanilla extract

6 oz. (1½ cups) cake flour

1 tsp. baking powder

1 tsp. kosher salt

FOR THE CORN CRUMBS

8 oz. (6 cups) Cap'n Crunch® cereal

¾ oz. (2 Tbs.) cornstarch

4 tsp. granulated sugar

½ tsp. kosher salt

5½ oz. (11 Tbs.) unsalted butter, melted and cooled slightly

3½ oz. white chocolate, chopped (½ cup)

continued on p. 208

This incredible cake requires some time to make the components. It needs to be frozen so the layers can set up properly, and then defrosted completely before serving. Plan on making it at least 4 days ahead.

MAKE THE CAKE

1. Position racks in the upper and lower thirds of the oven and heat the oven to 350°F. Spray three 8x2-inch round cake pans with cooking spray and line the bottoms with parchment.

2. In a stand mixer fitted with the paddle attachment, beat the butter and both sugars on medium speed until fluffy, 2 to 3 minutes. Scrape the bowl with a rubber spatula.

3. On low speed, add the eggs one at a time, mixing for about 20 seconds after each addition. Return the mixer to medium speed and beat until homogenous and fluffy, about 3 minutes. Scrape the bowl.

4. Combine the buttermilk, oil, and vanilla in a 1-cup measuring cup. With the mixer on low speed, slowly add the buttermilk mixture. Increase the speed to medium and beat until the batter is almost white and twice the volume of the original fluffy butter and sugar mixture, 4 to 6 minutes. Scrape down the bowl.

5. With the mixer on low speed, slowly add the cake flour, baking powder, and salt. Mix just until incorporated, 45 to 60 seconds. Portion the batter evenly among the cake pans and smooth with a spatula.

6. Bake the cakes until they're golden brown, bouncy to the touch, and a tester inserted in the center of each comes out clean, 18 to 20 minutes (rotate and swap the pans' positions after 10 minutes). Cool the cakes in their pans on wire racks.

MAKE THE CORN CRUMBS

1. Reduce the oven temperature to 300°F. Line two rimmed baking sheets with parchment.

2. In a food processor, grind the cereal to a powder. Combine the cereal, cornstarch, sugar, and salt in a large bowl and mix with your hands. Add the melted butter and toss with a rubber spatula until the mixture is evenly moistened. Squeeze the crumbs with your hands to make small clumps no bigger than peas and sprinkle them evenly on the prepared baking sheets.

continued on p. 208

FOR THE CORN CREAM

- **3 cups fresh or thawed frozen yellow corn kernels (from about 4 ears of corn)**
- **1 tsp. unflavored gelatin powder**
- **5 Tbs. granulated sugar**
- **1 tsp. kosher salt**
- **5 Tbs. sour cream**
- **5 Tbs. heavy cream**
- **¾ oz. (3 Tbs. plus 2 tsp.) confectioners' sugar**

FOR ASSEMBLY

- **2 cups best-quality strawberry preserves**
- **1⅓ cups hulled and quartered ripe strawberries; more for garnish**

2. Bake until the crumbs are a shade darker, about 15 minutes (rotate the sheets after 8 minutes). Cool completely on racks.

3. While the crumbs cool, melt the white chocolate in the microwave in a small microwave-safe bowl, using 15-second high-power intervals. Let the melted chocolate cool until no longer hot to the touch.

4. Transfer the cooled crumbs to a large bowl and pour the melted white chocolate over them. Toss with your hands until the crumbs are enrobed in the chocolate. Continue tossing with your hands every 5 minutes until the white chocolate hardens and the crumbs are no longer sticky, 30 to 40 minutes total. Break up any clumps that are larger than peas.

MAKE THE CORN CREAM

1. Purée the corn with ⅓ cup water in a blender until smooth. Strain through a fine-mesh sieve set over a measuring cup, pressing on the solids, until you have 9 fl. oz. of corn juice.

2. Put 1 Tbs. water in a small bowl. Sprinkle the gelatin over the water and let bloom for 5 minutes.

3. Meanwhile, combine the corn juice, sugar, and salt in a small saucepan over medium-low heat. Bring the mixture to a simmer and whisk for 2 minutes to cook out the starch in the corn. (The mixture will thicken as it heats.) Remove from the heat, stir in the gelatin, transfer to a heatproof container, and freeze until set to a pudding-like consistency, 1 to 1½ hours.

4. In a large bowl, whip the sour cream, heavy cream, and confectioners' sugar with a whisk to very soft peaks, 2 to 3 minutes. Add the cold corn mixture and slowly whisk until the color is even. Refrigerate until ready to use.

ASSEMBLE THE CAKE

1. Assemble an 8-inch springform pan and make a parchment collar for it: Cut two 12x14-inch rectangular strips of parchment. Fold the two strips lengthwise to get two 6x14-inch strips. Line the inside of the pan with the strips, nestling them into each other with the folded edge on the top.

2. Release the edges of the cakes with a paring knife. Turn the cakes out onto a clean work surface. Fit one of the cake layers into the springform pan, trimming it to fit snugly if necessary. Use the back of a spoon to spread half the corn cream over the cake base in an even layer. Sprinkle half of the corn crumbs evenly over the corn cream.

3. In a medium bowl, whisk the strawberry preserves to loosen them. Use the back of a spoon to spread one-third of the preserves as evenly as possible over the corn crumbs. Sprinkle ⅔ cup of the fresh berries evenly across the preserves.

4. Set another cake round (trimmed as needed to fit) on top of the berries and gently press it down. Repeat the process with the remaining corn cream and corn crumbs, half of the remaining preserves, and the remaining ⅔ cup berries. Fit the remaining cake round atop the fresh berries and spread the remaining preserves over the cake.

5. Freeze the cake for a minimum of 12 hours to set it. (The cake will keep in the freezer for up to 2 weeks; wrap in plastic once frozen.)

6. One to two days before serving, remove the side of the pan and let the cake completely defrost in the refrigerator—this will take about 36 hours. Do not thaw at room temperature.

7. Just before serving, carefully remove the parchment collar and garnish the top of the cake with freshly hulled and quartered strawberries. Serve cold. *—Christina Tosi*

PER SERVING: 1,120 CALORIES | 9G PROTEIN | 164G CARB | 50G TOTAL FAT | 25G SAT FAT | 12G MONO FAT | 9G POLY FAT | 160MG CHOL | 700MG SODIUM | 3G FIBER

Make Ahead

The assembled cake (minus the fresh strawberry garnish) will keep in the freezer for up to 2 weeks; if you plan on freezing it this long, wrap it in plastic once it's completely frozen. Be sure to defrost it in the refrigerator as per the instructions in the recipe. Do not thaw at room temperature.

METRIC EQUIVALENTS

LIQUID/DRY MEASURES	
U.S.	METRIC
¼ teaspoon	1.25 milliliters
½ teaspoon	2.5 milliliters
1 teaspoon	5 milliliters
1 tablespoon (3 teaspoons)	15 milliliters
1 fluid ounce (2 tablespoons)	30 milliliters
¼ cup	60 milliliters
⅓ cup	80 milliliters
½ cup	120 milliliters
1 cup	240 milliliters
1 pint (2 cups)	480 milliliters
1 quart (4 cups; 32 ounces)	960 milliliters
1 gallon (4 quarts)	3.84 liters
1 ounce (by weight)	28 grams
1 pound	454 grams
2.2 pounds	1 kilogram

OVEN TEMPERATURES		
°F	GAS MARK	°C
250	½	120
275	1	140
300	2	150
325	3	165
350	4	180
375	5	190
400	6	200
425	7	220
450	8	230
475	9	240
500	10	260
550	Broil	290

CONTRIBUTORS

Karen Barker is a pastry chef and cookbook author. She co-owns Magnolia Grill in Durham, North Carolina. She won the James Beard Outstanding Pastry Chef Award in 2003.

Rose Levy Beranbaum is a cooking instructor, cookbook author, and baker extraordinaire. She is the author of nine cookbooks, including *The Cake Bible*, and most recently, *Rose's Heavenly Cakes*.

Flo Braker is the author of numerous cookbooks; her most recent is *Baking for All Occasions*.

Kay Cabrera is a pastry chef and wedding cake designer living in Hawaii.

Greg Case was a pastry chef at Dean & DeLuca in New York City and Hammersley's Bistro in Boston before setting out on his own. He owns the G. Case Baking Company in Somerville, Massachusetts.

Regan Daley is a food writer from Toronto, Canada. Her cookbook, *In the Sweet Kitchen*, won several awards, including the IACP's Award for Best Baking and Dessert Book and Best Overall Book.

Abigail Johnson Dodge, a former pastry chef, is a widely published food writer, cooking instructor, and *Fine Cooking* contributing editor. She has also written numerous cookbooks; her latest is *Mini Treats & Hand-Held Sweets*.

Maryellen Driscoll is a *Fine Cooking* contributing editor. She and her husband own Free Bird Farm, located in upstate New York.

Keri Fisher is a food writer and cookbook author who worked in restaurants in Florida and Boston.

Gale Gand is founding pastry chef and partner at Tru restaurant in Chicago. She has won numerous James Beard Awards and published award-winning cookbooks, including *Just a Bite* and *Short and Sweet*. She was also the host of *Sweet Dreams*, the daily baking show on Food Network and the Cooking Channel.

Heather Ho was an executive pastry chef at Windows on the World restaurant in New York City.

Fany Gerson is a pastry chef and Mexican-food expert. Her books are *My Sweet Mexico* and *Paletas*.

David Guas is a pastry chef, restaurant consultant, and cooking teacher. David is the chef-owner of Bayou Bakery in Arlington, Virginia, as well as the author of *DamGoodSweet*.

Martha Holmberg is a cookbook author and food writer based in Portland, Oregon. Her latest book is *Fresh Food Nation*.

Yasmin Lozada-Hissom is pastry chef of Duo Restaurant and co-owner of Spuntino, both in Denver, Colorado.

Wendy Kalen is a food writer who has contributed recipes to *Fine Cooking, Cooking Light, Food & Wine*, and many other magazines.

Jeanne Kelley, the author of the award-winning cookbook *Blue Eggs and Yellow Tomatoes*, is a food writer, food stylist, and recipe developer.

Elinor Klivans, a former pastry chef, has written numerous cookbooks; her latest is *Slice & Bake Cookies*. Klivans also writes for the *Washington Post*, *Real Food*, *Fresh*, and *Cooking Pleasures*.

Lori Longbotham is a recipe developer and cookbook author whose books include *Luscious Coconut Desserts* and *Luscious Creamy Desserts*.

Emily Luchetti is the executive pastry chef at Farallon and Water Bar in San Francisco.

Barbara Lynch is the James Beard Award-winning chef-owner of Barbara Lynch Gruppo, which includes seven restaurants and food businesses in Boston: No. Nine Park, B & G Oyster, The Butcher Shop, Sportello, Plum, Drink, and Stir.

Kimberly Y. Masibay is a *Fine Cooking* contributing editor.

Alice Medrich is a three-time Cookbook of the Year Award winner and teacher. Her latest book is *Seriously Bitter Sweet*.

Jehangir Mehta opened Graffiti in New York City after working in numerous NYC restaurants including Aix, Compass, and Jean-Georges.

Jill O'Connor is a pastry chef, food writer, and author of six cookbooks, including *Sticky, Chewy, Messy, Gooey*.

Aimee Olexy owns three restaurants in the Philadephila area: Talula's Garden, Talula's Table, and Talula's Daily.

David Page and Barbara Shinn are owners of Shinn Estate Vineyards and Farmhouse, a Long Island, New York, winery and bed and breakfast. The former owners of Home restaurant in New York City are also the authors of the James Beard Award–nominated cookbook *Recipes from Home*.

Greg Patent, a baker, teacher, and James Beard Award winner for *Baking in America* studies and writes about food and cooking. He hosts *The Food Guys* on Montana public radio and blogs at thebakingwizard.com.

Liz Pearson worked as the kitchen director for *Saveur* magazine before moving back to her native Texas, where she is a freelance food writer and recipe.

Randall Price is Resident Chef at La Varenne's Chateau du Fey and cooks for private clients in Paris and the Auvergne.

Rebecca Rather is a baker and owner of the Rather Sweet Bakery café in Fredericksburg, Texas. She is the author of *The Pastry Queen*.

Nicole Rees, author of *Baking Unplugged*, is a food scientist and professional baker. She is the research and development manager for a baking ingredient company in Wilsonville, Oregon.

Katherine Eastman Seeley runs a catering company, Sweet & Savory, and also is a recipe developer and tester.

Maria Helm Sinskey is a noted chef, cookbook author, and culinary director at her family's winery, Robert Sinskey Vineyards, in Napa Valley, California. She is a frequent contributor to *Food & Wine*, *Bon Appetit*, and *Fine Cooking* magazines. Her cookbook *Family Meals* was a 2010 IACP Cookbook Award Winner. Maria's accolades include *Food & Wine's* Best New Chef 1996 and *San Francisco Magazine's* Rising Star Chef 1996.

Christina Tosi is the chef, owner, and founder of Momofuku Milk Bar. She is the 2012 recipient of the James Beard Rising Star Chef award.

Julia Usher is a pastry chef, writer, and stylist whose work has appeared in *Vera Wang on Weddings*, *Bon Appétit*, *Better Homes and Gardens*, and more. She is a contributing editor at *Dessert Professional* as well as a director of the IACP.

Carole Walter is a master baker, cooking instructor, and author of many cookbooks, including *Great Coffee Cakes*, which is based on years of studying with pastry chefs in France, Austria, Italy, Denmark, and the United States as well as two decades of teaching baking classes. Her latest book is *Great Cakes, Pies, Cookies, Muffins & More*.

Carolyn Weil, a former pastry chef, is a food writer and teacher.

Joanne Weir is a James Beard Award–winning cookbook author, chef, cooking teacher, and television personality. Her latest book is *Joanne Weir's Cooking Confidence*, the companion book to her public television show of the same name. She is also executive chef of Copita restaurant in northern California.

Shelley Wiseman is senior food editor at *Fine Cooking*.

INDEX